ORSON
WELLES

Orson Welles in the early 1970s. (*Academy of Motion Picture Arts & Sciences*)

ORSON WELLES

by

Joseph McBride

Revised and Expanded Edition

DA CAPO PRESS • NEW YORK

Library of Congress Cataloging in Publication Data

McBride, Joseph.
    Orson Welles / by Joseph McBride.—Rev. and expanded ed.
        p.   cm.
    Filmography: p.
    Includes bibliographical references.
    ISBN 0-306-80674-6 (alk. paper)
    1. Welles, Orson, 1915—Criticism and interpretation. I. Title.
PN1998.3.W45M32   1996
791.43′0233′092—dc20   95-48194
                                                                  CIP

First Da Capo Press edition 1996

This Da Capo Press paperback edition of *Orson Welles*
is a completely revised and expanded version of the book
published in New York in 1972. It is published by arrangement
with the author.

Published by Da Capo Press, Inc.
A Subsidiary of Plenum Publishing Corporation
233 Spring Street, New York, N.Y. 10013

Manufactured in the United States of America

For Linda Kavanagh and our daughter,
Jessica McBride

Orson Welles is an animal made for the screen and the stage. When he steps before a camera, it is as if the rest of the world ceases to exist. He is a citizen of the screen.

—Jean Renoir, in conversation
with the author, 1970

Contents

Preface to the Revised Edition:
Your Friendly Neighborhood Grocery Store   vii

1. No Wine Before Its Time   1
2. Apprentice Work   23
3. *Citizen Kane*   31
4. *The Magnificent Ambersons*   53
5. Picking Up the Pieces: *Journey Into Fear,*
   It's All True, and *The Stranger*   89
6. *The Lady from Shanghai*   103
7. Welles and Shakespeare: *Macbeth* and *Othello*   111
8. *Mr. Arkadin*   129
9. *The Fountain of Youth*   137
10. *Touch of Evil*   145
11. *The Trial*   155
12. *Chimes at Midnight*   163
13. *The Immortal Story*   175
14. *F for Fake*   181
15. The Other Side of Orson Welles   191

Filmography   215
Selected Bibliography   237
Acknowledgments   241

Preface to the Revised Edition:
Your Friendly Neighborhood Grocery Store

When Orson Welles received the American Film Institute's Life Achievement Award in 1975, an honor he accepted "in the name of all the mavericks," he told the Hollywood audience that he remained "not only your obedient servant, but also, in this age of supermarkets, your friendly neighborhood grocery store." With the unceasing proliferation of books on Welles in recent years, I find I have much that same feeling in putting together this volume, a revised and updated edition of my 1972 book *Orson Welles*. First published as part of the British Film Institute's Cinema One series, mine was only the third critical study of Welles's films published in English, following two small volumes by Peter Bogdanovich (1961) and Peter Cowie (1965) sharing a common title, *The Cinema of Orson Welles*. When I started writing this book in 1966, at the age of nineteen, I was motivated largely by the fact that, aside from the work of such French critics as André Bazin and Maurice Bessy, precious little else in the way of serious analysis had been written even on such early Welles classics as *Citizen Kane* and *The Magnificent Ambersons*, let alone on such later career landmarks as *Touch of Evil* and *Chimes at Midnight*. Today, however, the shelves are loaded with Welles biographies, critical studies and anthologies, and in-depth studies of individual films, including important archeological findings on his lost or mutilated works.

Welles's death in 1985 has only increased the flow of writing on his multifaceted creativity. Some of these books—along with articles in newspapers, magazines and scholarly journals—have greatly enlarged our understanding of Welles's life and work, drawing on newly available films and research materials. Two fascinating unproduced Welles screenplays, *The Big Brass Ring* and *The Cradle Will Rock*, also have been published since his death. Welles unfortunately never wrote more than a few pages of his promised autobiography, but we are lucky to have his extended commentary on his own career in his interview book with Peter Bogdanovich, *This Is Orson Welles*, itself a long-"lost," legendary work that finally was published in 1992.

In reading these recent books and articles, I have been pleased to find that my own relatively short volume, essayistic in style and devoted to analyzing the essential themes of a body of work that at the time was little understood, has been useful to many of the scholars who have come after me, enlarging upon or challenging my basic premises. So in dusting off and refurbishing a book that has been out of print for some sixteen years, I can't help feeling like the proprietor of a small, slightly unfashionable, but friendly neighborhood grocery store that has had to struggle to keep open for business, due to the better-stocked competition from the glistening chain stores on the better-travelled streets around the corner. What I can continue to offer, I feel, is personalized service, my own idiosyncratic selection of stock, and some leisurely one-on-one conversation—one critic's impassioned, youthful viewpoint on the filmmaker who most shaped his ideas of what filmmaking can be.

Writing this book over a four-year period in student rooming houses at the University of Wisconsin in Madison, Wisconsin, I felt an intense personal kinship with the youthful Orson Welles. My first viewing of *Citizen Kane* at college in the fall of 1966 changed my life, as *Kane* has changed the lives of so many other young *cinéastes*: watching this monumental film made by a twenty-five-year-old newcomer to Hollywood, I felt that anything was possible in movies. My feeling of sharing common ground with Orson Welles became a literal one when I discovered, to my astonished delight, that he had been born in nearby Kenosha, Wisconsin, and that he had been studied as a child prodigy in Madison ("Cartoonist, Actor,

Poet and only 10," a local paper headlined). I wrote much of this book a few blocks from the site of the only public school Welles ever attended (Washington Grade School), and I watched Welles movies on the UW campus, situated directly across Lake Mendota from the summer camp Welles attended in 1925 (Camp Indianola). Welles later told me that he had fled Madison ("a wonderful city") during the dead of night by canoe and train after a camp counselor tried to molest him, and that his only memory of Kenosha was the bleak day of his mother's funeral. "I'm not ashamed of being from Wisconsin," he said. "Just of being from Kenosha. It's a terrible place."

Spellbound by *Kane*, and fortunate to have the opportunity to see several other Welles films in a festival at the student union, I soon dropped out of the university, deferred my plans to write novels, and decided to concentrate on making student movies and writing film criticism and screenplays. After becoming president of the Wisconsin Film Society, I enjoyed access to a 16mm print of *Kane*, which I watched more than sixty times while writing this book. My first plan was to write a book-length study of *Kane*, but after I realized that there was a need for a more thorough study in English of Welles's body of work, my ambition for the book expanded. The *Kane* chapter, my first magazine article on Welles, initially appeared in the Fall 1968 issue of *Film Heritage*, and later that year in an anthology I edited for the Wisconsin Film Society Press, *Persistence of Vision: A Collection of Film Criticism*, along with my chapter on *The Magnificent Ambersons* and some preliminary thoughts on *Chimes at Midnight*. I published other parts of my work in progress in *Film Quarterly* and the BFI magazine *Sight and Sound*, under the mentorship of those magazines' editors, Ernest Callenbach and Penelope Houston; I also am grateful to Penelope for accepting and editing my book for the Cinema One series. I was able to bring various Welles films to Madison for showing to our loyal and forbearing film society membership; other films I had to track down more laboriously, by travelling on the Greyhound or Badger buses to Milwaukee and Chicago. In those benighted days before the videotape revolution, I had to take notes in darkened theaters, classrooms, screening rooms, and living rooms as I watched Welles's films over and over again to ensure that I understood their slightest nuances and quoted them correctly. I never finished college, because I was too busy writing this book. But it was worth it.

In the summer of 1970, with the manuscript of *Orson Welles* virtually completed, I made my first trip to Hollywood, to interview John Ford for a critical study of his films that I was writing with Michael Wilmington. There I looked up Peter Bogdanovich, whose largely unheralded directorial debut film, *Targets*, I much admired. Fortuitously, at the time I met Bogdanovich, he was helping Welles find *cinéastes* to appear in a film he was about to start shooting about Hollywood, *The Other Side of the Wind*. By the end of my first incredible week in Hollywood, I had not only interviewed John Ford and Jean Renoir, but thanks to Bogdanovich, I had met the elusive Orson Welles and was acting under his direction. The story of that experience, which lasted for six years and gave me the opportunity to get to know Welles in person and as a collaborator, is told in the final chapter of this book.

Although a few scenes from *The Other Side of the Wind* have been shown in public, the film still hasn't been released or fully edited. It is part of the extensive list of uncompleted or unreleased Welles films that Jonathan Rosenbaum described in his 1986 *Sight and Sound* article "The Invisible Orson Welles: A First Inventory." Rosenbaum, who edited *This Is Orson Welles* and has published several other invaluable articles on Welles, is foremost among the scholars who have done admirable work over the last decade or so in attempting to reconstruct and explicate the many gaps in Welles's career. Robert Stam, whose insightful research on *It's All True* appeared in the 1989 Welles issue of the film journal *Persistence of Vision*, defined the biggest challenge facing Welles scholars in apposite but perhaps unintentionally humorous language: "All discussion of *It's All True* spirals around an absent center—the missing text." Since then, part of that "missing text" has been reconstituted and triumphantly released as the 1993 documentary *It's All True: Based on an Unfinished Film by Orson Welles*. Other missing Welles texts have been filtering out, in whole or in part, and more are sure to come, however slowly. So the task of analyzing Welles's career will keep scholars busy for many years, since, in a very real sense, Orson Welles's career is far from finished. Even after his death, he continues to astonish us with his artistic fecundity and the endless variety of his work.

This book, then, remains a provisional text. It takes account of the archival and scholarly investigations and restorations that have occurred since 1972, while rethinking some of its original views in the light of subsequent discoveries and critical debate. When I set about the task of preparing a revised edition at the suggestion of Da Capo Press's editor, Yuval Taylor, I had not read the book for many years. I was unsure how I would feel about it today, since it was written by a much younger and greener man, barely out of high school, writing about films as an enthusiast in a distant Midwestern outpost, without the long experience of Hollywood ahead of him to educate him about the harsher realities of the film business. I was pleasantly surprised to find that, by and large, my *Orson Welles* held up well with the passage of time and that I recognized a closer kinship with the writer than I had expected. Aside from the occasional wince caused by a stylistic "jejunosity" (to borrow a word coined by Woody Allen), my analyses of Welles's films still struck me as cogently argued, even if I might express myself much differently if I were to start writing the book from scratch today. I have tried (mostly successfully) to resist that temptation, for as Graham Greene wrote in his autobiography *A Sort of Life*, "There is a fashion today among many of my contemporaries to treat the events of their past with irony. It is a legitimate method of self-defense. 'Look how absurd I was when I was young' forestalls cruel criticism, but it falsifies history. . . . Those emotions were real when we felt them. Why should we be more ashamed of them than of the indifference of old age? I have tried . . . to feel them, as I felt them then, without irony." Though I am only of middle age now, and still capable of experiencing those feelings as I watch Welles's films, the particular tone of youthful passion that invigorated my *Orson Welles* in 1972 seems worthy of retention, so I have decided to keep the language of the book as close to the original version as possible, while revising, augmenting, or eliminating some passages I no longer find valid or which needed clarification in light of more recent scholarship.

The reader will find that, for example, my first attempt at a scene-by-scene reconstruction of Welles's intentions for *The Magnificent Ambersons* (which I based on the shooting script) has been extensively updated in light of Robert L. Carringer's further research into the same subject, published in his 1993 book *The Magnificent Ambersons: A Reconstruction*. Although I disagree with many of Carringer's critical views on the film, his research has helped me be more precise about the differences between the original Welles version and RKO's mutilated release version (Carringer also has done excellent research on *Kane* for his 1985 book *The Making of "Citizen Kane"*). My evaluation of Welles's *Macbeth* has changed considerably in light of the 1980 restoration of Welles's original version, and I have revised my section on the film accordingly. The release of a longer version of *Touch of Evil* in the mid-1970s also occasioned some rethinking of my views, and I have written an entirely new section on *It's All True*, based on watching the 1993 documentary and on information from the research conducted by Robert Stam and by the documentary's researcher, Catherine Benamou (who also wrote about the film in the journal *Persistence of Vision*). Time has enabled me to recognize more virtues in Welles's *The Stranger* than were apparent when I was younger and perhaps a bit less generous toward Welles's rare artistic failures as a director. I have added chapters on Welles's extraordinary 1958 television film *The Fountain of Youth* (first published in the Winter 1971/72 issue of *Sight and Sound*) and on the last major film he completed, *F for Fake* (1974). The concluding chapter on the making of *The Other Side of the Wind* is drawn from the first edition of this book and from my article in the July-August 1976 issue of *American Film*. The opening chapter of this edition, "No Wine Before Its Time," gives an overview of Welles's career from my current perspective; it is adapted from an article I wrote for *The New York Review of Books* (May 13, 1993), "The Lost Kingdom of Orson Welles," which takes as its springboard Welles's autobiographical colloquy with Bogdanovich in *This Is Orson Welles*.

That book, by the way, has done much to clarify Welles's intentions as a filmmaker, and Rosenbaum's 131-page chronology of Welles's career is the current state of the art in that area of research, supplanting my own 35-page "A Catalogue of Orson Welles's Career," which served as an appendix to the 1972 edition of this book (Bret Wood's workmanlike 1990 book *Orson Welles: A Bio-Bibliography* is also useful, containing a wealth of information uncollected elsewhere). For this volume, I have replaced my original appendix with a much shorter one listing the credits for the films Welles directed and the titles of the films in which he acted. For those readers interested in a detailed analysis of Welles's checkered career as a film and television actor, my 1977 book *Orson Welles: Actor and Director* remains the only book-length study of that subject. The present volume does not address most of Welles's extensive work in theater or radio; Simon Callow's 1995 biography of Welles's early years, *Orson Welles: The Road to Xanadu*, brilliantly evokes Welles's theater work in the 1920s and 1930s, as well as giving a vivid sense of his radio career. Much research remains to be done on Welles's work in television, which is represented here by chapters on *The Fountain of Youth* and *The Immortal Story* (the latter was premiered on French television simultaneously with its theatrical release).

One of my conversations with Orson Welles I most fondly remember took place in a Hollywood television studio in 1978, when I was an audience member and observer during the taping of a segment for his unsold pilot for a television talk show, an experience I wrote about in an article for *Film Comment*, "All's Welles" (November/December 1978). While his technicians were scurrying around in a break from the shooting, Welles, perched on a chair in the middle of the studio, spied me jotting something on a pad of paper. He cocked an eyebrow quizzically in my direction and glared at me facetiously, addressing me by the name of my comical film critic character in *The Other Side of the Wind*: "Mister Pister . . . taking notes for his *third volume?*" At the time, I thought I might never write another book on Welles. But now that I've had the benefit of seventeen more years to take notes, think about his films, and revise my original work on Welles, I find that I have written that "third volume" he was wondering about.

JOSEPH MCBRIDE
Los Angeles, California
July 1995

1. No Wine Before Its Time

A certain great and powerful king once asked a poet,
"What can I give you of all that I have?" He wisely replied, "Anything, sir . . . except your secret."

—Orson Welles, epigraph to *Mr. Arkadin*

One of Orson Welles's best stories, though not one of his best
films, *Mr. Arkadin* (1955) tells of an aging tycoon of mysterious
origins who becomes terminally anxious that the guilty secrets
of his past will come to light. He hires a venal adventurer to
seek out the people who still remember the truth—and then
has them systematically killed. When it becomes clear that the
scheme has failed and the truth has been unmasked, Arkadin
kills himself by jumping from his plane, vanishing (literally)
into thin air.

Though filmed in Welles's most grandiloquently baroque
manner and studded with dazzling performances from such
character actors as Akim Tamiroff, Katina Paxinou, and Michael Redgrave, *Mr. Arkadin* falls far short of *Citizen Kane* as a
meditation on biography, not only because of wholesale reworking by other hands ("More completely than any other
picture of mine has been hurt by anybody, *Arkadin* was destroyed," Welles told his biographer Barbara Leaming), but
also because of its curiously indifferent portrayals of the two
central characters. Hiding behind egregiously phony beard
and makeup as Gregory Arkadin, Welles seems determined to
keep him as hollow and insubstantial a character as possible,

a symbol rather than a human being, as if illustrating too literally Jorge Luis Borges's description of *Citizen Kane*: "a centerless labyrinth." Welles allows Robert Arden to play Guy Van Stratten, Arkadin's researcher, as an utter fool, devoid of any but the most self-serving motives. Arkadin's contempt for Van Stratten is matched by the director, who displays wrath at those who dare to reveal the darkest secrets of others, even if they've been invited to do so. The emotional "No Trespassing" sign Welles erected in *Arkadin* helps explain why he was so skittish about having his own life probed by interviewers, and why he never managed to write a full-fledged autobiography.

In 1968, Peter Bogdanovich, then a young film journalist and budding director with one undeservedly obscure B-movie (*Targets*) to his name, was invited by Welles to interview him for "a nice little book" intended to "set the record straight" about his life and work. It was a chance to explore and understand the mysteries of a filmmaker long absent from the American scene, a man whose life had become as quasi-mythical as those of his protagonists. But Bogdanovich found that the unexpectedly lengthy and contentious process took on unsettling resemblances to *Mr. Arkadin*: "There were times when I seemed to play a variation of Van Stratten to Welles' personal version of Arkadin, because during our talks (on or off the record), he would get particularly agitated and annoyed about connections made between his work and his own life." Their fragmentary but fascinating interviews, edited by Jonathan Rosenbaum and belatedly (*very* belatedly) published in 1992 as *This Is Orson Welles*, follow the jigsaw-puzzle method Welles favored in approaching the mysteries of a great man's life, but they reveal as much about Welles's stubborn resistance to the autobiographical impulse as they do about the man and his films.

During the seven years in which those interviews were conducted and in the remaining years of his life, Welles was seen by the public mostly in embarrassingly silly television appearances, trading quips with Johnny Carson, clowning with Dean Martin, doing magic tricks for Merv Griffin, and serving as a commercial pitchman who vowed to "sell no wine before its time." Even as his youthful triumph with *Citizen Kane* became the subject of increasing reverence, the living Orson Welles became a national mockery: the butt of Carson's fat jokes and, even more damagingly, the object of condescension from those who felt that he was "wasting his talent."

Made with virtually unprecedented artistic freedom when Welles was only twenty-five, *Kane* became both his glory and his curse: everything after it couldn't help seeming like an anticlimax, no matter what else he achieved. In retrospect, all of Welles's later problems could be traced back to their roots in that too-early success, the unrealistic expectations it raised, and the virulent reaction against it by Hearst and Hollywood. *Kane* barely escaped being burned to placate the powerful publisher who served as the partial model for its central character, and though the film was a critical sensation, RKO had trouble finding theaters willing to play it. "Nobody would book it—they were scared," Welles recalled.

Welles's second feature, his adaptation of Booth Tarkington's *The Magnificent Ambersons*, might have surpassed the artistic achievement of *Kane* if it had not been mutilated by the panicky and increasingly hostile studio following a disastrous preview in Pomona. This Midwestern equivalent of Chekhov's *The Cherry Orchard*—a somber tale of a city that "befouled itself and darkened its sky" with the coming of the automobile—had the misfortune to be released when audiences were flocking to sunny fare as an escape from the dark headlines of World War II. After being cut by forty-three minutes and partially reshot, *Ambersons* was dumped onto the market on a double bill with the Lupe Velez comedy *Mexican Spitfire Sees a Ghost*, and soon was pulled from distribution. Bogdanovich has described its cutting as "the greatest artistic tragedy in the movies," and Welles lamented, "They destroyed *Ambersons*, and the picture itself destroyed me."

Welles was recalled from South America, where he was in the midst of shooting a goodwill documentary for RKO and the U.S. government, *It's All True*. With that film forcibly taken from him and abandoned, he was stripped of his studio contract and sent on the road for a lifetime as what he called a "a migratory worker. I go where the jobs are, like a cherry picker. . . . I had luck as no one had. Afterwards, I had the worst bad luck in the history of the cinema, but that is in the order of things: I had to pay for having had the best luck in the history of the cinema."

The major achievements with which Welles followed *Kane* and *Ambersons* also tended to fall into the category of *film maudit*—whether because of bizarre filming difficulties (*Othello*, recently "restored" in a crisp new print but with its music and dialogue altered in ways that would have appalled the director); reworking and contemptuous burial by the front office (*Touch of Evil*, which can be seen in a longer version containing more of Welles's footage as well as more scenes interpolated by a studio hack director); or because of repeated attacks by the *New York Times'* Bosley Crowther, who almost singlehandedly scared off U.S. exhibitors (*Chimes at Midnight*, which the philistine pundit called "a confusing patchwork of scenes and characters" with a "fuzzy and incomprehensible" soundtrack).

Chimes at Midnight (1966) is based on Shakespeare's cycle of plays about King Henry IV, Prince Hal (later Henry V), and his corpulent boon companion, Sir John Falstaff, whom Welles called "one of the only great characters in all dramatic literature who is essentially *good*." Anticipating his own end, Falstaff tells Hal with urgent warmth, "[B]anish plump Jack, and banish all the world!" I've always felt that line—indeed, Welles's whole glorious performance as Falstaff—was Welles's own passionate rebuff to those who used his girth to belittle him. Not only was Falstaff a character Welles was born to play, but *Chimes* was a film he had spent much of his life preparing to direct. He first played Falstaff when he was a boy, at the Todd School in Woodstock, Illinois; at the age of twenty-three he played the role again in his 1939 Theatre Guild/Mercury Theater condensation of several of Shakespeare's history plays, *Five Kings*. Telescoping and editing Shakespeare further for his and Hilton Edwards's 1960 Belfast and Dublin stage production titled *Chimes at Midnight*, and finally for the film version, Welles sharpened his focus on the larger-than-life figure of Falstaff and on the themes that concerned him most. He poured into the rich, melancholy story a lifetime of thoughts and feelings about such profound matters as old age and mortality, the betrayal of love and friendship, and the true meaning of honor, fatherhood, and kingly responsibility.

For all its virtuosity, and even while performing the rare feat of believably conjuring up a long-vanished world, *Chimes* resolutely avoids "technical surprises or shocks," Welles said, because "everything of importance in the film should be found on the faces." In *Chimes at Midnight*, as in the similarly elegiac *The Magnificent Ambersons*, Welles's usually dominant camera remains the servant of his characters: for, as he remarked, "There is a more personal feeling in those films, a deeper emotion."

The first time I saw *Chimes* was on the last night of its five-day run in Chicago in 1967; the theater was scheduled to turn into a soft-core porno house the following day, so I sat through it three times that night, not knowing when I would ever be able to see again the film I considered (and still do) Welles's masterpiece. I remember how the grizzled old winos who made up much of the audience reveled in Falstaff's humor, not fazed by the Elizabethan language; if Welles's film could please these groundlings, it could have pleased anybody, I felt at the time, but it was not to be. Welles's last chance for popular success had passed, and his career would be increasingly marginalized from that time forward, despite his valiant efforts to reclaim his reputation. The only two theatrical films Welles managed to complete in the last seventeen years of his life, *F for Fake* (1974) and *Filming "Othello"* (1978), are delightful intellectual divertissements, but since they fell into the hard-to-book category of "film essays," they barely left a trace in this country.

Most of Welles's creative energies in his later years were invested in shooting an ambitious film that hasn't (yet) reached the screen, *The Other Side of the Wind*, writing scripts that never made it before the camera, and trying to raise completion money from people who feared his largely undeserved reputation as a wastrel. That reputation, I can't help thinking, stemmed as much from his corpulence as from his track record as a director; if you're a maverick filmmaker weighing close to four hundred pounds and constantly in need of money, people are going to assume (however irrationally) that you've been gobbling up the equivalent of a movie each year.

In fact, despite his occasional budget overruns, Welles was a remarkably economical director who invested much of his own money into his work and performed cinematic miracles with meager resources. He proudly told me he used only 180 extras for the magnificent Battle of Shrewsbury sequence in *Chimes at Midnight*, an overwhelming distillation of the horrors of war into a percussively edited five-minute montage which moves from the glorious spectacle of charging knights to the ignominious agony of hand-to-hand combat in the muddy battleground. Welles's entire body of work no doubt cost less than one of today's monstrously budgeted extravaganzas. The real problem with Welles was that though he functioned in a popular art form he was not the sort of ambidextrous popular artist who, as he once said of John Huston, "can make a masterpiece or turn you out a blockbuster—or *both.*"

In the view of critic and biographer Charles Higham, whose books on Welles are riddled with factual errors and reductive judgments, Welles's problems in later years all boiled down to a crippling "fear of completion." This is a facile explanation that leaves out much in the way of historical and cultural context but nevertheless contains a germ of truth. After returning to Hollywood filmmaking for the first time in more than a decade, hoping to exorcise the RKO experience, Welles was lastingly traumatized by Universal's takeover of *Touch of Evil* (1958) and his dismissal from the final stages of cutting while the studio tried to reduce the complexity of his unorthodox style.[1] He never directed another Hollywood stu-

---

[1] A lengthy excerpt from Welles's fifty-eight-page memorandum to Universal studio chief Edward Muhl about the cutting appeared in the Fall 1992 issue of *Film Quarterly*. Welles's eloquent blend of diplomatic cajolery and sarcasm in arguing for his "jealous sentiments of ownership" is heartbreaking to read: "That I was denied even the right to consultation with you is a hard fact strongly hinting that, of all people, I must be the least welcome as a critic. In spite of this—and in fairness to a picture which you now describe as 'exceptionally entertaining'—I must ask that you open your mind for a moment to

dio film, and resisted some of the occasional offers that came his way to do so, while others he didn't resist never came to fruition; he told me in 1971 that John Calley, when he was production head of Warner Bros. in the late Sixties, called him in and offered to let him direct any film he wanted. "I told him I couldn't do it, because I can't get up at six o'clock every morning," Welles admitted. That sounds flippant, but the fact was that Welles was temperamentally unable to work on an assembly line. As a member of the ensemble cast of *The Other Side of the Wind* throughout its six years of production (1970-76), I saw firsthand that he preferred to work on his own schedule, as only Chaplin before him was able to do, because Chaplin also invested his own money in his films: Welles took days off when he felt like it, to think about the next scenes or simply to nap and gather his energies—and then he'd wear out his young crews by working eighteen hours straight, day after day, night after night, until *they* dropped or rebelled.

Welles's reputation for not completing films began with his ill-fated departure for Brazil in early 1942 to make *It's All True*, leaving the postproduction of *Ambersons* in the hands of subordinates who proved unable or unwilling to stand up to studio pressure. Although Welles unquestionably bears a large share of the responsibility for what happened in his absence, it is simplistic to blame the *Ambersons* debacle primarily on his self-destructive tendencies, as Robert L. Carringer does in his 1993 book *The Magnificent Ambersons: A Reconstruction*. Carringer, like Higham before him, downplays the combined effect of the inhospitable wartime mood and the other powerful factors that were operating against *Ambersons*: Welles's feeling of patriotic obligation to make *It's All True* because of his draft-deferred status; his simultaneous conflicts with RKO over that film; a disruptive change of studio administrations; and the studio's reneging on promises to keep him involved in the

---

this opinion from the man who, after all, made the picture." Muhl turned a deaf ear to many of the suggestions made by Welles in the memo.

cutting of *Ambersons* by long distance, even though he had surrendered the right of final cut in his contract.

It's All True, a three-part film about peasant life in Brazil and Mexico, had to be hastily started in time for the Rio Carnival, and experienced a myriad of production calamities on the far-flung locations, including the death of a leading cast member when a raft capsized. Welles was blamed, largely unfairly, for most of what went wrong. But RKO's displeasure with *Ambersons* and with *It's All True*'s sympathetic treatment of impoverished blacks and mestizos were the decisive factors in the studio's decision to pull the plug on the offbeat film: RKO's unit production manager on *It's All True*, Lynn Shores, complained to the Brazilian Department of Press and Propaganda that Welles's "continued exploitation of the negro [sic] and the low class element in and around Rio" was "in very bad taste." Shores reported to RKO that Welles had been shooting in "some very dirty and disreputable nigger neighborhoods throughout the city," and described one week's worth of samba footage as "just carnival nigger singing and dancing, of which we already have piles." Although *It's All True* was long considered a lost film (some of it literally was dumped into the Pacific Ocean), a partial restoration—including the stunning, virtually complete *Four Men on a Raft* segment and a documentary history of the production—was released by Paramount in 1993.

Hollywood always looked askance at Welles after his firing by RKO, occasionally tossing him an offbeat crime thriller to direct (*The Stranger, The Lady from Shanghai, Touch of Evil*), but greenlighting only one of his pet projects (*Macbeth*, filmed with panache as a Republic quickie), while giving him more frequent employment as a prematurely aged, glowering character actor. His many years in European exile after the late 1940s saw him, out of necessity, embracing what François Truffaut called "his position as an avant-garde director," evolving a looser, even more daringly idiosyncratic style in such films as *Othello, Mr. Arkadin, The Trial,* and *Chimes at Midnight,* breaking out of studio sets into expressionistically transformed natural surroundings and relying more on elaborate sleight-of-hand montage than on the long takes he favored at RKO.

While his output abroad was intermittent, his difficulties completing films did not become chronic until his later years, when old stories about his youthful misadventures scared away potential investors and the films he did start shooting often were bedevilled with financial and legal problems, some of his own making, since he was never a good businessman.

But whatever anxiety Welles undoubtedly felt about his career, no "fear of completion" or surrender to feelings of victimization stopped him from continuing to shoot film until the very day of his death, while continually pouring into his work the money he earned by making himself a figure of ridicule on TV shows, in other people's movies, and in even more demeaning commercial appearances. He paid a high price in public derision for his tenacity in continuing to make his own mostly unseen movies: the jokes gradually became conventional journalistic wisdom.

Anyone under the illusion that Welles was slothful or creatively dormant at any time of his life should start by browsing through *This Is Orson Welles*'s exhaustive, and exhausting, 131-page chronology of Welles's career, which takes the reader almost day-by-day from 1918, when the subject was three ("Makes his stage debut as walk-on in *Samson and Delilah* at the Chicago Opera"), to October 10, 1985, when he was seventy ("OW dies of a heart attack early in the morning at his house in Hollywood while typing stage directions for the material he plans to shoot with [his cameraman, Gary Graver] at UCLA later today"). The vast body of work listed in films, TV, theater, radio, recordings, journalism, literature, and other fields would be enough for several normal lifetimes. To Welles's great credit, his work has a gloriously unpredictable diversity, and if he had been allowed to make some of his unmade film projects, it would have been even more impossible to pigeonhole him.

Those of us who have written about Welles have only begun to describe the full richness of his career, in part because his career still is not finished. Much of Welles's late work was left uncompleted when he died—notably *The Other Side of the Wind*, his satirical meditation on filmmaking and machismo,

with John Huston playing an aging, Hemingwayesque director. Welles managed to put together only a partial rough cut
of the film before he died, but he did shoot virtually all the
footage he needed, and efforts are still underway to have the
film released. (My two accounts of the filming, written in 1970
and 1976, are contained in Chapter 15 of this book, along with
some afterthoughts from today's perspective.)

Like the unfinished Welles movies—which also include a
thriller called *The Deep* and a shortened version of *The Merchant of Venice*, as well as his decades-in-the-works adaptation
of *Don Quixote*[2]—*This Is Orson Welles*, based on Bogdanovich's
interviews with Welles between 1968 and 1975, had a checkered, somewhat mysterious past. The book was put aside after
Welles decided he wanted to write his memoirs first (he never
wrote more than a few pages before he died) and it seemed
destined to be buried, like Rosebud, in some dusty warehouse
before being tossed in the fire after Welles's death because of
an unpaid storage bill. "I thought from the mid-Seventies that
we'd never see it," Bogdanovich told me. "It was Orson's idea

---

[2]A version of *Don Quixote* assembled by Jess Franco and first shown publicly
in Spain in 1992 suffers from the film's erratic production and post-production
history. The print quality (unlike that of scenes shown elsewhere) is poor, the
editing (only partly by Welles) is often ragged and indulgent, some important
scenes are missing, and the soundtrack of the English-language version is an
off-putting mélange of dubbed voices. Since the actors playing Don Quixote
and Sancho Panza (Francisco Reiguera and Akim Tamiroff) both died before
Welles could finish the film, their voices had to be supplied by the director
and other actors. Even if Welles had finished it, his sometimes inspired, sometimes slapdash *Quixote* clearly would not have been the masterwork we might
have hoped it would be. But Tamiroff's bountiful embodiment of the earthy
Sancho is the performance of his life, and the cadaverous Reiguera looks like
a Gustave Doré illustration of Quixote sprung magically to life. Welles's adventurous visual style mixes formal compositions reminiscent of John Ford
and El Greco with playful *nouvelle vague*-ish scenes of the Don and Sancho
wandering bemusedly through the alien landscape of Franco's Spain. Sancho
even meets up with Welles and becomes an extra in the film we are watching,
but Quixote rails against the tools of filmmaking as "demonic instruments"
and rides off disgustedly for the Moon, the last frontier where "there may still
be room for knight errantry." Welles's *Quixote* is his wry, melancholic valen-
tine to Cervantes's blinkered visionary, whom the filmmaker loves for fighting
wrongs with "so much heart and so few means," and to the Don's profoundly
human squire, "a personality marvelous even in his stupidity."

to do it, Orson's idea how to do it, and his idea not to publish it, so I couldn't really argue."

For such a notorious egoist, Welles showed a surprising resistance to the confessional genre of literature, going only so far in the field of formal autobiography as to produce haunting fragments for the French *Vogue*'s Christmas 1982 issue. Those reminiscences of his mother and father, suffused with equal amounts of wonderment and gloom, have the tantalizing effect of a door being briefly cracked open onto the darkest recesses of Welles's psyche, and then as quickly being closed. The seriocomic word-picture of his father, the eccentric businessman, inventor, and *bon vivant* Richard Welles, ends with a startling and mysterious *coup de théâtre*: Welles confesses that as a child he was "convinced—as I am now—that I had killed my father. (I'll try to write about this later.)"

With such a topic looming on the horizon, it's little wonder Welles resisted the autobiographical impulse his admirers and vicissitudes of fortune might otherwise have dictated. Another reason Welles may have avoided doing so was to avoid dealing candidly with his own sexuality. In his shrewdly analytical 1995 biography *Orson Welles: The Road to Xanadu*, Simon Callow persuasively identifies an "area of sexual ambiguity [which] persists throughout the early part of Welles's life, striking a note of considerable complexity." That note can be heard echoing between the lines of the intense male relationships that form the dramatic center of Welles's work. The theme of sexual ambiguity emerged more openly in such late Welles projects as *The Other Side of the Wind* and his unproduced but posthumously published screenplay *The Big Brass Ring*. But rather than exploring the complexity of his own life history through the medium of autobiography, Welles, as Callow observes, chose instead "to rewrite history in his ongoing memoir, the story of his life as relayed to the press of the world over many years." Welles spoke frequently about homosexuality to Barbara Leaming for her 1985 *Orson Welles: A Biography*, but only to keep denying that he ever succumbed in his youth to what he portrayed as the constant advances of older men: "From my earliest childhood I was the Lillie Langtry of the older homosexual set. Everybody wanted me. I had a very bad way of turning these guys off. I thought it would embarrass them if I said I wasn't homosexual, that that would be a rebuke, so I always had a headache. You know, I was like an eternal virgin."

The sheer volume of the reminiscences Welles gave to Leaming for her biography—which the subject was promoting with the author in his last TV appearance on *The Merv Griffin Show* the night before his death—seems to have overwhelmed Leaming, who uncritically adopted Welles's point of view throughout. Welles's apparent generosity was, in fact, a smokescreen to keep Leaming (or a less malleable biographer) from probing more deeply. "I think there is a movie in the story of somebody who's getting a biography written about him," Welles told her. "I think finally the biographer comes with a pistol and shoots the subject." Leaming's entertaining but mostly superficial book may have been all Welles thought he owed the public, but it left the reader yearning for something more substantial.

This Is Orson Welles, despite its major and incidental pleasures, doesn't live up to the all-embracing autobiographical promise of its title. It's too loosely structured and too concentrated on filmmaking to be entirely satisfying as a substitute autobiography of a man with such a multifaceted personality. Welles imposed the book's free-associating organizing principle, and Rosenbaum's editing sometimes seems weighed down by the disorderliness of the material. But given the subject's brilliance as a raconteur, it probably would have been foolish to have stopped him from following his own conversational course in order to rearrange the book into a tidy chronological package. "I like digressions, don't you?" Welles remarks while discussing a joke cut by RKO from *The Magnificent Ambersons.* "Look at Gogol. Read the first few pages of *Dead Souls* again and you'll see how one mad little digression can give reverberation and density to ordinary narrative." The digressions into subjects that relate only tangentially (or not at all) to filmmaking—*The War of the Worlds,* comic books, FDR—or Welles's ruminations on such diverse literary sources as Shakespeare, Tarkington, and Bram Stoker are so compelling to make one wish for more, not less, of such asides, drawing from other aspects of Welles's personality. Such as his comment on why he was happiest as an actor on radio: "It's as close as you can get, and still get paid for it, to the great, private joy of singing in the bathtub. The microphone's a friend, you know. The camera's a critic." Or his reflection on history: "This hand that touches you now once touched the hand of Sarah Bernhardt—can you imagine that? . . . When she was young, Mademoiselle Bernhardt had taken the hand of Madame George, who had been the mistress of *Napoleon!* . . . Peter —*just three handshakes from Napoleon!* It's not that the world is so small, but that history is so short. Four or five very old men could join hands and take you right back to Shakespeare." (Callow reports, however, that it was not Welles but his actor friend Micheál MacLiammóir who in fact touched the hand of Sarah Bernhardt. Welles could not resist appropriating the event for his own observation.)

The virtue of the rambling style of *This Is Orson Welles* is that it allows the reader the opportunity of eavesdropping for a few hours on a great conversationalist. In the four-hour companion package of audio tapes, the pleasure can be savored even more palpably. Welles's magisterial baritone and his great convulsing, Falstaffian laugh, accompanied by the intimate sounds of his match lighting a cigar and ice cubes clinking in his glass of Scotch, are preserved in these highlights from their conversations. After the tapes were transcribed, Bogdanovich edited them, added contextual material from production memoranda and other documents, and sent each chapter to Welles, "typed as he had requested, the left side of the page blank for him to rewrite. Eventually, a few months later, a chapter would come back, thoroughly revised, heavily rewritten at times (including some of my own remarks). I understood Orson occasionally altered things for dramatic purposes, and if it was good for the 'cause' to have me a little more gauche or pushy, why would it matter?"

Welles shaped the book in much the same way he edited his films: Welles's film footage, as Truffaut once put it, was "shot by an exhibitionist and edited by a censor," attaining an intensified musical intricacy and dialectical tension in the process. The book's careful reshaping from the more spontaneous raw material not only gives the illusion of a free-flowing conversation but also allows Welles to skip over or obfuscate topics he doesn't want to explore more fully or precisely.

Welles's often merciless ragging of Bogdanovich—a very good sport and cheerful masochist—served as a sort of rough draft for the film that was germinating in Welles's mind at the time their interviews began and whose start of production, as the tapes of the interviews reveal, was triggered by something Bogdanovich said to Welles about Hollywood's neglect of old directors. *The Other Side of the Wind* is centered around a birthday party for the legendary director played by John Huston, and it mocks and decries the interview process by which overly possessive film buffs, in Welles's view, simultaneously worship and assault their idols. When the film started shooting, Bogdanovich and I were cast as a pair of fatuous interviewers (Charles Higgam [*sic*] and Mr. Pister) who follow Huston's Jake Hannaford around, peppering him with incessant questions. During one scene in Hannaford's car, I ask him, "In the body of your film work, how would you relate the trauma of your father's suicide?"—and get thrown out of the car in retaliation.

When Bogdanovich became a celebrated director himself with *The Last Picture Show* in 1971, he helped Welles with the independent production of *The Other Side of the Wind*, even letting him live at his Bel-Air mansion and shoot parts of the film there when Bogdanovich was in Europe making Daisy Miller. But the tensions between him and Welles increased considerably, especially after Bogdanovich tried and failed to find Welles a directing job in the Hollywood studios. Welles recast Bogdanovich in *The Other Side of the Wind* as a Prince Hal–like director and left me with most of the arcane and intrusive film-buff questions.

Welles's resentment of what he saw as the curse of overly intellectualized probing of the artist's mind comes across throughout the Bogdanovich interviews. "He felt like certain comics do, that if you have to explain a joke, it must be bad," Bogdanovich reports. When Bogdanovich prods him to verbalize "the meaning of the exchange of looks [among] Prince Hal and the king and Falstaff over Percy's body"—one of the most beautiful, purely visual scenes in *Chimes at Midnight*—Welles replies with exasperation, "If that isn't clear, it speaks pretty badly for me." He repeatedly mocks Bogdanovich for asking "one of those searching, penetrating questions I thought we'd avoid," and admits, "The whole purpose of a book like this is what I quarrel with." When Bogdanovich tries "to argue about your impatience with the search for themes," Welles responds, "Luckily, we know almost nothing about Shakespeare and very little about Cervantes. And that makes it so much easier to understand their works. . . . It's an egocentric, romantic, nineteenth-century conception that the artist is more interesting and more important than his art."

But Bogdanovich was unrelenting in his quest for connections between Welles's inner life and his work.

> Bogdanovich: Why did you decide to begin *Othello* with the funeral?
>
> Welles: Why not? [*Laughs*] I don't know. Have another drink.
>
> Bogdanovich: Well, it couldn't be coincidental that *Kane, Othello,* and *Mr. Arkadin* all begin with the death of the leading character. . . .
>
> Welles: Just shows a certain weakness of invention on the part of the filmmaker.
>
> Bogdanovich: You can give me a better answer than that.
>
> Welles: Peter, I'm no good at this sort of stuff. I either go cryptic or philistine.

Of course, Welles doth protest too much, for no filmmaker was ever more articulate, or less of a philistine. When he turned his mind to it, as he did for much of his time with Bogdanovich, Welles could give the kind of interview that justifies the existence of the process. A powerful example: when Bogdanovich made Welles "so sick, I couldn't sleep" by telling him about John Ford and the other old directors who couldn't find work in the "with-it" Hollywood of the late 1960s—the discussion that led Welles to start filming *The Other Side of the Wind*—Welles exploded: "It's so *awful*. I think it's just terrible what happens to old people. But the public isn't interested in that—never has been. That's why *Lear* has always been a play people hate."

"You don't think Lear became senile?" asks Bogdanovich.

And Welles responds, "He became senile by giving *power* away. The only thing that keeps people alive in their old age is power. . . . But take power away from de Gaulle or Churchill or Tito or Mao or Ho or any of these old men who run the world—in this world that belongs only to young people—and you'll see a 'babbling, slippered pantaloon.'

"It's only in your twenties and in your seventies and eighties that you do the greatest work. The enemy of society is the middle class, and the enemy of life is middle age. Youth and old age are great times—and we must treasure old age and give genius the capacity to function in old age—and not send them away. . . . "

Such moments of unguarded passion are all too rare in *This Is Orson Welles*. Some of Welles's sparring exchanges with Bogdanovich are wry and revealing—especially the running joke about Bogdanovich deviously steering the protesting Welles back to the painful (to him) subject of *Citizen Kane*—but more often we share the interviewer's frustration over Welles's reticence, which ultimately becomes exasperating. Reading this book helps us understand why Welles never was able to complete a conventional autobiography. His participation in this enterprise seems half-hearted; he sits for a lengthy session of analysis but displays an almost neurotic aversion to introspection, evidently stemming from an ingrained fear of having to share his deepest feelings to the public, or from a self-protective need to portray himself as "a centerless labyrinth."

Welles's films show some of the same ambivalence toward the necessary process of artistic self-revelation; the twin roles of exhibitionist and censor always vied for his attention. Despite his reputation as a ham, which stemmed in part from the inescapable largeness of his body and voice, Welles never seemed entirely comfortable as an actor, and (especially in later years) he accepted parts mainly to make money to finance his directing ventures. He frequently seemed overly studied, guarded, and stiff on screen, taking refuge behind theatrical floridity and tongue-in-cheek jocularity. He worried that he seldom "really felt" what he was playing, and he almost never (except as Harry Lime in Carol Reed's *The Third Man*) appeared on screen without a false nose and other makeup to transform his appearance. It was no coincidence that Harry Lime was the character he most detested of all those he played on screen: "I hate Harry Lime," he said. "He has no passion; he is cold; he is Lucifer, the fallen angel." And he told Bogdanovich, "I read once—Norman Mailer wrote something or other—that, when I was young, I was the most beautiful man anybody had ever seen. Yes! Made up for *Citizen Kane!*" Hiding his naked face was a lifelong obsession for Welles, as if he had a terrible secret to hide, something shameful to cover up—something for which his face was his actor's metaphor. He used makeup as "camouflage" to fend off invasion of his emotional privacy, just as, at the age of ten, he scared off bullies at Washington Grade School in Madison, Wisconsin, by carrying his makeup kit to school and making himself up with a bloody face.

In the films he directed, Welles typically played emotionally barricaded, self-disguising characters whose moral makeup was far removed from his own, or whose flaws exaggerated his own more pardonable vices and failings for dramatic effect. He hid behind the grotesque corpulence of the corrupt cop Hank Quinlan in *Touch of Evil*, the waxen face and walrus mustache of the moribund Macao merchant Mr. Clay in *The Immortal Story*, or the protean features of Charles Foster Kane, revealing his feelings about their moral dilemmas less through his acting than through his intricately rhetorical and frequently ironic camerawork, giving himself a dual presence in the films. Rarely did he allow himself to express a naked emotion on screen through his acting alone, although when he did so as Falstaff, in the great rejection scene when Prince Hal/King Henry V (Keith Baxter) says "I know thee not, old man"—a scene devastating in its simplicity—it became the defining moment of his career.

Bogdanovich recalls the "strangely conspiratorial quality Orson and I fell into almost at once," and it was the younger man's ability to discern the areas of greatest emotional vulnerability in Welles that made Welles try to retreat so vehemently from the revelations demanded of him. "Orson had been burned in so many places in his emotional and personal life, he was afraid of being hurt again," Bogdanovich realized. "He preferred to talk about something new, something that wasn't in the past, something that was possible to change."

Bogdanovich's patient wheedling, his willingness to put up with so much mockery, and his thorough grounding in Welles's work counterbalance his limitations as an interviewer, which are most glaringly seen in his lack of awareness of the sociopolitical aspects of Welles's work: of *Ambersons,* he confesses to Welles, "You know, it wasn't until about the fourth or fifth time I'd seen the picture that I saw any social points." But Bogdanovich's tenacious cajoling of his recalcitrant subject arose from a fervent curiosity about Welles which wouldn't take "no comment" for an answer.

"No, Peter, I have no 'Rosebuds,'" Welles insists when Bogdanovich probes into Welles's cinematic reflections of his relationship with his mother, whose death when he was nine caused him lifelong emotional devastation. But that line triggers the book's most moving personal reminiscence, about the young Orson's stays with his father, who in his later years owned the picturesque Sheffield House Hotel in Grand Detour, Illinois:

"Well, where I do see some kind of 'Rosebud,' perhaps, is in that world of Grand Detour. A childhood there was like a childhood back in the 1870s. No electric light, horse-drawn buggies—a completely anachronistic, old-fashioned, early-Tarkington, rural kind of life, with a country store that had above it a ballroom with an old dance floor with springs in it, so that folks would feel light on their feet. When I was little, nobody had danced up there for many years, but I used to sneak up at night and dance by moonlight with the dust rising from the floor. . . . Grand Detour was one of those lost worlds, one of those Edens that you get thrown out of. . . . I feel as though I've had a childhood in the last century from those short summers."

Welles's reverie about this "marvelous little corner in time," his own personal Twilight Zone—which he readily concedes found lasting resonance in *Ambersons* and his other work— comes to a painfully abrupt end when his memory inevitably turns to the fire that destroyed his father's hotel two years before Richard Welles's death in 1930. "Can I go now?" Welles asks Bogdanovich, and you can hear the childish plaintiveness in his voice as the chapter closes.

Strikingly similar in mood to the autobiographical frag- ments about his childhood in the French *Vogue*, this story shows what we lost when Welles found that he couldn't write a book about his life. In bringing the Grand Detour story to an elliptical conclusion, Welles barely elaborates on what his soli- tary dance in the moonlight meant to him, although we can take that dance as an image for the odd, lonely childhood that shaped him as an artist and to which he kept retreating sym- bolically for his cinematic "lost Edens"—as geographically dis- parate as Mrs. Kane's Colorado boardinghouse, the Amber- sons' Indianapolis mansion, Don Quixote's Spain, Falstaff's Merrie Old England. Perhaps Welles never allowed us closer to his "secret" than he did in his mysterious reference to his responsibility for his father's death, which may have been the prototype for all the betrayals of close friends and flawed fa- ther figures in his films.

Although Richard Welles's death certificate says he died of natural causes (chronic heart and kidney disease) in a Chicago hotel, Higham's 1985 biography *Orson Welles: The Rise and Fall of an American Genius* and Frank Brady's *Citizen Welles* (1989) report that the elder Welles might have been a suicide, and Callow's biography judges those "persistent rumors" to be "perfectly feasible." According to Barbara Leaming, "the young Orson told people that he was present at his father's suicide," but she thinks that didn't literally happen and that Welles's claim "only reflected his own intense guilt . . . at hav- ing betrayed Dick when he needed him." As Callow comments, "What matters here is not proof one way or the other (quite obviously he did not physically kill his father) but the fact that he felt that he was, at the deepest level, responsible for his father's death. He was already riven with guilt about him." Welles felt his alcoholic father "drank himself to death," and he blamed himself for pushing Dick Welles over the edge by listening to the advice of friends and refusing to see his father again unless he stopped drinking. This story calls to mind Peto's epitaph on Falstaff in *Chimes at Midnight:* "The King has killed his heart." Welles subsequently considered his action "inexcusable," telling Leaming, "I don't want to forgive myself. That's why I hate psychoanalysis. I think if you're guilty of something you should live with it."

Welles's reminiscences of his father and Grand Detour reverberate in *This Is Orson Welles* when Bogdanovich succeeds in eliciting from Welles a precise definition of his work's thematic core. In a exchange on the gracefulness of Tarkington's lost Eden, Bogdanovich asks, "That's the thing you admire most, isn't it? That and gallantry. Isn't *Ambersons* as much a story of the end of chivalry—the end of gallantry—as *Chimes at Midnight?*" Welles corrects him by saying, "Peter, what interests me is the *idea* of these dated old virtues. And why they still seem to speak to us when, by all logic, they're so hopelessly irrelevant. That's why I've been obsessed so long with *Don Quixote.*" Welles was, in many ways, his own best critic, pointing the way for professional critics to see his work more clearly and precisely.

In talking with Bogdanovich about Joseph Cotten's character in *Citizen Kane,* drama critic Jedediah Leland, who in the bitterness of his old age muses that he might have served both as Charlie Kane's "stooge" and as his only friend, Welles points out, "I'm a totally different kind of person from Jed Leland. I'm not a friend of the hero." When dealing with Welles and other legendary directors, the young Bogdanovich cast himself in the role of "friend of the hero," and his surprisingly intense argument with Welles about Jed Leland is one of this book's most revealing passages.

Welles vehemently objects to Bogdanovich's notion that Leland betrayed Kane by writing his negative review of Kane's pathetically inept opera-singing mistress, Susan Alexander (Dorothy Comingore). "He didn't betray Kane," Welles says of Jed Leland. "Kane betrayed him. Because he was not the man he pretended to be. . . . If there was any betrayal, it was on Kane's part, because he signed a Declaration of Principles which he never kept." "Then why," wonders Bogdanovich, "is there a feeling that Leland is petty and mean to Kane in the scene when he gets drunk? . . . [M]aybe one feels that Leland could have afforded to write a good review." "Not and been a man of principle," Welles insists. "Then why do I somewhat dislike Leland?" asks Bogdanovich. "Because he likes principles more than the man," Welles replies, "and he doesn't have the size as a person to love Kane for his faults."

I suspect that Bogdanovich may have been thinking of that exchange when he wrote, "There are quite a few things I didn't agree with Orson about in those days, but most assuredly I do now. Age and experience." The Bogdanovich who wrote those words in his conciliatory introduction to what Welles initially proposed as "a nice little book" now has the size as a person to love Welles for *his* faults. Welles displayed jealousy over his protégé's commercial success, resented the failure of Bogdanovich's efforts to help him find work in Hollywood, and feuded with him over their book, which, Bogdanovich relates, eventually became "lost somewhere in the depths of a storage facility while I was going through a personal and financial crisis."

When Welles accused Bogdanovich of saving the manuscript to release only after his death, Bogdanovich retrieved it and sent it back to him "with a note saying, in effect, it was his life, and here it was for him to do with as he saw fit." Welles was "very touched" by the gesture. Bogdanovich writes of their last conversation over the telephone, shortly before Welles's death: "We had been laughing, and then I said something about having made some terrible mistakes. He said, suddenly serious, that *he* had made so *many* mistakes, and that it seemed to be almost impossible to go through life without making an incredible number of them.... I came to realize our last conversation had been a kind of apology from both of us for having made mistakes about each other."

Though it might have seemed so to Welles, and to Bogdanovich at many times over the years because of the obstacles Welles placed in the way of its publication, *This Is Orson Welles* is not one of their mistakes, but a fitting, if imperfect, memorial to their complex and passionate friendship. As such the book is a further reflection of a central theme of Welles's work, the troubled relationship between surrogate father and rebellious son, and the tendency for that friendship to end in misunderstanding and feelings of betrayal. But as the book's editor, Jonathan Rosenbaum, writes elsewhere, "It somehow seems fitting that in order to piece together Orson Welles's autobiography, we have to turn to his creative work."

2. Apprentice Work

Welles seldom volunteered to interviewers that he did any experimentation in film before coming to Hollywood, undoubtedly preferring the world to think that he burst full-blown on the scene with *Citizen Kane*. To an interviewer who asked him how he arrived at *Kane*'s "cinematic innovations," he replied airily, "I owe it to my ignorance. If this word seems inadequate to you, replace it with innocence." But Welles was not really a filmic innocent.

When I started my research into Welles's career in the late 1960s, I found a few mentions in print, largely unheeded by film historians, of a 16mm film he shot in July 1938 for use in a Mercury Theatre stage production, William Gillette's farce *Too Much Johnson*. The silent slapstick comedy film was never shown publicly. Shortly before the summer tryout of the play opened in Connecticut, the Mercury discovered that Paramount owned the film rights, for which it expected to be paid if the film was shown with the play on Broadway; not only that, but the theater used for the tryout did not have a fireproofed projection booth; and in the end the play never made it to New York anyway. Welles shot what was planned to be a twenty-minute filmed prologue to the play, and ten-minute sequences to introduce the second and third acts. Included in the cast of the film were Joseph Cotten, Edgar Barrier, Arlene Francis, John Houseman, Marc Blitzstein, Judith Tuvim (later known as Judy Holliday), and Virginia Nicolson, Welles's first wife (using the stage name Anna Stafford); Welles appeared briefly as a Keystone Kop. The story concerned an 1890s New York rake (Cotten) who is chased to Cuba by his mistress's husband. As Welles told Bogdanovich, "*Too Much Johnson* had an elaborate farce plot that required a lot of old-fashioned, boring exposition to set it up. The idea was to take all that out and do the explaining in a movie. That way you could start right with the slamming doors."

Sadly, the only copy of the film was destroyed in an August 1970 fire at Welles's villa in Madrid which also consumed several unpublished books and unproduced scripts. Welles was sanguine about the loss when I met him three weeks later. "It's probably a good thing," he said. "I never cared much for possessions, but over the years I accumulated a few. Now I can tell everybody how great those scripts were! I wish you could have seen *Too Much Johnson*, though. It was a beautiful film. We created a sort of dream Cuba in New York. I looked at it four years ago and the print was in wonderful condition. You know, I never [fully] edited it. I meant to put it together to give to J. Cotten as a Christmas present one year, but I never got around to it." Welles also assembled a five-minute film from stock footage as prologue to his 1939 vaudeville show, *The Green Goddess*, "depicting an air crash in the Himalayas," according to his associate Richard Wilson; and he shot test scenes for one day in 1939 while preparing his abortive RKO production of Joseph Conrad's *Heart of Darkness*.

Even earlier Welles experiments on film have come to light. Welles told Bogdanovich that his very first movie was a "documentary" made when he was nine years old (i.e., around 1924), during a visit to St. Peter's Basilica in Vatican City. Welles sarcastically described it as "a highly artistic study . . . featuring Significant Architectural Detail. This was handheld throughout, mind you, so it was really way ahead of its time. I got fascinated with that fountain—Antonioni at the very summit of his powers never held a single shot so long. Then, to my horror, the very instant I'd run out of film, the great doors of the cathedral were flung open and, with a mighty fanfare of trumpets, out came the Pope on a palanquin surrounded by Swiss Guards and a hundred cardinals. Well, with an empty camera, you could say I missed the parade. After that experience, I retired as a filmmaker."

The next time Welles used a movie camera, apparently, was in May 1933, while staging a production of Shakespeare's comedy *Twelfth Night* at the Todd School in Woodstock, Illinois, from which he had graduated in 1930. Welles filmed most of the dress rehearsal of the play, in which he appeared as Malvolio. The film was shot in color with a silent-movie camera from a fixed camera position in the auditorium, and a short excerpt was preserved by his schoolmaster Roger Hill and Hill's wife, Hortense. Its existence was revealed by Richard France in his 1977 book *The Theatre of Orson Welles*, which notes that Welles's set design for the play featured "a twelve-foot-high storybook with pages that turned to provide the scene changes," an idea borrowed from a Kenneth MacGowan stage production that Roger Hill had seen in Chicago. In the film, France writes, "A small backdrop is completely covered with a bright stylized rendering of a London street. The style is vaguely post-Impressionistic, and above all one notices the vivid patterns of unrealistic coloring. . . . Welles also narrated the film, and his voice sounds very much as it does today."

In 1969, thanks to a tip from film historian Russell Merritt, I was able to unearth an extremely interesting little piece of Welles juvenilia, made in 1934. A silent film called *The Hearts of Age*, it was preserved in an obscure private collection (I made the first public disclosure of the film's existence in a Spring 1970 article in *Film Quarterly*, "Welles Before *Kane*," upon which this chapter is based). *The Hearts of Age* runs about four minutes and stars Welles and Virginia Nicolson (whose name is spelled Nicholson in the credits); Welles was co-director with a college student named William Vance. The copy I saw, until that time the only one extant, was the original black-and-white 16mm print. It was donated, as part of the Vance collection, to the Greenwich, Connecticut, Public Library. The sound of the splices clicking through the projector was nerve-racking—though the film was in remarkably good condition—but my apprehension about projecting it was more than assuaged by the excitement of discovery. Access to the film subsequently was given to the American Film Institute, and a duplicate negative for preservation was lodged in the Library of Congress; the film has since been released on videotape.

The credit cards list only the title and the actors, but they are in Welles's handwriting. The film was made when he was nineteen, during the six-week "Summer Festival of Drama" he sponsored in 1934 at the Todd School. William Vance, who also produced *The Hearts of Age* and makes a brief appearance in it, was a college student when he met Welles; he later went on to produce and direct television commercials. I saw a ten-minute adaptation of *Dr. Jekyll and Mr Hyde*, made in 1932, which Vance stars in and directed. It is nothing more than a crude and rather risible student movie. *The Hearts of Age* is something more, however. Although Welles told me it could hardly be considered directorial experience, since it was just "a Sunday afternoon home movie," there are many flourishes which point unmistakably to his later work. A few of the shots are eerily prophetic of *Kane*, and the film shows even more than *Kane* the extent to which Welles was under the spell of German theatrical and cinematic expressionism. If some of the camerawork is perfunctory (especially when Welles is not on the screen), many of the shots are beautifully lit and composed, and the general lack of coherence is almost offset by the humor of Welles's performance.

Welles poked gentle fun at me for taking the film seriously, since it was intended, he said, as a rib on Jean Cocteau's *Blood of a Poet* and the whole surrealist school. The character he plays is an old man, apparently a figure of death, and I had taken this to be a foreshadowing of his later fascination with age and corruption. But there was a simpler explanation: he was copying the appearance of the doctor in *The Cabinet of Dr. Caligari*. In any case, the film belongs in the same genre as the "serious" avant-garde shorts of the period. The surrealist movement was itself largely a joke against respectable art, and it's often impossible to draw the line between pretension and put-on in a film such as Man Ray's *Les Mystères du Château du Dé*. Explaining why he made *The Hearts of Age*, Welles told Bogdanovich, "I don't care much for surrealism on the screen. Never did. . . . But it was a put-on."

"It was all a joke," Virginia Nicolson confirmed to Richard France. "There was no script. Orson simply amused himself thinking up totally unrelated sequences to be shot à la grand guignol. Bill Vance, who owned both film and camera, was a movie fiend in those days and went around shooting reel after reel of happenings mainly invented by Orson over a drink."

It would be foolish to try to discuss *The Hearts of Age* as anything but juvenilia, but it does show a vigorous, unguarded, *personal* approach even in its facetious steals from other movies. *Citizen Kane*, we should remember, is also the product of youthful eclecticism. That is part of its charm; its strength, like that of the first *nouvelle vague* films, comes from the integration of these divergent styles into a coherent framework, each part appropriate to the drama. We can see in *The Hearts of Age* that Welles, like many young artists, had to work a penchant for playful in-joking out of his system before being able to create a unified work.

At first the film seems hopelessly muddled. The first shot is of a spinning Christmas tree ball (*Kane!*), which is later repeated and then echoed again when a white-robed figure walks past stroking a globe. After the opening shot, we see a quick montage (much too quick for comfort, with that projector churning away) of bells ringing, some of the shots in negative (the influence of F. W. Murnau's *Nosferatu*). Then we see an old lady—Virginia Nicolson in grotesque makeup—rocking back and forth. The camera, smoothly hand-held in contrast to the jerky camerawork in *Dr. Jekyll*, pulls slowly back to show that she is suggestively straddling a ringing bell. The next shots reveal a man in blackface (Edgerton Paul), wigged and dressed in a lacy little boy's costume incongruously completed by football knickers, pulling the bell-rope, with the old lady on the roof above him. After the second shot of the spinning ball, we see a tilted shot of a gravestone with three elongated shadows moving slowly on the ground behind it, and then a grave marker tilted in the opposite direction with a hand grasped around it.

A shadow hand rings a shadow bell, hazy latticework lighting all around it; in the next shot, the hand-bell falls harshly to the ground, no longer a shadow now. That the nineteen-year-old Welles could conjure up such sophisticated lighting effects shows the influence of several years of theatrical experience, not only with the Todd School's student company as an actor, director, and designer, but also as an actor with Dublin's Gate Theatre company, whose productions (directed by Hilton Edwards) were strongly influenced by German expressionism.

From the ominously falling hand-bell, Welles returns to the old lady riding the larger bell with an obscenely pained expression as the blackfaced man tugs spiritedly away. She opens an umbrella over her head (Welles was also fond of Keaton, who liked to fool around with umbrellas when it wasn't raining). We see a hand spinning a globe in closeup, and then a striking shot, worthy of Murnau: a gray tombstone, dizzily tilted, with a shadow hand creeping up it (a *white* shadow, because the shot is in negative) and beckoning with a long finger, while a corporeal hand crawls along the edge of the stone. We see a piano keyboard—a flashforward, as it turns out—and then Orson Welles opening a door over a rickety flight of stairs.

It is always a strange experience to stumble back upon an early screen appearance of one of the *monstres sacrés.* The shock of that unforeseen entrance is not only the shock of recognition, it is like a glimpse of a Platonic form. We are watching a privileged drama; every step, every gesture, is hazardous and exciting, because what is at stake is the formation of a legend. Sometimes we are startled, as when we see Chaplin without tramp's costume as a suave, top-hatted villain. Does he know what we know? Or are we witness to the very moments in which the great secret makes itself known? It is enchanting to see Katharine Hepburn sweep down a staircase in *A Bill of Divorcement*, Cukor's camera whipping across an entire room to intercept her flight; but how would we react if we could see Garbo in the advertising film she made for a department store, demonstrating how not to dress? With a bravura that will come to be known as his, Welles the director delays Welles the actor from appearing until we are sufficiently expectant of a grand entrance, an apparition that will transfix our attention.

Whatever doubts we might have as to Welles's self-awareness are immediately dispelled by his appearance, mincing
and leering, in a sort of comic Irishman costume, his face grotesquely aged like the lady's, his hairline masked and a wispy
clown wig protruding from his temples. He starts down the
stairs, bowing to the old lady. He carries a top-hat and a
cane—later to be the talisman of other Wellesian characters,
from Bannister in *The Lady from Shanghai* to Mr. Clay in *The
Immortal Story*. He descends the stairs from a variety of angles,
intercut with the old lady watching warily. Then Welles shows
the character walking down the steps three times in succession, a common enough affectation but appropriate here to un-
derscore the fateful nature of the character's arrival. Presently
we are treated to quick appearances of Virginia Nicolson as a
Keystone Kop and William Vance as an Indian wrapped in a
blanket (making a face into the camera as he passes), neither
of which has much connection with the already rather tenuous
story.

It becomes clear that Welles's character is a death-figure, for
he disturbs the indefatigably rocking old lady by appearing all
over the rooftop of an adjoining building—and making a
choking gesture with his cane for the man in blackface, a gesture echoed twenty-four years later by Quinlan in *Touch of
Evil*. One of those quaintly symbolic inserts dear to Griffith
and Stroheim interrupts the action: a hand pouring coins from
a shell, and a broom sweeping the money away. (Later we will
see a hand dropping a crumpled five-dollar bill to the floor,
but nothing else will come of it.) Death appears at the window, leering coyly and dangling two heart-shaped lollipops,
tortuously wrapped around each other. These especially infu-
riate the old lady, who accelerates her rocking. From the smiling Death, Welles cuts to a skull, to a yanking rope, to a pair
of feet hanging in mid-air, and to the head of the black-faced
bellringer, dangling in a noose. Then we see a drawing of the
hanged bellringer, and soon a hand enters the frame and
draws a little bell as signature in the corner.

There is a startling transition to Death walking into a darkened room (the underworld?) carrying a candelabrum. He
places it on a piano and starts to play, the camera tilted wildly

to the right as he pounds furiously away: very much *The Phantom of the Opera*. We see his fingers coming closer and closer to the camera. Abruptly the pianist hits a wrong note and stops. He plunks at the keys, bending his head owlishly to test the sound (a good job of miming by Welles). He gets up and discovers that the old lady is lying dead inside the piano. Death opens the piano bench and takes out, instead of sheet music, a pile of thin slabs, shaped like tombstones. He shuffles through them: "Sleeping," "At Rest," "In Peace," "With the Lord," and "The End," leaving the last behind. He sits down again to play, undulating deliriously. We see the bell again, and then his hands playing the piano. Then the slab, "The End."

3. Citizen Kane

In one of the tales of Chesterton, "The Head of Caesar," I believe, the hero observes that nothing is more frightening than a centerless labyrinth. This film is just that labyrinth.

—Jorge Luis Borges

A Moralist Against Morality

Orson Welles's first act in his first feature film, *Citizen Kane*, was to die, and most of his other films also begin with intimations of that strange moment in which a legendary life becomes a lifeless legend. Dramatizing the process by which legend is created—and destroyed—was central both to Welles's public persona and to the deepest sources of his creative power. Such a theme came naturally to an artist who began as a child prodigy, made the cover of *Time* when he was only 23, and shortly thereafter found himself a household word as a result of his *War of the Worlds* radio hoax. From *Citizen Kane*, an examination into legend which finds the possibility of definition illusory, to *Chimes at Midnight*, *The Immortal Story*, and *F for Fake*, which turn the idea of legend into a monstrous, melancholy *jeu d'esprit*, Welles spent his career exploring the contradictions of human nature.

While assessing his own work, Welles once described himself as "a moralist against morality." In the same interview, he elaborated: "In reality, I am a man of ideas; yes, above all else—I am even more a man of ideas than a moralist, I suppose." It is clear that Welles's films are not moralistic in the sense that Howard Hawks's are, for example—as fables of exemplary behavior; and just as clearly, they are not anarchistic and behavioristic like Jean Renoir's. In a Welles film there is, for the most part, an extreme dissonance between the characters' actions and emotions and the underlying moral framework.

Welles will be as chivalrous to his characters as Renoir, but he will not allow the characters' actions to determine the form of the film. Instead, he will go so far as to construct a geometrical pattern of counterpoints and visual ironies, in *Kane*, to bind his hero into a system which makes him seem, from our contemplative vantage point, almost powerless. Or, in *The Magnificent Ambersons* and most of his later films, he will use a godlike narrator to detach us from the struggles of the hero; in most of his films he distorts chronological structure, beginning the film with scenes which depict or imply the hero's destruction, thus placing his subsequent actions in an ironic parenthesis. His opening scenes often contain a poetic or literal "synopsis" of the story which is to follow. *Kane* has its newsreel, *The Ambersons* its quasi-documentary on the town, *Macbeth* the witches' convocation, *Othello* its funeral procession and caging of Iago, *The Trial* its parable of the law, *Chimes at Midnight* the conversation between the two old men, Falstaff and Shallow, recounting their lives. These overviews serve a function similar in some ways to that of the chorus in a Greek tragedy: acquainting us with the broad outlines of the myth so that we will be aware of the consequences inherent in the hero's actions *as* he carries them out, and placing us in an exalted moral position which enables us to maintain a concurrent emotional sympathy and ideological detachment.

Welles, however, was no determinist. The structural similarity to Greek tragedy, and the resulting evocation of a dimly realized fate which becomes clear to the hero only at the moment of destruction, should not obscure the deeper allegiances of his moral position. The "fate" metaphor is not the core of his position; it is a framework, a device which throws the hero's true responsibilities into relief. Welles is a deeply rhetorical artist, but an ironist, not a polemicist. In *The Trial*, for example, he seems to be making the best possible case for the worst character he can imagine as still capable of heroism. Kane is most charming at his most morally odious moments—starting a war, harassing innocent citizens with captivating arrogance—and most pathetic in his moments of tenderness. Power, intellect, and charm came so easily to Welles himself that he tended to view them less as virtues than as moral temptations.

But beyond masking an inability to lead a simple, stable emotional life, power and its attendant anxieties tend to plague the Welles hero past the point of futile compensation into the realm of gratuitous brutality. And with this comes a horrible sense of guilt—not the sentimental regret for being less than perfect, but the knowledge that emotional vulnerability has been the excuse for endlessly enlarging malignity, an obsession which thrusts its cause deeper and deeper into the subconscious and necessitates a greater and greater hypocrisy. Self-deception and the struggle against awareness are the tragic flaws of Welles's hero. The climax in a Welles film is the unmasking of the hero by a younger man, his best friend or surrogate son, who sees in the hero's face the shame of guilt and corruption, and thus is able to recognize it in himself.

The creation of myth is not only a means by which the Welles hero conceals his moral weakness from himself and others; it is also the creation of a more easily manageable rationale for his actions. Kane justifies his abuse of friendship with his self-sufficiency as a legend, but underneath this is a deeper cause he will not admit, and which finally destroys him. He deludes himself into thinking that he has become a prisoner to his legend, and no longer personally responsible (the sense of determinism), just as Joseph K. in *The Trial* excuses himself as the victim of a universal conspiracy. It is only when the myth is exposed as sham that he comes to face the guilt within himself. The same pattern is repeated, with an increasingly melancholic self-awareness, for all of Welles's heroes, until in *Chimes at Midnight* the mask of deception becomes painfully candid. Falstaff is not only the hero of the tragedy; he seems to incorporate within himself the soul of the tragedian as well. He is a liar who expects no one to believe his lies, and so exaggerates them to the point of absurdity. The lies are no longer lies but a desperate confession.

And if *The Immortal Story* seems both the most intimately personal and the most theatrical work of Welles's career, the paradox is inevitable. Welles is the most theatrical of film directors, even more so than Cukor, Ophüls, or Bergman. His dual presence as both author and hero is all but essential to his work. *The Trial* suffers because of an excessive and stifling distance between Welles and his hero; Welles appears in the film as the hero's nemesis, and the moral rhetoric involved almost swamps any possibility of sympathy with the hero. In *The Magnificent Ambersons*, his only feature film in which he does not appear (other than the still uncompleted *The Other Side of the Wind*), the hero closely resembles Welles, and the metamorphosis is immeasurably smoother. When Welles appears on the screen, he feels the necessity to surround himself with baroque distortions of the real world. The time is out of joint the moment he steps on. And we always know the source of the distortion; from the very beginnings of his career, Welles flaunted his command of his media. In the puppet theater plays of his boyhood, he would supply the voices of all the characters himself. An idle boy's amusement? In *The Trial*, Welles not only plays the Advocate but narrates the film and dubs in the voices of eleven other characters, creating an eerie sense of omnipresence. In his radio plays he would often interrupt the narrative to make comments both on the characters and on the medium itself. Time and again on the stage he dramatized his position as cosmic ringmaster; when he did a musical version of *Around the World in Eighty Days*, he trotted out a kitchen sink just to prove that he had not forgotten.

Throughout his films, the moral presence of Welles makes itself felt through the eye of the camera. In a Welles film the camera is a character. In his script for the unmade *Heart of Darkness*, his first Hollywood project, this is literally true—the camera was to have been Marlow. In *Kane* the camera shadows the reporter, whose face we never see completely. The intricate camera movements and long takes characteristic of Welles (although more so in his Hollywood studio films than in his independent work) help to immerse us in the maze-like ironies of his scenes. The camera is the audience, and the longer it moves without the distancing device of a cut, the more we are made aware of its (our) shifting relationship to the characters. Welles comments: "I believe, thinking about my films, that they are based not so much on pursuit as on a search. If we are looking for something, the labyrinth is the most favorable location for the search. I do not know why, but my films are all for the most part a physical search." Perhaps because they are also a moral search, an inquiry by the audience into the truth about the legendary hero.

While retaining the freedom to use rapid montage for physical immediacy (as in the battle sequence of *Chimes at Midnight*) or for intellectual comment (as in the ending sequence of *Touch of Evil*), Welles tends to prolong the tension among the characters and camera as long as possible, to approximate the intimacy of a theatrical experience. The long take, like the deep-focus photography of which Welles is fond, helps persuade us of the dramatic reality of the scene—a necessary counterpoint to the moral distancing—and in respecting the integrity of time and space, it asserts the moral unity of what is shown. Though the event—for example the long uninterrupted snow scene in *Kane* or the tortuous interrogation scenes in *Touch of Evil*—may be highly dialectical in emotions and ideas, the integrality of the mise-en-scène functions as a metaphor for the inevitability of the actions' coincidence. The camera creates a moral labyrinth in which the characters must struggle, ironically unaware of the depth of their dilemma. An excellent example is the long dolly shot in *Ambersons* moving along with George and Lucy as they argue in their carriage. We see the characters' feelings ("identify" with them), but the ceaseless variation of the distance between the camera and the carriage also distances us from them. This distortion, a contrapuntal actor-camera movement, a montage *within* the shot, helps to explain the mixture of compassion and irony omnipresent in Welles's films.

The intellectual and emotional complexity of Welles's work stems from his willingness to confront and explore the implications of his own legendary image, in which he finds reflections of the duality of human nature. "As he himself is a poet, a humanist, a liberal," François Truffaut observed, "... one can see that this good and non-violent man was caught in a contradiction between his own personal feelings and those he has to portray in the parts given him because of his physique. He has resolved the contradiction by becoming a moralistic director, always showing the angel within the beast, the heart in the monster, the secret of the tyrant. This has led him to invent an acting style revealing the fragility behind power, the sensitivity behind strength.... The weakness of the strong, this is the subject that all of Orson Welles's films have in common."

Citizen Kane

"Movies," said Welles in 1970, "should be rough." But he began his movie career thirty years earlier by making a fanatically precise *objet d'art* which left not the tiniest detail to chance ... *Citizen Kane*. Youth was the time for Welles to explore the surfaces of illusion. The newspaper magnate Charles Foster Kane creates a world in his own image; when the image is shattered, nothing is left but vanity and death. *Kane* is ostensibly an attempt to resolve the complexities of a legendary man's character—it unfolds as a search for the meaning of his dying word, "Rosebud"—but it is actually a piece of prestidigitation which makes the character disappear behind a flourish of artifice and mystery. At the end, the secret to Kane's personality is as hermetically sealed as the snowy image inside the glass ball which he drops, and shatters, when he dies at the beginning. Like *The War of the Worlds*, *Kane* has tended to overshadow its creator's subsequent achievements, those "rougher" works which go beyond the tricks of theater to a more intimate exploration of character. Welles was trying to make the Last Word in movies, looting Hollywood for its finest techniques and technicians to build himself an immortal monument. It is the scope of his youthful presumption that keeps *Kane* perpetually fresh and exciting.

Although Welles and his screenwriting collaborator, former newspaperman Herman J. Mankiewicz, based Charles Foster

Kane on a number of sources, including *Chicago Tribune* publisher Robert McCormick and financier Samuel Insull, Kane's overriding resemblance to the newspaper magnate William Randolph Hearst was obvious to most viewers when the film appeared, and a reading of W. A. Swanberg's biography *Citizen Hearst* demonstrates the extent to which the film borrows from the life of "the great yellow journalist." Because of the Hearst papers' blacklisting of the film, and the Hollywood studios' anxiety over possible ramifications for the rest of the industry, *Kane* narrowly escaped being burned to placate the powerful publisher. No doubt for legal reasons, Welles usually confined himself to ironic comments about Hearst, such as his 1941 remark, "Some fine day, if Mr. Hearst isn't frightfully careful, I'm going to make a film that's *really* based on his life." To Bogdanovich, Welles insisted that "the real story of Hearst is quite different from Kane's. And Hearst himself—as a *man*, I mean—was *very* different. . . . I found myself alone with [Hearst] in an elevator in the Fairmont Hotel on the night *Kane* was opening in San Francisco. He and my father had been chums, so I introduced myself and asked him if he'd like to come to the opening of the picture. He didn't answer. And as he was getting off at his floor, I said, 'Charles Foster Kane would have *accepted*.' No reply . . . And Kane *would* have, you know. That was his style—just as he finished Jed Leland's bad review of Susan as an opera singer."

Kane is of course an autonomous dramatic character, existing apart from any reference to Hearst, but there is value in noting where the characters of Kane and his prototype intersect, and where they diverge. It is where they diverge that the film most resembles autobiography. Hearst, for example, lived with his parents until he was nineteen and continued to see them, but Welles's mother died when he was nine—Kane is eight when his guardian, the banker Walter Parks Thatcher (George Coulouris), takes him from his mother—and Welles's alcoholic father died when Orson was fifteen. Welles shied from that comparison as well ("I have no Rosebuds"), but there were more points of contact than he would acknowledge.

There also has been a long-standing controversy over the authorship of *Kane*'s script. It flared up in 1971 when Pauline

Kael published a long article in *The New Yorker* claiming that Mankiewicz was in fact almost entirely responsible for the script from idea to final draft.[1] Kael admitted to me that she had deliberately avoided talking to Welles or his partisans, and Welles commented later, "She never sought me out. She knew it would spoil her copy. 'Orson Welles, on the other hand, insists that . . . Welles maintains, however . . .' It would have been boring for her rhetoric." In speaking to Bogdanovich for *This Is Orson Welles*—well before Kael's aspersions first appeared in *The New Yorker*—Welles, far from minimizing Mankiewicz's contributions to the script of *Citizen Kane*, described them as "enormous." He also noted that John Houseman "made some very important contributions" to the script. Asked how the script of *Kane* originated, Welles replied, "I'd been nursing an old notion—the idea of telling the same thing several times—and showing exactly the same scene from wholly different points of view. Basically, the idea Rashomon used later on. Mank liked it, so we started searching for the man it was going to be about. Some big American figure—couldn't be a politician, because you'd have to pinpoint him. Howard Hughes was the first idea. But we got pretty quickly to the press lords."

And in a November 17, 1971, letter to the London *Times* explaining how he and Mankiewicz had worked on the script for *Kane*, Welles wrote, "The initial ideas for this film and its basic structure were the result of direct collaboration between us; after this we separated and there were two screenplays; one written by Mr. Mankiewicz, in Victorville, and the other, in Beverly Hills, by myself. . . . The final version of the screenplay . . . was drawn from both sources." Bogdanovich found corroboration for Welles's account from such people as

---

[1]Kael's article, which originally appeared in the February 20 and 27, 1971, issues of *The New Yorker*, was reprinted in *The "Citizen Kane" Book* (1971) and in her 1994 collection *For Keeps*. For further rebuttals, see my article, "Rough Sledding with Pauline Kael" in *Film Heritage*, Fall 1971; Andrew Sarris's "Citizen Kael vs. Citizen Kane," *The Village Voice*, April 15, May 27, and June 3, 1971; Bogdanovich's article "The *Kane* Mutiny," *Esquire*, October 1972 (reprinted in *Focus on Orson Welles*, edited by Ronald Gottesman, 1976, and excerpted in *This Is Orson Welles*); and Robert L. Carringer's thoroughly researched 1985 book *The Making of "Citizen Kane."*

Welles's secretary, Katherine Trosper, and the film's associate producer, Richard Barr (formerly Richard Baer), both of whom attested to the fact that (as Trosper put it) "Orson was always writing and rewriting." John Houseman, who worked as Mankiewicz's editor during the scriptwriting, had a bitter falling-out with Welles and frequently claimed in later years that Mankiewicz was the sole writer of *Kane*. But shortly after working with Mankiewicz on the script, Houseman cabled Mankiewicz: "Received your cut version and several new scenes of Orson's. . . . After much careful reading I like all Orson's scenes including new montages and Chicago opera scenes with exception of Kane Emily sequence." And Houseman said in 1969 that after he and Mankiewicz finished their work, "Orson took over and visualised the script. He added a great deal of material himself, and later he and Herman had a dreadful row over the screen credit. As far as I could judge, the co-billing was correct. The *Citizen Kane* script was the product of both of them."

The ironic part of the controversy is that, in the end, it doesn't much matter what exact percentages of the script Welles and Mankiewicz wrote. Kael herself acknowledged that the greatness of the film is in the direction: "*Kane* does something so well, and with such spirit, that the fulness and completeness of it continue to elate us. The formal elements themselves produce elation; we are kept aware of how mar- vellously worked out the ideas are." The final version of the script is a model of screenwriting, for it doesn't attempt to direct the film on paper; it reads almost like a play, setting each scene briefly, with a few atmospheric suggestions, and following with dialogue and a minimum of technical notes. As Houseman said, "Orson turned *Kane* into a film; the dynamics and the tensions are his, and the brilliant cinematic effects—all those visual and aural tensions that add up to make *Citizen Kane* one of the world's great movies—those were pure Orson Welles."

Kane's death at the film's inception occurs in a fantastic, dreamlike context to which the audience has no orientation. The jump-cut from the death to the newsreel continues the disorientation. Though the newsreel shows the events of

Kane's life in their relation to historical time, placing his first wife's death in 1918, his death in 1941, etc., it is only when we are shown the *News on the March* reporters conferring in the projection room that we are placed in a coherent time system. Now the film's present tense, the prosaic, antiromantic aspect, is introduced. A system has been created in which all of Kane's actions are now in the past tense—and hence no longer of any effect. Welles's use of time counterpoints Kane's apparently powerful actions with the audience's foreknowledge that those actions will fail and that he will remain as he was shown at the beginning of the two hours: destroyed. The events of his life as we will see them exist in a limbo of moral futility.

When the newsreel ends, we see the beam throwing it to the screen, then hands turning off the projector, which halts with a whir. It is as if the movie world has been declared void, but only "as if," for *Citizen Kane* continues. Welles wants to shock us out of our acceptance of the newsreel as truth about Kane, and to shock us visually by showing Rawlston, the newsreel editor (Philip Van Zandt), standing and waving his arms in the very light with which the newsreel has just been shown. Welles keeps Rawlston's face in shadow—as he does throughout the film with Thompson (William Alland), the *auteur* and narrator of the newsreel—to emphasize the distance necessary to the artist's inquiry. We see Thompson and are thus able to "identify" with his viewpoint, but since we never see him completely, we are forced to temper our sympathy with irony. Kane's face is completely in shadow at his most selfless moment, when he reads the Declaration of Principles and signs it, pausing before he says "Kane," and giving an odd hollowness to the word. The shifting reportorial attitudes of Kane, Leland, and Thompson form a running ironic motif about the possibility of presenting truth "objectively."

Rawlston tells Thompson, "It isn't enough to tell us what a man did. You've got to tell us *who he was.*" Overriding Thompson's protests and the wisecracks of the other reporters—among whom, without makeup, are Joseph Cotten (who also plays Jedediah Leland) and Erskine Sanford (also the old *Inquirer* editor, Carter)—Rawlston sends Thompson out in quest of Rosebud: "Maybe he told us all about himself on his deathbed." To which another reporter calls out, "Yeah, and maybe he didn't." Cotten is heard muttering "Rosebud" in a mocking tone of voice, just as he will do later as Leland at the end of Thompson's search; his presence here as a sort of Leland *doppelgänger* suggests that the search is doomed to failure—Thompson will be running around in circles. The reporter, who stands for the audience, also stands for the artist approaching the contradictions of his subject matter. Intrigued, or rather forced, to speculate on the meaning of a word or an action, he goes in closer search of the possible implications of the clue. In the course of seeking further development of his preliminary image, he finds both support and negation of it, gradually modifying it and then abandoning his search just short of finding a definitive solution to the problem. The reporter goes as far as he can—within feet, in fact, of Rosebud—but he never does reach it. Welles and the audience do "find" Rosebud, of course, but this, as we shall see, only demonstrates that Thompson was correct in accepting Kane's contradictions and not judging him.

"With me," Welles once said, "the visual is a solution to what the poetic and musical form dictates. I don't begin with the visual and then try to find a poetry or music and try to stick it in the picture. The picture has to follow it. And again, people tend to think that my first preoccupation is with the simple plastic effects of the cinema. But to me they all come out of an interior rhythm, which is like the shape of music or the shape of poetry. I don't go around like a collector picking up beautiful images and pasting them together. . . . I believe in the film as a poetic medium. I don't think it competes with painting, or with ballet—the visual side of films is a key to poetry. There is no picture which justifies itself, no matter how beautiful, striking, horrific, tender . . . it doesn't mean anything unless it makes poetry possible. And that suggests something, because poetry should make your hair stand up on your skin, should suggest things, evoke more than you see. The danger in the cinema is that you see everything, because it's a camera. So what you have to do is to manage to evoke, to incant, to raise up things which are not really there. . . . And the interior conception of the author, above all, must have a single shape."

The rest of the film is colored by what we have seen in the newsreel, the first statement we have received about Kane. The reporter's subsequent inquiries are for him and for us a kind of criticism of the magniloquent *News on the March* (and of the documentary approach?). What we saw in the newsreel undoubtedly happened to Kane; he did live in the castle we are shown, did make the speeches we hear, etc. But the camera also lies ("There is no picture which justifies itself"), and we are not yet able to go beyond the surface to comprehend the "interior rhythm," the poetry, of Kane's life. The image is suspect in *Kane;* each moment in the musical pattern of the film has significance only in the context of all the other moments, past and to come. What is on the screen at a given moment is not definitive but is part of a state of mind shared by the author and his audience. Kane's actions are seen in two forms: in *précis* in the newsreel, more fully in the subsequent parts of the film. The tension of the structure is a fusion of suspense and mystery, a kind of metaphysical tension: suspense in that we (with Thompson) have foreknowledge of the actions we see Kane perform; mystery in that we are trying to discover the "secret" behind them, Rosebud. Kane's life as we see it follows the scheme of classical tragedy, but it does not follow the *form* of classical tragedy. His end, in fact, comes at the very beginning of the film. We see his other actions out of order, through the reporter's eyes. The negation of the idea of Aristotelian chronology as it applies to Kane implies a deterministic suspension of the laws of cause and effect. The fugal structure of the film makes us see his life not as the strong, simple, straightforward action of classical tragedy but as a futile, cyclical "theme and variations."

Significantly, neither of Kane's closest friends, Leland and Bernstein (Everett Sloane), appears in the newsreel. The script called for them to be present in the shots of Kane's wedding to his first wife, Emily Monroe Norton (Ruth Warrick), but Welles wisely omitted them. "All I saw on that screen is that Charles Foster Kane is dead—I know that, I read the papers," Rawlston jokingly comments. What we saw obviously is the product of a man who has no personal acquaintance with his subject. All Thompson has done is to read the papers and look at the newsreel footage. But for a brief section of "bootlegged" footage of the elderly Kane being wheeled through his rose garden, the newsreel has shown us only what Kane did for the public's eye. We even see him trying to smash the camera of an *Inquirer* photographer after his marriage to his second wife, Susan Alexander (Dorothy Comingore)! The inclusion of the bootlegged footage, like the one sequence in Hitchcock's *Rear Window* shot outside of the hero's perspective, helps to ensure our awareness of the perceptual strategy involved. A title in the newsreel fills the screen with the paradoxically true and false words, "Few private lives were more public."

Thompson's search is a chronological, Aristotelian drama. He changes during the beginning-to-end frame of the film, a period of something more than a week from Kane's death to the end of his research into Kane's life. The climax of Thompson's drama comes when he tells the elderly Bernstein that Leland has "nothing particular the matter with him, they tell me, just . . . ," and makes an embarrassed pause. Bernstein finishes the sentence for him: "Just old age," and adds, "It's the only disease, Mr. Thompson, that you don't look forward to being cured of." Thereafter Thompson is less and less detached, and finally he is repelled by the callousness shown by Kane's butler. He is seeing himself as he had been at the beginning of the search. Like Leland, like Kane himself, Thompson is an innocent cruelly brought to recognize corruption. The sobering effect of age is constantly brought home in the juxtapositions of the young and old Kane, the young and old Leland, the young Thompson and the old Bernstein and Leland.

The counterpoint between Thompson's dramatic growth and Kane's futile attempts to change the course of his life contributes subconsciously to the irony of the film, just as the absolute symmetry of the film's construction maintains a constant ironic counterpoint to the utter lack of order in Kane's life. To give just one example of the hundreds of symmetrical devices, the photograph of Kane, Emily, and their son used in the paper when the mother and son die in an automobile accident appears in the newsreel immediately after Kane and Emily strike a pose for their wedding picture. Then, much later, we see the actual taking of the photograph—at the moment before Emily sends the boy home in the car and tells Kane that they are going to Susan's apartment: where Kane will decide to end the marriage. It takes dozens of viewings to become fully conscious of this kind of subliminal metaphor, though one does sense its operation. We feel what Gertrude Stein called "the pleasure of concentrating on the final simplicity of excessive complication."

In the doggedness of Thompson's search and in its final futility, Welles is mocking the audience's hope for a pat solution to Kane's life. Leland mocks it: "Rosebud? Yeah, I saw that in the *Inquirer*. Well, I never believed anything I saw in the *Inquirer*. Anything else?" Thompson alone of the reporters who gather in Xanadu at the end realizes that there is, finally, no solution. Someone tells him that if he had found out what Rosebud meant, it would have explained everything. Facing the camera, though still in shadow and with the camera receding from him, he says, "No, I don't think so. No. Mr. Kane was a man who got everything he wanted and then lost it. Maybe Rosebud was something he couldn't get or something he lost, but anyway it wouldn't have *explained* anything. No, I guess Rosebud is just a piece in a jigsaw puzzle—a missing piece."

Then the missing piece is filled in, but what may we make of the completed puzzle? Welles's camera leaves Thompson for majestic tracking shots over the vast pile of objects Kane has spent his life in accumulating . . . among them a headless statue of Venus, linked in an earlier camera movement with his mother's stove. From the high shots of the pile, we move in to a privileged shot: Rosebud, Kane's childhood sled, filling the screen, burning. Dwight Macdonald was a typical viewer in stating that this shot gave him "a big thrill," though he couldn't explain why. With the shot we see the "solution" for which we and Thompson have been searching, and we realize that it does in fact solve nothing. Thompson is dignified by our realization that we had to see Rosebud to reach his understanding.

But is it possible, as some viewers feel, that the reporter's speech is ironic, that seeing the emotionally potent image of the burning sled makes us realize that there *is* an explanation? Hardly, for the revelation of Rosebud, far from explaining the mystery of Kane's futile existence, adds another dimension to it. If Welles had not shown us Rosebud, we would have continued to think that there could be a solution, and that Thompson is merely unable to find it. We would be left to conjure up our own solutions. Instead, by recalling Kane's expulsion from his childhood home and his use of the sled as a weapon against his guardian, Thatcher, Welles is completing the cycle of Kane's life by going back to the starting-point—to the moment when he still had a chance. Despite the suggestions of a Lost Eden in the scene of Kane's expulsion from his home (the snow, the long unbroken tracking shot, the huge caressing closeup of mother and child), it is important to remember that Kane's childhood was far from idyllic.

When we first see the child, vignetted through a window in the distance, he is playing by himself in the snow, as solitary and helpless as in his old age. The family tensions are sketched in quickly and cryptically: the mother (Agnes Moorehead) is domineering but anguished as she commits her son to Thatcher; the father (Harry Shannon) is pathetic and clumsy in his objections. Why is she sending Charles away? To get him away from his father, who apparently abuses the boy when drunk? Perhaps. But more likely, given the aura of helplessness with which Welles surrounds the entire family, it is simply that the accident which made the Kanes suddenly rich (a defaulting boarder left them stock in a booming silver mine) has created its own fateful logic—Charles must "get ahead." What gives the brief leave-taking scene its mystery and poignancy is precisely this feeling of predetermination. The sled with which little Kane blindly and instinctively lashes out at his fate becomes a symbol not of what his life was but what it could have been. The journey away from home is evoked in a haunting shot of the sled lying half buried in the snow as a mournful train whistle blows on the soundtrack.

When the elderly Kane clutches the glass ball and murmurs "Rosebud," it is at the moment when Susan (who reminded him of his mother) leaves him. An astonishing and all but invisible touch connects the childhood scene with the beginning of Kane's affair with Susan. When Mrs. Kane sits down at the table to sign the papers giving Charles to Thatcher, the camera makes an infinitesimal pan to the right, revealing in the background, on a table, the glass ball. Years later, in Susan's apartment, the ball appears again, hidden among a clutter of bric-à-brac on a table, with the magical illogic of a poetic metaphor. When Susan leaves Xanadu, Kane discovers the ball among Susan's belongings, and it will be with him on his deathbed. What makes Kane's last word and the image of the sled so powerful is this entire undercurrent of suggestions—suggestions which point at something illusory, unattained, and perhaps unattainable.

Though Welles himself was prone to apologize for Rosebud—"It's a gimmick, really, and rather dollar-book Freud"—we should trust the tale, not the teller, and consider also the shots following those of the burning sled: smoke rising from the castle and dissolving into the dark sky, a dissolve to our initial position behind the "No Trespassing" sign, and then a dissolve to Xanadu seen again from behind the giant "K," altered now by the darkness of the window behind which Kane died, dawn light faintly shining on the clouds around the castle, and the smoke rising from above it. The repetition of two perspectives from the enigmatic opening sequence (which the script describes as "Ankor Wat, the night the last King died") forces us to acknowledge that although Kane's dilemma has been illuminated, the evidence is still open to consideration, and the mystery remains. As Robin Wood observed of the psychiatrist's explanation of Norman Bates at the end of *Psycho*: "The psychiatrist, glib and complacent, reassures us. But Hitchcock crystallizes this for us merely to force us to reject it. We shall see on reflection that the 'explanation' ignores as much as it explains." Hitchcock then shows us Norman, whom we "understand," sitting wrapped in a womb-like blanket, irretrievably irrational; and then the car withdrawing from the swamp. Similarly, the last sequence of *Kane*, under which merge the two counterpointed motifs of the musical score—the "power" motif in brass and the "Rosebud" motif on the vibraphone, as composer Bernard Herrmann described them—resolves the situation into perfect ambiguity.

Thompson's cockiness has been supplanted with humility. He now has an empathy with Kane which was only perfunctorily expressed in *News on the March*. By vicariously experiencing the events he represented in his newsreel, he has come to understand that Kane was more than "an emperor of newsprint." In a speech included in the final version of the script but not in the film, Thompson has this to say to a reporter who asks him what he has discovered: "Well—it's become a very clear picture. He was the most honest man who ever lived, with a streak of crookedness a yard wide. He was a liberal and a reactionary. He was a loving husband—and both his wives left him. He had a gift for friendship such as few men have—and he broke his oldest friend's heart like you'd throw away a cigarette you were through with. Outside of that—" This is best out of the film, since it merely puts into words what is so powerfully made felt through the sight and sound of the ending scenes. But it is a hint of the film's method, the constant ironic undercutting of the audience's search for a solution.

The title itself expresses the central paradox. "Citizenship," alliance with effective human society, is the goal to which Kane/Cain vainly aspires. He speaks the word "citizens" twice, at the times in which his purest societal impulses are manifested, but moments also of the highest irony: when he is reading the Declaration of Principles—"I will also provide them with a fighting and tireless champion of their rights as citizens, and as human beings"—and when he is delivering his campaign speech to the "decent, ordinary citizens." Welles undercuts the spirit of Kane's high-minded speech by cutting to the dandyish Leland on the words "the working man and the slum child" and to Bernstein and his underworld associates applauding after the words "the underprivileged, the underpaid, and the underfed."

Citizen represents the heroic, effective aspect of Kane; *Kane* represents his foredoomed, predetermined aspect. Our heroic conception of Kane as a tragically flawed character marching through time to his doom is tempered with an understanding that he was not in complete control of the events of his life, that some force has ordered them. Thompson's presence further emphasizes this tension, as do Gregg Toland's use of deep-focus photography, the recurrence of low-angle shots, and the virtual absence of closeups, strategies which tend to integrate the character into the milieu. The most explicit expression of determinism in the film comes when Susan leaves Kane. The screeching cockatoo flies past the camera, and we see Kane standing in shock at the door of her room in the extreme background. In medium shot, he pivots mechanically back into the room, and Welles cuts to a low-angled shot of the rest of the motion; Kane moves like a marionette, a feeling intensified by the formalizing device of changing the angle of a continuous motion. The lowness of the angle abstracts him into a shape, non-rational, a phenomenon of milieu.

The sense of determinism gives the film an increasingly cold, hard feeling, which is conveyed both in the way Welles plays Charles Foster Kane and in the way he directs the character. As Kane's megalomania begins to reach Hearstian dimensions, blunting his youthful idealism, Kane's boyish swagger begins to stiffen. His face becomes less mobile, his carriage more rigid. Kane begins to seem more like a statue than a human being, Welles implying in this concrete manner that the willful exercise of great power saps the humanity of a man. Welles frequently stages Kane's most emotional scenes in shadow, in profile, or in extreme long shot, as if to convey his growing retreat into his own private, antisocial world. In the later scenes at Xanadu, this leads to a sometimes excessive emotional distance from the character that makes the film seem overly rhetorical. But it is a method absolutely central to Welles's conception of character: the men he plays always have an inner core of humanity that becomes more and more ossified as their rampant egotism drives them farther away from the social constraints governing the conduct of civilized men.

The last time Kane is seen on screen, in the scene in which he smashes Susan's bedroom after she leaves him, the private emotions Kane has been hiding behind his mask-like façade finally burst forth in a sudden frenzy. Typically, it is an emotional expression he can only make in solitude. This infantile tantrum ends with Kane's finding the glass ball and murmuring "Rosebud," thus taking the character full circle by giving him the same line as both exit and entrance. Welles's face at this point, though encased in the heaviest makeup he wears in the film, is an almost frightfully candid picture of grief and desolation, the eyes dissolved in tears, staring zombie-like and unseeing past the shocked assemblage of servants outside the door.

(William Alland, who plays Thompson, made a telling comment on the shooting of this scene: "Orson never liked himself as an actor. He had the idea that he should have been feeling more, that he intellectualized too much and never achieved the emotion of losing himself in a part. When he came to the furniture-breaking scene, he set up four cameras, because he obviously couldn't do the scene many times. He did the scene just twice, and each time he threw himself into the action with a fervor I had never seen in him. It was absolutely electric; you felt as if you were in the presence of a man coming apart. Orson staggered out of the set with his hands bleeding and his face flushed. He almost swooned, yet he was exultant. 'I really felt it,' he exclaimed. 'I really felt it!'")

Given the example of Thompson's newsreel, it might be assumed that the events of Kane's life included in each of the other narrators' flashbacks—the Thatcher manuscript and the recollections of Bernstein, Leland, Susan, and Raymond the butler (Paul Stewart)—are grouped together not by chance but for metaphorical reasons. Such is the case. Thatcher's section has to do entirely with power plays: his taking Charles away from his parents, his giving Kane a substitute sled, Kane's retaliation by means of his newspaper, and finally Thatcher's taking of the newspaper from Kane and Kane telling him, "I always gagged on that silver spoon."

Bernstein is childlike. His flashback shows an idealized Kane and contains most of the triumphal moments of Kane's career. Of all the characters in the film, Bernstein remains the best-disposed towards Kane, who demanded nothing from him but camaraderie. The placement of events in Bernstein's section also equates him with the beginnings of Kane's newspaper and political careers ... the days when he was conquering the world. Bernstein and the more skeptical Leland are repeatedly seen facing each other in profile across the frame, and their radical opposition dramatizes the difference between the emotional demands they make on Kane. The last time the two are together, on the night of the disastrous opera, Bernstein faces Leland and tells him in a strange and moving tone, "I guess that'll show you." As the script indicates, the line is delivered "with a kind of quiet passion, rather than triumph."

If the selfless Bernstein is equated with loyalty, Leland, the romantic idealist, is equated with love and disillusionment. In his flashback, we see all the phases of Kane's love life, from the idyllic beginning of marriage to the meeting with Susan, the confrontation with political boss Jim Gettys (Ray Collins) in Susan's apartment, the resultant rupture from Emily, the marriage to the "singer," and finally Susan's and Kane's humiliations in the opera and Kane's reading of Leland's review with a hollow laugh that sounds more like a sob. Since he is a romantic, Leland feels and remembers all of the emotional extremes the other characters are prone to remember only selectively. In Bernstein's flashback, for example, we see Emily only in awestricken long-shot, but in Leland's we see the marriage dissolving from tenderness to coldness, in the breakfast montage; Susan's flashback shows only the catastrophic moments of her relationship with Kane, but Leland's shows the catastrophe and the courtship. Time and again, Welles emphasizes Leland's brooding presence in showing the progress of Kane's love life. His face is held in a lap dissolve over the start of the breakfast montage, and again over the end of the montage. "It was a marriage just like any other marriage," is his melancholy comment. Again, when he tells about Kane meeting Susan, his face is held for several seconds over the rainy street. Finally, when Leland walks away from Thompson between the arms of two callous nurses, there occurs the most profound device of the film: he vanishes into the billboard picture of Susan, a visual suggestion that Kane has displaced his love for Leland onto her.

In Leland's first scene with Thompson at the hospital, the script calls for the camera to move, after a few lines, from

Thompson's face to Leland's, but Welles had decided to keep the reporter's face constantly out of direct sight of the camera. So we share Thompson's obsessive stare at Leland. Welles's transposition of the lines, "I can remember absolutely everything, young man. That's my curse. That's one of the greatest curses ever inflicted on the human race, memory," from a position later in the speech to the very opening of the scene has an important effect on our view of Leland—as an embodiment of Kane's past, the physical presence of his memory, a living Rosebud, the better part of his nature. Seen in this perspective, Leland's action in refusing to answer Kane's letter from Xanadu is the last refusal of Kane's conscience to accept his gesture of reconciliation. Leland's monologue is Joycean in its tragicomic caesuras (from ". . . We do believe in *something*" to "You're absolutely *sure* you haven't got a cigar?"); all the more so in the lines as Cotten speaks them.

Leland is never seen with a woman, though there is a hint of an infatuation with Emily: "I can tell you about Emily. I went to dancing school with Emily. I was very graceful.—We were talking about the first Mrs. Kane." The script did in fact contain a scene (in a brothel) in which Kane tries unsuccessfully to interest Leland in a girl. He ignores her and challenges Kane about dragging the country into war. Leland personifies Kane's loving impulses, and he is undone by his candor. He tells Kane what he thinks about Susan, and is punished, like Cordelia in *King Lear*, like Falstaff, for loving too freely and simply. Nor can Leland help telling the truth in his review of Susan Alexander, even though he knows it will end both his newspaper career and his friendship with Charlie Kane. As Welles insisted to Bogdanovich, it was not Leland who betrayed Kane: "Kane betrayed him. Because he was not the man he pretended to be." But Leland, as a result, becomes an embittered, spiteful old man, for, as Welles put it, "he likes principles more than the man, and he doesn't have the size as a person to love Kane for his faults." Kane tells lies, overreaches, creates a myth about himself, and finally crushes the *alter ego* who questions the human effect of that power. Leland's presence emphasizes the limits of Kane's ability to love. He plays Abel to Kane.

Young George Orson Welles. (*Lilly Library, Indiana University, Bloomington, Indiana*)

Welles made a film of this production of Shakespeare's *Twelfth Night*, which he designed and directed at the Todd School in Woodstock, Illinois, in May 1933. (*Lilly Library, Indiana University, Bloomington, Indiana*)

Joseph Cotten with Virginia Nicolson (left) in Welles's uncompleted 1938 film *Too Much Johnson*, made to accompany a Mercury Theatre production of the period farce by William Gillette. (*Lilly Library, Indiana University, Bloomington, Indiana*)

The nineteen-year-old Welles as Death in *The Hearts of Age*, a 1934 short he codirected with William Vance.

Virginia Nicolson made up as an old lady in *The Hearts of Age*.

Welles as Charles Foster Kane in *Citizen Kane* (1941), which François Truffaut called "the Film of Films." (*RKO/Turner*)

Before shooting the room-smashing scene in *Citizen Kane,* Welles confers with cinematographer Gregg Toland. (*RKO/Turner*)

"Rosebud": the death of Charles Foster Kane.

The reporter (William Alland) and editor (Philip Van Zandt) of *News on the March*.

Charlie Kane's Lost Eden: Buddy Swan as the young Kane, with Agnes Moorehead and Harry Shannon as his parents and George Coulouris as his top-hatted guardian, Walter Parks Thatcher.

An example of Toland's deep-focus technique in *Citizen Kane*: Jedediah Leland (Joseph Cotten) and Mr. Bernstein (Everett Sloane) in the foreground, with Kane and chorus girls in equally sharp focus in the background.

The disastrous opera debut of Susan Alexander Kane (Dorothy Comingore).

Kane destroying Susan's bedroom after she walks out of his life.

Xanadu: the detritus of a lifetime.

"And now, Major Amberson was engaged in the profoundest thinking of his life": Richard Bennett in *The Magnificent Ambersons* (1942), based on Booth Tarkington's novel about a doomed Midwestern family. (*RKO/Turner*)

Inventor Eugene Morgan (Joseph Cotten) and his horseless carriage in an early scene from *The Magnificent Ambersons.*

"The last of the great, long-remembered dances that 'everybody talked about'": George Amberson Minafer (Tim Holt) and Lucy Morgan (Anne Baxter) on a landing of the Amberson mansion, with Fanny Minafer (Agnes Moorehead) and Eugene on the dance floor in the background.

The tragic Aunt Fanny reacting to the rekindled romance of Isabel Amberson (Dolores Costello) and Eugene during their visit to the Morgan automobile factory.

The end of an era: irising out on the automobile ride in the snow.

One of the scenes cut from *The Magnificent Ambersons* by RKO: George sits uneasily with his mother in the drawing-room of the Amberson mansion, a picture of his late father between them. (*Lilly Library, Indiana University, Bloomington, Indiana*)

The original ending sequence in the boarding house: Fanny Minafer's bleak reunion with Eugene. (*Lilly Library, Indiana University, Bloomington, Indiana*)

"The end of the communication between people": Fanny and Eugene. (*Lilly Library, Indiana University, Bloomington, Indiana*)

A frame enlargement from the original ending sequence of *The Magnificent Ambersons*, which Welles considered "much the best scene in the movie." (*Lilly Library, Indiana University, Bloomington, Indiana*)

Welles played Colonel Haki in the Mercury Production of *Journey Into Fear* (1943), with Everett Sloane (far right) and Joseph Cotten (second from right). (*RKO/Turner*)

Welles in the Brazilian fishing village of Fortaleza, directing the *Four Men on a Raft* segment of his ill-fated documentary *It's All True* (1942). (*Paramount*)

The heroic *jangadeiros* in *Four Men on a Raft*: from left, Raimundo Correia Lima ("Tatá"); Jerônimo Andre de Souza ("Jerônimo"), partially hidden; Manuel Pereira da Silva ("Manuel Preto"); and Manuel Olimpio Meira ("Jacaré"). (*Paramount*)

Welles and cinematographer George Fanto (at camera) filming *Four Men on a Raft* on the coast of Brazil. (*Lilly Library, Indiana University, Bloomington, Indiana*)

The Story of Samba (Carnaval) segment of *It's All True* was filmed in both Technicolor and black-and-white in Rio de Janeiro. (*Lilly Library, Indiana University, Bloomington, Indiana*)

4. The Magnificent Ambersons

> It was a much better picture than *Kane*—if they'd just
> left it as it was.
>
> —Orson Welles

> Showmanship in place of genius: a new deal at RKO.
>
> —RKO trade advertisement, 1942

If, as has been said, the lost footage of Erich Von Stroheim's
original eight-hour version of *Greed* is the cinematic equivalent
of the Holy Grail, then the cinematic equivalent of the lost Ark
of the Covenant surely must be the lost footage of *The Magnificent Ambersons.*[1]

Describing *Ambersons* as "a mutilated masterpiece," François Truffaut wrote in 1972, "It hasn't had the repercussions of
Citizen Kane; and in any theater today, moreover, there will be
half as many spectators for *Ambersons.* Yet each time I see this

---

[1] I made the first attempt at a verbal reconstruction of Welles's original version
of *Ambersons*, using the final shooting script, in my book *Persistence of Vision:
A Collection of Film Criticism* (1968) and in the first edition of this book (1972).
This chapter has been revised with information from Robert L. Carringer's
complete transcription of the original Welles version (based on the studio cutting continuity, dated March 12, 1942) in *The Magnificent Ambersons: A Reconstruction* (1993), and from the thirty-six-page appendix by Peter Bogdanovich
and Jonathan Rosenbaum reconstructing the missing scenes in *This Is Orson
Welles* (1992). Bogdanovich and Rosenbaum convey a more vivid sense of the
lost footage than Carringer does, with the help of some frame enlargements
(preserved by Welles) to which Carringer evidently lacked access.

film it has a greater emotional effect on me. I believe that in shooting *Citizen Kane* Orson Welles was more anxious about the medium, while in *Ambersons* he seems to have been excited primarily by the characters."

Welles felt unusually close to his source material, Booth Tarkington's 1918 novel. He claimed that Tarkington was a friend of his father and used him as the model for inventor Eugene Morgan (the Joseph Cotten character). Welles's father, Richard Welles, was a fabulous Midwestern character who "tried very hard to invent the automobile," as his son put it. Richard Welles's actual inventions, according to Simon Callow's biography of Orson Welles, "were largely confined to the business in which he worked, and that was the lamp trade"; he was treasurer and general secretary of the Badger Brass Manufacturing Co. in Kenosha, Wisconsin, a firm that had a great success manufacturing the Solar acetylene bicycle lamp (which was invented, however, by someone else). "At the turn of the century," Orson recalled, "my father began making bicycle lamps because he thought there was no future in the automotive business. He made a fortune in spite of himself, inasmuch as the automobile manufacturers bought the lamps for their cars." The last of the Amberson fortune is squandered on automobile headlights. Furthermore, the doomed romance between Eugene and Isabel Amberson in Tarkington's novel resembled that of Welles's father and mother, and the Oedipal intensity of the mother-son relationship also struck a deep chord in the filmmaker. Although Welles's boyhood in some ways resembled Kane's, the *enfant terrible* George Orson Welles was closer to the spoiled rich kid George Amberson Minafer.

Bred in genteel Midland towns (George in Indianapolis, Welles in Kenosha), the boys were exceptional, George Minafer as the last of the aristocrats, Welles as an artistic *wunderkind;* and both grew up with a natural sense of arrogance and entitlement. The bumptious George Minafer is Charlie Kane given a decade's reprieve. Kane's snow scene is brief, tense, claustrophobic, punctuated by small, sharp camera movements. His childhood is over in minutes. George's Eden lasts years longer, and his expulsion is delayed for thirty minutes on the screen. The camera movements in his film are longer, more graceful, his snow scene more relaxed. As Truffaut commented, "This film was made in violent contrast to *Citizen Kane,* almost as if by another filmmaker who detested the first and wanted to give him a lesson in modesty."

George Amberson Minafer's innocence ends with a long iris-out, a tribute both to the conventions of an earlier, more graceful age of movies—the silent movies with which Welles grew up—and to the passing of an age, the end of the old agrarian way of life with the coming of the automobile to a Midwestern city that "befouled itself and darkened its sky." As *Chimes at Midnight* is a lament for the *conception* of Merrie England, *Ambersons,* Welles said, is a lament "not so much for the epoch as for the sense of moral values which are destroyed."

Tarkington's novel, which won a Pulitzer Prize in 1919, had been filmed once before, as *Pampered Youth,* a 1925 silent directed by David Smith. Ben Alexander played George as a boy, and Cullen Landis was George as a young man. Welles adapted Tarkington's *Seventeen* and *Clarence* for the radio, and on October 29, 1939, presented his radio adaptation of *Ambersons,* starring himself as George and Walter Huston as Eugene Morgan; to convince RKO to let him make the film in 1941, Welles played a recording of that broadcast for studio president George J. Schaefer. Welles was too mature-looking to repeat the role of George on screen, assigning it to cowboy actor Tim Holt, whose honorable efforts in the role have been underappreciated.

Welles took exceptional care with the soundtrack for the film. Robert Wise, who edited Welles's first two features, recalls that Welles was nervous about recording some loops needed for post-synchronization on *Kane.* After the looping was done, however, he was so taken with the process that he decided to make a preproduction recording of the dialogue for *Ambersons* and have the actors synchronize their lips and motions to it. The first day of shooting was a fiasco: the actors could hardly act, let alone synchronize. Wise says that everyone but Welles and the actors found the whole matter hilarious, and it was abandoned by lunchtime.

Unsuccessful though it was, the experiment in "radio sound" furthered Welles's work. Howard Hawks had developed rapid-fire overlapping dialogue, notably in *His Girl Friday* (1940), and Alfred Hitchcock had experimented with aural montage as early as *Blackmail* (1929). Welles used such techniques with even greater audacity and density in both *Kane* and *Ambersons,* and he encouraged composer Bernard Herrmann, who had first worked with him in radio, in the use of what Herrmann called "radio scoring" for films. As Herrmann explained in a 1941 *New York Times* article, that meant "musical cues which last only a few seconds.... [I]n radio drama, every scene must be bridged by some sort of sound device, so that even five seconds of music becomes a vital instrument in telling the ear that the scene is shifting." Herrmann conceived of some scenes in *Kane,* such as the breakfast montage, as "ballet suites," and Welles cut them to match the music. Herrmann worked closely with Welles on new uses of sound effects and orchestration, and in *Ambersons* the two carried their experiments to a new degree. Lengthy sections are almost continuously underscored with music, while overlapping dialogue is made to serve new dramatic functions. (Unfortunately, when RKO recut *Ambersons,* it also brought in studio composer Roy Webb to redo parts of Herrmann's elegiac score, in an attempt to make it more conventional and less "somber," and Herrmann refused to let his name be used in the credits.)

Welles wrote most of the script of *Ambersons* in a nine-day stint on King Vidor's yacht, aided by his radio experience with dramatizing the book. Shooting began on October 28, 1941. At night he was acting in Norman Foster's *Journey Into Fear,* a Mercury production for which he directed several scenes and helped Joseph Cotten write the script. On Sundays he was appearing on his *Orson Welles Show* for CBS Radio; and, with the outbreak of World War II, he also was preparing to leave for South America to shoot *It's All True,* his goodwill documentary undertaken at the urgent request of the U.S. government. Welles finished shooting *Ambersons* on January

31, 1942, and after working with Wise on the editing for three days and nights in a Miami studio, the director left for South America on February 4. He took along a rough cut of *Ambersons* and continued to work on the editing from Rio by telephone, cable, and shortwave radio. However, because of wartime travel restrictions, Wise was unable to join Welles in Rio with the workprint so that the director could make final adjustments, as had been agreed.

On March 17, RKO, which was becoming anxious about both the production problems of *It's All True* and the commercial potential of *The Magnificent Ambersons*, gave *Ambersons* a sneak preview in Pomona, California. The studio, in part with Welles's acquiescence, had already removed several sequences from the director's original cut, which ran a hundred and thirty-one minutes (some of the cut sequences were later restored for the release version); according to Robert Carringer's research, the Pomona version ran about a hundred and ten minutes. Many in the preview audience—comprised mostly of young people attracted by the main feature, the wartime musical *The Fleet's In*—reacted negatively to *Ambersons*, finding it slow, overly grim, and unintentionally comic. One person who filled out a preview card called it "the worst picture I ever saw," and another patron complained, "We do not need trouble pictures, especially now. . . . Make pictures to make us forget, not remember." Other cards called it "A horrible distorted dream . . . as bad if not worse than *Citizen Kane* . . . It stinks." But many other people in the audience responded favorably. "I think it was the best picture I have ever seen," one audience member commented, and another wrote, "I was disgusted with the way some people received this picture which truly brings art to the picture industry." Still another viewer declared, "This picture is magnificent. The direction, acting, photography, and special effects are the best the cinema has yet offered. It is unfortunate that the American public, as represented at this theater, are unable to appreciate fine art."

The studio held a second preview before an older, more upscale crowd on March 19 in Pasadena. The film by then had undergone further changes, with some scenes restored and others eliminated, bringing the running time to a hundred and seventeen minutes, according to Carringer (Bogdanovich's account gives a running time of a hundred and fifteen minutes). This time the reaction was much better, with only eighteen unfavorable preview cards out of eighty-five. As Bogdanovich has written, "Had the film remained in this form, it would still have been fairly close to Welles's version; despite the deletion of seventeen minutes, the spirit of the work was not diminished. Above all, no new scenes had been shot and the crucial 'last act' was still intact. But nothing evidently could erase the memory of the first preview, and panic set in." On March 21, Schaefer wrote Welles, "Never in all my experience in the industry have I taken so much punishment or suffered as I did at the Pomona preview . . . especially in the realization that we have over $1,000,000 tied up. It was just like getting one sock in the jaw after another for over two hours." The studio subsequently exercised its contractual right to take over the editing (Welles had final cut on *Kane*, but had to waive that right in order to make *Ambersons*). Robert Wise was ordered to make further cuts, and Joseph Cotten and Welles's business manager, Jack Moss, also participated in the reediting process. Welles's ending was scrapped, a new ending was shot by assistant director Freddie Fleck, other scenes were redone by Wise, Fleck, and Moss, and the last two reels were wholly reshuffled. Welles sent frantic cables from Rio, alternately trying to stop the wholesale reworking of the film and making his own editing suggestions in the hope of salvaging his basic conception. But the studio ignored him. Two more sneaks finally convinced the studio to release *Ambersons*—now down to its present length of eighty-eight minutes—and it was dumped onto the market on July 10 at two Los Angeles theaters, on a double bill with the Lupe Velez comedy *Mexican Spitfire Sees a Ghost*.

While the reworking of *Ambersons* was underway, RKO had undergone a change in hierarchy, and Schaefer was deposed, in part because of his sponsorship of Welles. One of the first moves taken by new studio head Charles Koerner was to order Welles to return from Brazil. Before leaving he shot the *Four Men on a Raft* sequence in Fortaleza with a crew of five, at a production cost of only $10,000. But Koerner stripped him of his contract and the *It's All True* footage, to which he was denied access. Welles's Mercury staff were given twenty-four hours to vacate their offices—nine days before the opening of *Ambersons*—and the studio also took over the editing of *Journey Into Fear.*

Welles was dismayed over Joseph Cotten's involvement in the studio's recutting of *Ambersons,* describing him to biographer Barbara Leaming as "my best friend who had become their ally." But Welles was most angry with Wise, whom he felt had seized the opportunity to advance his own directing ambitions over the ruin of *Ambersons;* Welles declared that "they let the studio janitor cut *The Magnificent Ambersons* in my absence." After publishing my first version of this chapter, I asked Welles if he thought I had been too hard on Wise in assigning him the principal blame for the studio's recutting, when in fact the situation was somewhat more complicated than that. Welles insisted, "You can *never* be too hard on Robert Wise."

"Of course I expected that there would be an uproar about a picture which, by any ordinary American standards, was much darker than anybody was making pictures," Welles told Leaming. "First I *charmed* them, you know, *then* I tore the thing to shreds . . . but I thought I had a movie so good—I was absolutely certain of its value, much more than of *Kane*—that I had absolutely no doubt that it would win through in spite of that industry fear of the dark movie. If you see the movie you'll see that it's like all the preparations for the betrayal of Falstaff [in *Chimes at Midnight*]. It's exactly like that, you know. It's a tremendous preparation for the boarding house with Aggie Moorehead and Joe Cotten [the original ending, desolate and Chekhovian], and the terrible walk of George Minafer when he gets his comeuppance. And without *that,* there wasn't any plot. It's all about some rich people fighting in their house. I'm an enemy of great length in a movie, but this *had* to have—a kind of awful pompous word—a certain epic quality. When you do a family and the change of American life because of the automobile, it has to have a kind of size to it."

RKO's advertising tried to mask the somberness of the story with empty-headed sensationalism focusing on the relationship between Eugene Morgan and George's mother, Isabel Amberson Minafer (Dolores Costello)—"Scandal played no favorites when that high-and-mighty Amberson girl fell in love once too often!" read the New York ad on the day of the premiere. *Ambersons* lost more than $600,000 at the box office, but the studio's perfunctory release, coupled with the butchery of the picture itself, made its failure a self-fulfilling prophecy. It's revealing to look back at the *Variety* box-office reports for the early weeks of the film's release, which demonstrate that its reputation as box-office poison is partly a myth, like so much else about Welles's career. In some situations, *Ambersons* started very well indeed. It was "holding up beyond expectations" in Los Angeles and doing "sensationally" in San Francisco; business was "nice" in New York and Baltimore, "good" in Denver and Omaha, "not bad" in Boston and Philadelphia, etc. In some places, such as Chicago and Cincinnati, it was playing "below expectations," and business undoubtedly was hurt by the mostly negative reviews. Overall, according to *Variety*, *Ambersons* had a "spotty" rather than a disastrous start. Since the film was quickly pulled in most places, it's clear that RKO never gave it a real chance to build an audience. Carringer concludes that after the early previews, the studio "in effect abandoned it."

But *The Magnificent Ambersons* was a movie for the ages, not a movie for 1942.

The frame is edged with soft-focus in the early shots, which have the feeling of old photographs coming magically to life. Manny Farber complained that the first shots are no more than a succession of "postcards" connected by narration, but the flow of the section depends on this kind of time-compressing exposition, disguised by the soft, whimsical music and by Welles's narration, which seems to caress the images with loving eloquence. Seen silently the montage would have less connective tissue, but with the soundtrack, the shots of the streetcar, the men in the bar, the rowboat, the stovepipe hat, and Eugene modeling clothes go by in smooth and natural succession. The extreme economy of this sequence is part of its beauty. The novel has a similar beginning—wry comments on the mores of the 1870s—but takes three chapters to get through George's childhood years. Given the advantage of being able to *show* the period evolving, Welles compressed George's first seventeen years into only a few minutes on screen (the studio tightened it even further, also rearranging part of the opening montage).

"The magnificence of the Ambersons began in 1873. Their splendor lasted throughout all the years that saw their Midland town spread and darken into a city . . ." In the first two sentences of narration, Welles summarizes the rise and eventual collapse of the Amberson dynasty, and the fate of their community. The use in early scenes of the townspeople as a chorus and the designation of an old gossip as a "prophetess" could hardly make the parallel with Greek tragedy more explicit; nor could the story's debt to *Oedipus Rex*, its tragic mother-son relationship, be more clear. By its very indirection, the poetic beginning heightens the tragedy that is to follow. What is left unsaid and what is treated playfully in the prologue to *Ambersons* will echo throughout the slowly darkening remainder of the film.

Young George's two rapid rides through the town in his pony cart at ages nine and seventeen (both slightly revised by the studio) foretell the later behavior of "Rides-Down-Everything," as Eugene's daughter Lucy (Anne Baxter) refers to George. Welles tells us that "George Amberson Minafer, the major's one grandson, was a princely terror," as we see his cart gradually approaching the camera in extreme long shot. As George drives out of the frame left, Welles cuts to him driving left through a laborer's sand pile, then shows him driving away from the camera and through the town as if he owns it. "There were people, grown people they were," the narration continues, "who expressed themselves longingly— they did hope to see the day, they said, when that boy would get his comeuppance."

As he did with Rosebud several times in the early parts of *Kane*, Welles mocks his own central motif. He cuts to a couple on the street: "His *what?*" asks the lady. "His come*up*pance," answers the gentleman in his most determined tones. "Something's bound to take him down some day; I only want to *be* there." This is one of the first indications of the slight variation in attitude between the novel and the film: Welles's distance from the characters is slightly greater than Tarkington's, a fact which no doubt accounted for much of the tittering of audiences unable to see the satire. When Eugene falls through the bass viol early in the film, Welles is telling how the instruments of the serenade will "presently release their melodies to the dulcet stars"; Tarkington used the line with softer irony in referring to the popular songs of the day.

In the second ride through the town, the speed of the carriage is greatly increased: the cutting is more rapid, smaller portions of the right-to-left arc are used, and the effect is that George has indeed returned from college "with the same stuffing." Just after George has snapped his whip at another laborer, the camera pans from ground level right with the carriage, and the spinning hub veers close to the camera in a succinct visual metaphor for George's hubris. (RKO removed Welles's following scene, which perhaps unnecessarily showed George returning to his old boyhood club, the Friends of the Ace, and bullying his way back into its presidency.)

Welles's Hollywood enemies attributed the success of *Kane* to Gregg Toland, the great photographer who worked closely with him in planning the shots and the texture of the film. By the time *Ambersons* went on the floor, Toland was under contract to Samuel Goldwyn, so Welles turned to Stanley Cortez, who took Toland's work with deep-focus further and helped the director conjure up the three-dimensionality of a bygone world. But despite Cortez's training in low-budget pictures, which Welles thought would help speed up the production, Cortez took the opportunity of his first A-picture to become painstakingly deliberate in his working methods. He proved too slow for Welles, so the exasperated director turned to cameraman Harry J. Wild for much of the filming. Cortez also irritated Welles with his pretentious manner of discussing cinematography by drawing analogies with other art forms, including such comments as "Orson, I see Major Amberson as

Rembrandt's *An Old Man Seated"* and "Orson, doesn't this scene remind you of Respighi's *Fountains of Rome?"*

André Bazin has dealt at length with the psychological and dialectical advantages of giving equal focal stress to each object in a scene; with Toland's processes, objects two hundred feet from the camera are as sharp as those in the extreme foreground. The director can choreograph his scenes with great subtlety, changing the audience's viewpoint without the intervention of a cut. Bazin found that the deep-focus work of Jean Renoir, and of Toland for William Wyler and Welles, represented a revolution in film style, an assertion of the integrality of space and time in direct opposition to the classical theories of montage.

Toland stated simply that it obviated the "loss of realism" due to breaking a scene up into "long and short angles." Welles has stressed the gain in ambiguity: "The public may choose, with its eyes, what it wants to see of a shot. I don't like to force it." The recurrent use of low angles in *Ambersons*, though seldom as deliberately obtrusive as in *Kane*, places further emphasis on the characters' relation to their surroundings. Cortez and Wild also achieved a chiaroscuro reminiscent of period daguerrotypes and of Billy Bitzer's photography for Griffith. The counterpoint between the almost documentary immediacy of the exteriors of *The Magnificent Ambersons* (in itself a kind of stylization) and the meticulous stylization of the camera movement, action, and dialogue contributes much of the film's power. As James Agee perceptively remarked in his *Time* review, the film is shot "from a viewpoint so fresh that it creates a visual suspense in the very act of clarification."

The predominance of the city and the baroque furnishings of the mansion, and the implicit family-mansion metaphor, impart a strong determinism to the story. George could hardly have helped growing up that way ("They-Couldn't-Help-It" is Lucy's name for the woods inhabited by Chief "Rides-Down-Everything"). Welles's meticulous use of settings—the idyllic snowy fields with only telephone wires intruding, the somnolent little town providing a backdrop for George and Lucy's carriage ride, and the bustling, noisy city they later walk

through (and the dirty metropolis George walks through
alone)—all this carries the story of the town along with the
story of the family. The film still has the epic quality Welles
was seeking, though it has been lessened by the recutting.
Most damaging were the studio's excisions of many of
Welles's references to the polluting effect of the automobile. At
a time when factories were being pushed to maximum capacity for the war effort, Welles's radical critique of the American
myth of "progress"—demonstrating how, as Major Amberson
feared, the automobile came to "change the face of the
land"—was judged too potent for the mass audience in that
summer of '42.

On George's return home, Welles tells us, "cards were out
for a ball in his honor, and this"—slight ironic pause—"pag-
eant of the tenantry was the last of the great, long-remembered dances that 'everybody talked about.'" In its original
form, the ball sequence, as Welles told Leaming, "was the
greatest *tour de force* of my career"; despite some studio tam-
pering, it remains one of his most dazzling achievements.

After a distant shot of the mansion lit up for the ball, a
slow dissolve reveals Eugene and Lucy Morgan, seen from
behind, entering the house. The camera follows. The physical
feeling in this shot is extraordinary: servants open the doors
on either side, smiling broadly as they pull hard against the
wind; Sam the butler (J. Louis Johnson) bows and takes
Eugene's hat; couples pass in front of the camera while in
the background the party is in full gaiety (the camera all the
time tracking in). Inside the gaudily opulent Amberson mansion, an architectural monstrosity that the neighbors consider
"the pride of the town," the characters in the story are
resplendently framed by shiny black walnut balustrades and
staircases; a sparkling, gently swaying cut-glass chandelier
and flickering gas lights hanging from ornate ceilings; and
enough vines and flowers to decorate the most rococo funeral parlor.

When Eugene and Lucy arrive, a cut to an opposite viewpoint starts a slow tracking shot toward George and Isabel's
receiving line. A lavishly decorated Christmas tree sweeps by

on the left as the camera approaches Uncle John Minafer (Charles Phipps), a loud bumpkin telling Major Amberson (Richard Bennett) how he'll be laid out in this very hall "when his time comes," and telling George, "There was a time though in your fourth month when you was so puny nobody thought you'd live." This line is tossed off, but in it lies a key to George's megalomania, an explanation of the absurd affection Isabel will lavish on him until her death. On her deathbed she will ask George if he has had enough to eat and if he has caught a cold on the trip home. One is reminded of the first words of Mrs. Kane: "Be careful, Charles! Pull your muffler around your neck, Charles!" As she says the words Charles reflexively does pull his muffler around his neck. George's reaction to his uncle's untactful line here, however, is a fierce "M'mber you v'ry well indeed!" The first real glimpse of George as a young man defines his character. His arch, elegant profile is set against the left of the frame as the camera stops tracking, and his face shows the ridiculous arrogance that is to doom his mother.

Eugene is now greeting Isabel, and Welles cuts to a shot of the three faces: George's wary on the left, Isabel's smiling, Eugene's in profile on the right. Immediately, wordlessly, the tension is established. When Eugene tells George that "from now on you're going to see a lot of me—I hope," the violins off-camera start a gay tune. When Isabel introduces George to Lucy a few seconds later, the musicians are in the midst of a transition which becomes a high, plaintive note the moment after Isabel says, "You don't remember her either, Georgie, but of course you *will*." The rest of the sequence is increasingly fluid: a long track back with George and Lucy through the ballroom, the camera craning up with them as they ascend the stairs (showing a violinist in the foreground playing the plaintive tune), a dissolve to a tracking shot of Lucy's suitors crisscrossing in front of George and the camera, a scene of George and Lucy on a landing with dancers visible below them, a soft-focus wipe to the family gathered around a punch bowl. But the sequence would have been even more fluid if the studio had not excised several shots featuring comedy relief from Uncle John (including the beginning part of the complex tracking shot of Lucy, George, and Lucy's suitors) and two inter-changes foreshadowing the fate of George and Isabel.

In the first conversation, Isabel says as she watches George and Lucy go to the dance floor, "Those children. It's touching. But of course they don't . . . it's touching." And George's uncle Jack Amberson (Ray Collins) comments, "Do you know what I think whenever I see these smooth triumphal young faces? I always think . . . oh, how you're going to catch it. Oh, yes. Life's got a special walloping for every mother's son of 'em." To which Isabel replies, "Maybe some of the mothers can take the walloping for them." After the scene at the punch bowl, Jack was to make an even more pointed commentary to Eugene about Isabel considering George "a little tin god on wheels. . . . My gosh! What does she see when she looks at him?" This was the beginning of what Carringer describes as "Perhaps the most lamented of all the lost footage: most of a four-minute, single-take, horseshoe-shaped tracking shot" in which the camera was to traverse much of the dance floor, gracefully interweaving dramatic and comedic strands of the story.

One reason for the cut, which occurs just after George and Lucy walk past the refreshment table and an elderly couple approach excitedly, was that the couple continued with a comical exchange about the town's latest delicacy—olives—in counterpoint with the serious discussion between Jack and Eugene. Chances are that the olive remarks caused guffaws at the preview, partially because it is here that Welles's satirical distance from his characters' Midwestern gaucherie is most apparent. "The result," Welles lamented, "was a useless jump in an otherwise unbroken scene." As it remains, the camera-work is dazzling enough—the camera still seems to dance away with Eugene and Isabel, stand still for George and Lucy's brief conversation, and then retreat as the two dance away on the wonderful exchange about George's ambition: to be a yachtsman.

The ball ends on a slow Sternbergian dissolve from Eugene and Isabel dancing in the foreground to the couple dancing in the extreme background after the rest of the dancers have gone. Here Welles's use of multilayered sound perspective is at its most dazzling. We hear, distantly, George and Lucy talking, then on a cut we hear them at normal volume; the music stops, in the foreground Eugene thanks Isabel, and from the audience's side of the camera we hear Jack: "Bravo! Bravissimo!" Again we hear Eugene, then Lucy and George in the background. This linear use of three sound perspectives creates a remarkable illusion of depth, and the mingling of voices in the subsequent leavetakings heightens the scene's breathless tension. The choreography is similarly punctuated: Jack walks towards George, the camera panning left; George's aunt, Fanny Minafer (Agnes Moorehead) runs in back of them; Isabel dashes in front of the camera. As the scene ends, Isabel is poised in the foreground between facing profiles of Lucy and George. The "flat" screen becomes surreally three-dimensioned.

The travelling shot of Eugene and Lucy driving home in his automobile was shorn by RKO of its ending moments, in which Eugene deflects her question about how Isabel came to marry the stodgy Wilbur Minafer (Don Dillaway). The studio also dropped a scene of Eugene and Lucy lightheartedly discussing George's strengths and weaknesses while parking the car in their stable. That scene originally followed the family argument in the upstairs hallway of the Amberson mansion, in which Welles uses sound montage for another kind of three-dimensional tension, with Fanny's, Jack's, and George's voices following each other in rapid irritated succession. Agnes Moorehead establishes Aunt Fanny's character as swiftly as she did Mrs. Kane's. Derisive laughter greeted Aunt Fanny at the Pomona preview in 1942, and at almost every showing of the film I attended in the 1960s, before the ascendance of the women's liberation movement, whose influence I believe finally silenced the hecklers. George Cukor, reacting to similar laughter at a screening of his *Little Women,* angrily called such a response "a bum's laugh." The ridicule of Aunt Fanny was an indication of how much of this tortured woman Moorehead compels the audience to see. It is a beautiful and harrowing performance, and it moves me greatly each time I see the film.

The daytime snow scene which now follows the hallway argument offers a humorous contrast between the grace of the sleigh (which soon capsizes) and the grotesque rumblings of Eugene Morgan's "broken-down chafing-dish." Gene's strenuous attempts to start the car with George's reluctant assistance are played out against a stylized backdrop that includes houses, fences, and telephone wires. As the scene plays in the release version, the automobile is still a diversion in the purity of the snow, and the jaunty riding song in the auto ("The Man Who Broke the Bank at Monte Carlo") epitomizes the spirit of the times as well as did "Oh, Mr. Kane!," which also marked the end of a carefree era. But the tone of the scene would have been radically different if RKO had not removed a lengthy discussion of the soot and smog brought by the automobile, pollution that is clearly visible as the characters ride through a new development of low-cost housing on land once owned by Major Amberson:

> *Isabel:*   When we get this far out you can see there's quite a little smoke hanging over town.
> *Jack:*   Yes, that's because the town's growing.
> *Eugene:*   Yes, and as it grows bigger it seems to get ashamed of itself so it makes that big cloud and hides in it.
> *Isabel:*   Oh, Eugene.
> *Eugene:*   You know, Isabel, I think it used to be nicer.
> *Isabel:*   That's because we were young.
> *Eugene:*   Maybe. It always used to be sunshiny, and the air wasn't like the air anywhere else. As I remember it, there always seemed to be gold dust in the air. . . .

The slow iris-out begins as the car and the singing diminish into the distance. The script has the film opening with an iris effect and the snow scene closing with a simple fade: the shifting was an inspired idea.

The *allegro* movement is over, and, even in the truncated release version, the gradual darkening has begun. With a fade-in we see the mansion doors (which had opened on the ball scene shortly before), but now there is a wreath on one and Eugene's shadow on the other. The music stops abruptly as the door clicks shut behind the Morgans—indoors the neighbors and relatives are filing around a coffin. Placing the camera in the coffin's position was done notably by Carl Dreyer in *Vampyr* (1931), but of course for a different effect. Here it serves to nullify our feelings—if any, since we have hardly seen him—for Wilbur Minafer, George's father, with whom, in Truffaut's theory about the subjective and objective uses of the camera, it is now impossible to identify.

A film in which the camera actually plays a character, as in Welles's unfilmed 1939 script of *Heart of Darkness* or in Robert Montgomery's *Lady in the Lake* (1946), is usually described as "subjective," but Truffaut argued that such a visual strategy represents the exact opposite of subjective filmmaking, which depends on the audience identifying with the feelings of a character. And the only way to identify with a character, Truffaut concluded, is to see the character. A classic example of the subjective camera—in that unconventional but suggestive definition—is the little boy's interview with the psychiatrist in Truffaut's *Les Quatre Cents Coups*: the camera holds on the boy's face for the whole interview, and we see his feelings. Applying Truffaut's theory to Welles's work helps us understand its complexity of tone. When the young Kane receives a Christmas sled from his guardian, for example, the camera tilts from his face to a grotesquely angled view of the towering Thatcher. In the same shot we see Charles and see Thatcher from the boy's angle—feeling as well the guardian's power over the boy. In *Ambersons'* funeral scene, our attention is not on Wilbur in his coffin but on the family around it, and particularly on Fanny, who moves towards the camera and is then shown in great closeup, her face streaked with tears, more for herself than for her brother. A pointed little chorus follows on a dissolve from Fanny's face: two grim townsmen, staring into the camera as the mourners had done in the previous scene, one of them saying, "Wilbur Minafer—quiet man—town'll hardly know he's gone" (filmed by Welles, it replaced a shot of Wilbur's tombstone used in the original cut).

The famous kitchen scene, which directly follows the events of Wilbur's death in the release version, actually takes place some months later (the studio cut a shot of George's college diploma that made clearer the passage of time). Welles seats the audience across from George as he stuffs himself, Fanny prodding him about Eugene's involvement with Isabel at his commencement, from which he has just returned. The camera makes two slight pans, one at the beginning and one at the end of the scene, and the effect is of eavesdropping on a confusing and revelatory confrontation between a person masking her emotions and another oblivious to them. We share each hesitation and gesture with the characters, prodded by no editorial device. The implication involved in showing the scene to us in its totality is that the hesitations are just as important as the gestures. The *mise-en-scène* is baroque: a clutter of pots hanging in the background, a giant stove in the left rear, long black shadows across the ceiling, a clutter of serving dishes, pitchers, and plates in the foreground. George stuffs himself relentlessly.

Welles has given an erroneous impression of this scene: "The actors were rehearsed for five weeks before we started the film. And on this scene at least four days, except that this scene was never written. No word of it was written—and we discussed everybody's life, each one's character, their background, their position at this moment in the story, what they would think about everything—and then sat down and cranked the camera, and every actor made up his lines as he went along. The scene lasts three and a half minutes or something in its entirety and was written by the actors as we went along. I'm very proud of them for it. It has an extraordinary effect, entirely due to their preparation for doing it."

A study of the novel and the screenplay contradicts Welles's remarks: with a few differences, the scene comprises the first part of Chapter Sixteen in the novel. Jack (a Falstaffian character whose name in the book is George Amberson) does not appear in this scene in the book; his lines are taken from a speech of his in Chapter Fifteen and from one of George Minafer's in Chapter Sixteen. And the scene *was* written out in the script—it covers pages sixty-four to sixty-eight. The only improvisations were the occasional lines about George's eating: "Quit bolting your food ... Don't eat so fast, George ... Want some more milk?—No, thanks ... You're going to get fat.—Can't help that!" But Welles is correct in his praise of the actors: the scene *seems* off-the-cuff because of their skillful interweaving of set dialogue and impromptu remarks.

The scene now ends with a fade-out on Jack's "I really don't know of anything much Fanny *has* got—except her feeling for Eugene," and a cut to a blacksmith hammering steel in Eugene's factory, the prelude to the intricately choreographed scene of Eugene giving a tour of his plant to Fanny, Isabel, Lucy, and George. But between these scenes, Welles originally interposed a night scene on the lawn of the mansion, one that introduces a motif suggesting affinities between the characters in *Ambersons* and those in Chekhov's *The Cherry Orchard.* George, looking out the window (as he now is on the fade-out), shouts "Holy cats!" and dashes outside to look at a row of excavations on the mansion lawn. He stands in the rain, furious; Jack arrives a moment later to shield him with an umbrella and to defend the Major's decision to break up the lot for housing. "But why didn't he sell something or other, rather than do a thing like this?" the uncomprehending George demands, and Jack replies, "I believe he has sold something or other, from time to time." The loss of the excavation scenes—and of later scenes which touch on the Major's thrift measures—robs the film of some of its most acute points of family-town conflict.

The factory scene, with its intense workmen pulling ropes and pushing automobiles, its car on display, and its process screen showing large machines in the background—all this clamor sets off most effectively the small focus of the scene: Fanny's anguished face turning slowly towards the camera as Isabel and Eugene reminisce about "the original Morgan Invincible," which stands behind them. A brief excised scene showed George and Lucy getting into their carriage and joking about their "sentimental" elders, with Eugene's automobile passing them as it emerges from the factory, Isabel and Fanny riding in the back seat.

The next scene in the released film is the brief conversation between Isabel and Eugene on the mansion lawn, which Welles had intended to come three scenes later. It is followed by George driving Lucy through the town in his carriage—the

continuation of the earlier scene that originally began outside
the factory. The disruption of continuity may not be entirely
apparent to the viewer, but it contributes to the uneasy feeling
that the conversation on the lawn seems out of place.

The release version jump-cuts from the carriage following
in the exhaust of Eugene's car to the carriage trotting steadily
along the street. This long, spectacular tracking shot, which
continues for blocks on RKO's smalltown street and gives a
powerfully realistic sense of time and place, is also a famous
example of Welles's camera vs. character counterpoint. At the
end of the shot the camera gains slowly on the carriage, and
we can see that the dolly has been rolling on streetcar tracks.
Welles goes so far to acknowledge the camera's involvement
in the scene as actually to show the wheel of the dolly (another carriage) in the lower left-hand corner of the screen.

The camera halts; George gallops the carriage out of the
frame right; the Major's buggy follows and a quick dissolve
shows Jack and the Major in conversation inside the buggy.
This procession of the generations—first the automobile, then
George, then the Major—is a superb visual metaphor. The
buggy scene, with the melancholic Major murmuring about
how the town "seems to be rolling right over" his heart, has
been truncated, and the reason was a reference to the excavations: the Major complaining about "those devilish workmen
yelling around my house and digging up my lawn."

The next scene retained in the film is the dinner-table argument, but the scene in the Major's buggy was to have lap-dis-
solved into a delicate late-summer evening's conversation on
the mansion verandah. Traffic lights pass on the street in the
background; the script indicates that bicycles and surreys were
to be flashing by, disrupted by an occasional noisy automobile,
and the new construction on the lawn has progressed, with
one house already completed. George is brooding, at first
oblivious to the conversation. Fanny tells Isabel that autos are
a fad, "Like roller skates. Besides, people just won't stand for
them after a while. I shouldn't be surprised to see a law
passed forbidding the sale of automobiles the way there is
with concealed weapons." When Isabel counters with a gentle
question about her sincerity in telling Eugene that she had en-

joyed the afternoon's drive, Fanny says that she "didn't say it so very enthusiastically," and that it "hardly seems time yet— to me" for anyone to get the idea that Eugene had pleased her.

A very uneasy pause in the conversation follows, the only sound Isabel's distracted whistling. Then Isabel notices that across the street, the old gossip Mrs. Johnson (Dorothy Vaughn) is spying on them from her bedroom window with a pair of opera glasses. Isabel goes inside, remarking, "It's cooler in the house, though it's really not warm anywhere, since nightfall. Summer's dying. How quickly it goes, once it begins to die." Fanny expresses reproach over Isabel's "queer" behavior, her violation of mourning Wilbur.

Not only did little seem to "happen" overtly in this most Chekhovian of scenes, prompting RKO to discard it even *before* the Pomona preview, but it ended with an element of fantasy that underscored George's emotional immaturity. While George sits brooding, Lucy (to quote Welles's shooting script) "appears in old-fashioned transparency (the shadowy ghost figure from the silents). She throws herself on the steps at his feet." The visionary Lucy begs George to forgive her and assures him that she will never again listen to her father's opinions. George solemnly pardons her, but then he pictures Lucy "as she probably really is at this moment; sitting on her own front porch in the moonlight with four or five boys, all of them laughing most likely, and some idiot probably playing a guitar." Realizing he has been talking to himself, George leaps up and yells, "Pardon nothing! Riffraff! Riffraff! Riffraff!" This was to have dissolved to the lawn scene, which RKO relocated to an earlier place in the picture.

The climax of the drama, George's tactless announcement that "Automobiles are a useless nuisance," comes in the dinner sequence, the next retained in the film and reportedly Welles's favorite in the film. This is George's first formal step. From this point on he is determined to wreck his mother's romance. The first few shots keep George in the background, on the periphery of the conversation. He blurts out his line off-screen while Eugene and the Major are shown talking; Welles cuts to Jack withdrawing his hand from the table, then to Isabel holding her breath, her head slightly back and her eyes partly closed. Only then does he show George, who repeats the insult and adds, "They'll never amount to anything but a nuisance and they had no business to be invented." After a reprimand from Jack (which in the novel is given by the Major, Jack being absent), George is shown in sullen isolation. In the background is a giant cross-bar shadow, similar to those which appear throughout *Kane* at the most ominous moments: the opening, the breakfast montage, Susan's suicide attempt, the ending. Welles also made extensive use of this visual motif in *Othello*, showing Iago's cage time and again during the course of the action.

"I'm not sure George is wrong about automobiles," Eugene replies to the insult with measured intensity. "With all their speed forward they may be a step backward in civilization. It may be that they won't add to the beauty of the world or the life of men's souls—I'm not sure. But automobiles have come, and almost all outward things are going to be different because of what they bring. They're going to alter war, and they're going to alter peace. And I think men's minds are going to be changed in subtle ways because of automobiles. And it may be that George is right. It may be that in ten or twenty years from now, if we can see the inward change in men by that time, I shouldn't be able to defend the gasoline engine, but would have to agree with George—that automobiles had no business to be invented."

Following Eugene's eloquent speech and his angry departure, Fanny accosts George in the hallway, expressing her anguished approval of his tactics. Welles employs one of the most powerfully sustained crane shots of his career as George follows Fanny through huge shadows and they halt on the first landing, the camera tilted slightly to the right as George shakes her with violent emotion. This is one of Agnes Moorehead's greatest scenes. She simultaneously conveys profound anger at George and sympathy for George, envy of Isabel, and devastating self-pity ("It's only old Fanny, so whatever she says, pick on her for it! Hammer her! Hammer her! It's only poor old lonely Fanny!"). She insists that the romance between Isabel and Eugene "never would have amounted to anything if Wilbur had lived," and George asks incredulously, "You mean Morgan might have married *you?*" She gulps—her head back, her fingers doing a nervous pirouette on the railing—and, with exquisite inflection, says, "No . . . because I don't know that . . . I'd have accepted him."

George dashes off, leaving Fanny terrified. As he grills the old gossip, Mrs. Johnson, the camera eavesdrops, reframing the characters five times in its almost complete revolution around the room. The transition from this scene is a visual shock like that of the screeching cockatoo in *Citizen Kane*: George in his dark suit strides out of the frame left—the white-dressed Mrs. Johnson stands outraged for a moment—then a cut to Jack's bath water streaming out of the tap as he and the tap make similar groaning sounds. Following George's argument with Jack about whether Isabel has the right to marry Eugene (somewhat abridged by RKO to lessen George's obnoxiousness), a scene was cut by RKO of George ostentatiously placing a framed picture of his father on a mantelpiece in the drawing-room, then moving it to a table. The next part of the sequence is retained in the released film: Eugene arriving, George watching from the window, George opening the door and ordering him to leave. "Perhaps you'll understand *this*," he says, and slams the door. For about ten seconds Morgan stands still, seen through the frosted glass. Then he leaves, and George goes back into the house, slamming the door of the entrance hall behind him. The studio cut the end of the sequence, in which Isabel finds George sitting in the drawing-room. Hearing the doorbell ring and being told by the maid that it was a peddler, she asks George what the earlier "peddler" (George's explanation to the maid) had been selling. "He didn't say," George answers. A tense moment follows after Isabel notices the picture George has placed on the table. She casually asks if it is Lucy, but then says, "Oh! That was nice of you, Georgie. I ought to have had it framed myself, when I gave it to you."

A short scene of George peering out the front door was to precede the scene of Isabel waiting in the drawing-room for Eugene to arrive. But in the film as it stands, the earlier scene of George walking away from Eugene at the door dissolves into Isabel waiting (the framed picture of Wilbur prominently on view). After Jack leads her through the hall to tell her what George has done, a ponderous upward tilt of the camera, underscored by a heavy musical chord and huge shadows, shows Fanny dashing down the stairs to keep George from disturbing his mother.

In the release version, a tilted shot of the empty hall (through which Jack and Isabel had walked moments earlier) bridges scenes of Eugene writing a letter to Isabel urging her to defy George, and Isabel reading the letter. The subsequent confrontation between mother and son was reshot by Robert Wise to tone down George's brutally forbidding reaction to Isabel's marriage plans. In Welles's scene, George calls Eugene's letter "simply the most offensive piece of writing that I've ever held in my hands," and tells her that in opposing the marriage he is "doing what my father would do if he were here." She capitulates—but not easily, not mawkishly, as she does in the scene now in the film. (In the script, Welles followed this confrontation with George self-consciously examining himself in a mirror and whispering Hamlet's speech beginning "'Tis not alone my inky cloak, good mother ..." That scene does not appear in the original cutting continuity.) Two brief scenes cut from the film were to show Isabel slipping a letter under George's door and him reading it; this is her final surrender to George, who frowns as he whispers (guiltily?), "Mother."

The long tracking shot along the street with George and Lucy, the film's next scene, is concerned not with a combat between two wills, as was their earlier trip through the town, but with Lucy's cool domination over George. Hence the camera maintains a *constant* distance from them. Welles's Stroheim-like naturalism dominates here—in the windows of the buildings behind them can be seen reflections of the buildings across the street, as in the earlier shot. But things are different: more people are on the sidewalks, the pedestrians' pace is faster, the traffic heavier (including several automobiles). The earlier shot had included more residences than stores: in place of the earlier scene's homely hardware store are a drapery shop, a large bank, a movie theater, a drugstore. A warehouse has acquired a second story since we saw it last. On the boards outside the theater are posters for a Gaston Méliès Western and for "Jack Holt in *Explosion*," a reference to Tim Holt's father, who started his long Western career in 1919, fourteen years after this scene takes place.

Lucy's rather puzzling indifference to George would be more understandable had the film not been reworked. Welles intended the scene to be in its present place, but it should be recalled that the last time Lucy was to have appeared was in the cut scene of George's "vision." There she was to have been seen being wooed by several other boys, and if that had remained, her subsequent attitude might have seemed less surprising. When George meets her on the street, he asks, "Haven't you —" and she cuts in, "Haven't I what?" He drops the matter and it is apparent that Eugene hasn't told her about what happened the day before (she wouldn't be speaking to George if he had). Her coolness to George in the release version is explained by her comments about the quarrel they had, and how they hadn't spoken to each other "all the way home from a long, long drive." But it is hard for the audience to connect this with the much earlier carriage ride through town. Lucy teases George about the absurdity of their earlier behavior, and the confused audience is left to speculate over whether she has or hasn't heard about Eugene's expulsion after all. And when George walks away and Welles cuts to a closeup of Lucy which includes only the dark parts of her outfit—her collar, hat, and muff—this tonal change, which would have been such an expressive formal effect had the film retained its original structure, only provides more confusion. And when she faints in the drugstore . . . Since this sequence is intended both as counterpoint to a much earlier scene and to refer to a scene which has been removed, it does not work.

The Welles version followed this with a comical scene of the drugstore clerk (Gus Schilling) recounting Lucy's fainting to some pals in a pool hall. Then came another night scene on the mansion verandah, this one between the Major and Fanny. Their dialogue is concerned with the decay of the town and the Major's financial problems, which he had tried to remedy

(without much luck) by having the houses built, and with
Fanny's and Jack's investment in the headlight company. The
dialogue shifts to an elliptical exchange about Isabel's desire
to return home, the Major telling Fanny, "She ought to come
while she can stand the journey."

Since this was removed, the fainting scene now fades to the
scene of Jack helping Lucy out of a chauffeur-driven car in
front of the Morgan mansion. Their dialogue has been redubbed. In Welles's version, Jack wondered if "history's going
on forever repeating itself" and mused, "Well, here's the Amberson mansion again, only it's Georgian instead of nonde-
script Romanesque; but it's just the same Amberson mansion
my father built long before you were born." As they entered
the house, the scene took on a darker overtone:

> Jack: You're pretty refreshingly out of the smoke up
> here.
> Lucy: Yes, until the smoke comes and we have to
> move out farther.
> Jack: No, no. You'll stay here. It'll be somebody else
> who'll move out farther.

The dialogue redubbed by the studio over the characters'
backs is the archest kind of plot exposition: "Mighty nice of
you, Lucy, you and Eugene, to have me over to your new
house my first day back.—You'll probably find the old town
rather dull after Paris." The studio had carefully removed all
the scenes dealing with the new houses on the lawn, and as a
consequence found itself with a five-year gap to explain (it is
now 1910, and the fainting scene occurred in 1905, just before
George and Isabel left for Europe). After Jack tells Eugene and
Lucy that the ailing Isabel wants to come home from abroad,
and the short scenes of Isabel arriving at the station and being
driven home ("Changed—so changed"), Welles had a scene in
the upstairs hall outside Isabel's bedroom.

The Major, querulous and bewildered, demands to see his
daughter, and when he is admitted into the room, Fanny tells
George that Eugene has arrived, wanting to see Isabel. George
abruptly refuses, ordering Fanny to blame the decision on the
doctor. This is followed in the Welles version by Fanny going

downstairs to Eugene and doing as George told her. Eugene asks Fanny if he "could only look into the room and see her for just a second," but he finally capitulates.

Both of those scenes were cut, and an awkward replacement scene was directed by Freddie Fleck, showing George refusing Morgan at the foot of the stairs, Morgan defying him, and then Fanny saying, "I don't think you should right now— the doctor said . . ." and breaking into tears. Jack agrees with her, and Eugene leaves, Fanny following him with her eyes. This change of emphasis is unfortunate. Shifting the final decision, however inconclusively, to a distraught Fanny and to Jack lessens one of the book's (and script's) most powerful themes, George's guilt over denying his mother's last request. A remnant of that theme can be seen in the next shot— George's face superimposed on the window as Eugene walks to his car, visually implying that it was George who ordered Fanny's and Jack's decision, despite the implication of Fleck's scene on the stairs.

The nurse's voice tells George that his mother wants to see him, and Welles immediately cuts from the superimposed shot of George's face to his actual face turning away from the window. This is a powerful effect, a visual shock that in its complete reversal of George's image shows how deeply he is shaken. (Compare this to the bullets shattering the mirror images of Bannister and his wife at the end of *The Lady from Shanghai.*) Achieving this effect allows Welles to understate the deathbed scene. George shows more shame than grief, the grief having been shown at the window, as he listens to his mother's pathetic questions. "Dear, did you—get something to eat?" "Yes, mother." "All you needed?" "Yes, mother." When she says she would have liked to have seen Eugene just once, George turns away in deep shame. Isabel's eyes strain to see him leave.

Welles's version showed George brokenly entering his bedroom, expressing grief over his mother's failing health to Jack and the Major. But in the release version, there is a lap-dissolve from Isabel's face directly into the scene of Fanny telling George of his mother's death. Although Welles maintained, "The full version made that sharp finish much more effective," it remains perhaps the most powerful single shot in Welles's entire body of work. Accompanied by the two contrasting musical motifs used in *Citizen Kane*—the deep brass of the "power" motif and the vibraphone "Rosebud" motif—the slow transition reveals the Major sleeping fitfully on George's bed. He suddenly awakes, the music hinting that he has been dreaming, and rises in terror. The camera makes an hallucinatory pull slightly away from him, Jack crosses in front of him, the camera holds on the Major for a moment and then pans right as he totters off towards Jack, who by now has almost left the frame—suddenly Fanny throws her arms around George, who is standing in the extreme foreground with his back to the camera: "George! She loved you! She loved you!" George's face is not shown, just his back, and Welles again achieves the objective-subjective fusion of the reporter's scenes in *Kane*. The two tiny camera movements achieve such a strong effect because of their careful timing with the characters' movements, with the shock of Fanny's entrance, and because of the surreal, dreamlike compression of the scene: once the Major wakes, it is over in seconds. Like Kane's hand entering the frame to slap Susan, it is an epiphany.

A fade-in flickers to show the Major seated in front of an unseen fireplace, the light of the flames playing on his face. He stares straight into the camera, which is at a slight low angle, like Mr. Clay ruminating on power and destiny many years later in *The Immortal Story*.

"And now," Welles narrates, "Major Amberson was engaged in the profoundest thinking of his life. And he realized that everything which had worried him or delighted him during this lifetime—all his buying and building and trading and banking—that it was all trifling and waste beside what concerned him now. For the Major knew now that he had to plan how to enter an unknown country, where he was not even sure of being recognized as an Amberson."

Richard Bennett, the splendid old stage star Welles had brought out of retirement to play the Major, died two years after the film was completed. He had trouble retaining his lines ("It must be in the sun ... There wasn't anything here, but the sun in the first place ... "), and his eyesight was so bad that he couldn't read from a blackboard during the scene. When the scene was shot, Welles stood just outside the frame and prompted Bennett every few words; later, when the sound was processed, Welles's voice was eliminated. This partially explains the pauses between the phrases, which have such a moving effect when combined with the somber music, the slow track forward, and the sculptural lighting on the Major's deeply lined face. The fadeout also flickers, an effect repeated several times during the film: the lighting on the character's face (here from the fire) is the strongest in the shot, so the dissolve or fade makes the face appear disembodied. (The Major's monologue was somewhat condensed by RKO, which also eliminated off-screen dialogue between Jack and Fanny about their investment in the failed headlight company.)

From this point, the structure of the film has been changed completely. The following is the structure of Welles's original version:

1. Major at fireside.
2. Major's and Isabel's tombstones.
3. Jack borrowing money from George and bidding him farewell at railroad station.
4. George takes his "last walk home" through "what seemed to be the strange streets of a strange city"; dissolves of buildings; the camera follows him to the darkened mansion; he kneels at his mother's bed and asks forgiveness.
5. George learning of the extent of their impoverishment from distraught Fanny in mansion kitchen and ballroom.
6. George refuses a job offer from the lawyer Roger Bronson (Erskine Sanford) and asks help in getting a job in a dynamite factory.
7. Eugene and Lucy walking in their garden, talking about Chief "Rides-Down-Everything."
8. George injured in auto accident.
9. Accident seen as newspaper story, below headline about "AUTOMOBILE BUTCHERY."

10.   Eugene in his factory reading story; leaves for hospital; arrives at hospital; exits hospital.

11.   Eugene visits Fanny at nighttime in her shabby-genteel boarding house. While other boarders eavesdrop and a phonograph plays a seriocomic vaudeville routine about a wealthy man's ruination (performed by Joseph Cotten and Norman Foster), Eugene and Fanny discuss Lucy and George (soon to be married). Fanny reacts with cold desolation as Eugene insensitively speaks to her of Isabel: "Fanny, you're the only person I'd tell this to, but it seemed to me as if someone else was in that room down there at the hospital, and that through me she had brought her boy under shelter again—that I'd been true at last to my true love." They exchange goodnights and Fanny rejoins the other boarders. Eugene gets into his car and drives off into the skyline of the changed city.

12.   Credit sequence, spoken by Welles over shots of Tarkington's novel, film equipment, production materials, and principal cast members. Ends with shot of microphone and Welles saying, "I wrote the script and directed it. My name is Orson Welles. This is a Mercury Production."

The following is the ending structure as it now stands:

1.   Major at fireside (abbreviated).
2.   Jack and George at station (abbreviated).
3.   Eugene and Lucy walking in garden.
4.   George with Fanny in mansion kitchen and ballroom (kitchen scene partly reshot by Jack Moss).
5.   George in Bronson's office.
6.   George walks through town; dissolves of buildings; he kneels at the bed and asks forgiveness (abbreviated, with different closing narration).
7.   George injured in auto accident (abbreviated).
8.   Accident seen as newspaper story (headline revised to "AUTO CASUALTIES MOUNT").
9.   Eugene in his study with Lucy; they leave for hospital (directed by Freddie Fleck).

10. Eugene and Fanny in hospital corridor (directed by Fleck).
11. Credit sequence (composer Bernard Herrmann's credit omitted).

The structure of the final sequences in Welles's original cut had the inevitability of classical tragedy, unfolding with a corresponding visual grace and fluidity. A static scene (Jack's farewell to George) was followed by a montage (George walking home), which was followed by a violent scene (Fanny's hysteria), and so forth. But the scenes as they stand now have only a haphazard chronological continuity, and seem jarringly disconnected from each other, with cavernous and bewildering gaps of storytelling logic. The scene which suffers the most from this displacement is the lovely shot of Eugene and Lucy walking through their garden, which in its present place seems a bit labored and coy. But as Welles intended it, as a meditative counterpoint to the intense dramatic scenes of George's repentance and Fanny's hysteria, it no doubt would have been most effective.

Furthermore, George's job at the dynamite factory seems to last an incongruously short time before he is injured in the auto accident, which in turn is weakened in effect. Welles's plan was for the garden scene to intervene between Bronson's office and the accident. The Morgans' talk would have conditioned the viewer's awareness that George has been on the job for some time, as indeed he has: the script indicates that a year has elapsed. The accident, in the novel's words, was "so commonplace and inconsequent that it was a comedy," but following immediately after his "comeuppance," that moving shot of him kneeling in the deserted house, the accident seems so *consequent* upon his "comeuppance" that it is absurd. But the audience doesn't have time to reflect on the melodramatic effect of its placement, for immediately after the newspaper inserts reporting the accident come the dismal ending scenes directed by assistant director Freddie Fleck. Reviewers of the day seemed oblivious to the studio's reworking of the film, but the perceptive Manny Farber, writing in *The Nation*, sensed that something was awry, attributing the "hearts-and-flowers finish" to "blundering editing."

The thematic reversal in these last two scenes, not to mention the stylistic letdown, is appalling. After a scene in Morgan's study in which Anne Baxter prods a hypnotized-looking
Joseph Cotten into striding out of the frame with her, we are
asked to agree, as Eugene informs Fanny outside George's
hospital room, that "everything's going to be all right." And,
thanks to the meretricious direction, Fanny seems to have become Eugene's "true love."

The book's woolly and rather protracted denouement has
Eugene going to a medium and believing for a while that he
has contacted Isabel, who tells him to "be kind." Then he returns home to see George, who asks his forgiveness. It ends
with the sentimental note that through Eugene, Isabel "had
brought her boy under shelter again. Her eyes would look
wistful no more."

Welles's final scene in the boarding house, on the other
hand, offered a devastating view of shattered lives, set
against the backdrop of an equally blighted city. He described to Bogdanovich what he was seeking in the agonizingly tense final scene between Agnes Moorehead and
Joseph Cotten: "If only you'd seen how she wrapped up the
whole story at the end. . . . Jo Cotten goes to see her after all
those years in a cheap boarding house and there's just nothing left between them at all. Everything is over—her feelings
and her world and his world; everything is buried under the
parking lots and the cars. That's what it was all about—the
deterioration of personality, the way people diminish with
age, and particularly with impecunious old age. The end of
the communication between people, as well as the end of an
era. Sure, it was pretty rough going for an audience—particularly in those days. But without question it was much the
best scene in the movie."

In slapping a new conclusion onto the story, RKO attempted to send the viewers out with the consolation of a
typical Hollywood happy ending—a strategy which, under the
bleak circumstances in which the characters find themselves,
seems truly grotesque. The film now ends with a beaming
Eugene telling Fanny in the hospital corridor that through him
Isabel had "brought her boy under shelter again and that I'd

been true at last to my true love." On these last words, the camera swings to Fanny's face, then back to include Eugene. The implication, reinforced by a sudden burst of music and a little sigh from Fanny, is that Eugene has loved her all along.

The power of individual scenes persists through the chaotic structure of the present ending sequence. Foremost is Agnes Moorehead's great scene in the kitchen and hall of the deserted mansion. Welles rehearsed her over and over until she gave a chillingly convincing portrait of hysteria. As George drags her through the hall, shaking her back to her senses, the camera tracks rapidly back with them through three rooms and into the dining room, gaining increasingly on them and finally pulling away to distance us from a scene of an intensity seldom equalled on film.

The dissolves of George walking through "the strange streets of a strange city" are done with the camera playing George: this objective effect reinforces the strangeness of the dirty buildings, telephone wires and rundown houses ("New Hope Apartments"). The montage was longer in Welles's cut, also including shots of shabby apartment buildings and tenements which once, the narration tells us, were the scenes of happy events in George's boyhood. The montage was to dissolve to shots entering the vacated and neglected mansion (taken from George's point of view), and the script indicates that these would be followed by a dissolve to an elaborate shot (still seen through George's eyes) in which the camera wanders slowly through the mansion. It recapitulates the drawing-room, the kitchen, returns up the staircase, stops for a moment, pans down to the heavy library doors (behind which Isabel had learned of Eugene's expulsion), and after a short pause pans back and continues, even more slowly, up the stairs to the second-floor hall and to the closed door of Isabel's room. The door swings open and we see that nothing has been changed. Then this extraordinary shot was to fade out.

The shot does not appear in the cutting continuity for Welles's original version of the film, however. Carringer speculates that Welles may have not been happy with the footage, which he assigned to Cortez to shoot on his own. During this part of the montage, the script indicates that the narrator was to have said:

> Tonight would be the last night that he and Fanny were to spend in the house which the Major had forgotten to deed to Isabel. Tomorrow they were to move out. Tomorrow everything would be gone. The very space in which tonight was still Isabel's room would be cut into new shapes by new walls and floors and ceilings. And if space itself can be haunted as memory is haunted, then it may be that some impressionable, overworked woman in a "kitchenette," after turning out the light, will seem to see a young man kneeling in the darkness, with arms outstretched through the wall, clutching at the covers of a shadowy bed. It may seem to her that she hears the faint cry, over and over...

At this point the screen was to fade into the dark shot of the back of George's head, which, as the camera retreats, reveals him kneeling in his mother's room, saying, "Mother, forgive me. God, forgive me." But the cutting continuity indicates that the narration was placed over the shot of George kneeling at the bed, with his lines coming at the end of the scene. In the release version, that narration has been dropped entirely and the scene begins with George's lines in voiceover. They are followed by an even more powerful piece of narration, which (surprisingly) is not in the original cutting continuity:

> Something had happened—a thing which, years ago, had been the eagerest hope of many, many good citizens of the town. And now it came at last: George Amberson Minafer had got his comeuppance. He'd got it three times filled—and running over. But those who had so longed for it were not there to see it, and they never knew it. Those who were still living had forgotten all about it and all about him.

"If Flaubert re-read *Don Quixote* each year," Truffaut once remarked, "why can't we re-see *The Ambersons* whenever possible?" The first half of the film is relatively intact, and enough of Welles's overall conception remains for it to be apparent from the film itself just how great it was before RKO got cold feet.

Despite the fact that the studio showed little more faith in the recut version than in the Welles version, Robert Wise has always attempted to justify the recutting as a matter of commercial necessity: "We had a picture with major problems, and I feel all of us tried sincerely to keep the best of Welles's concept and still lick the problem. Since Ambersons has become something of a classic, I think it's now apparent we didn't 'mutilate' Orson's film." Wise felt that World War II had prevented the audience's interest in the film's subject matter. While it's likely that such a corrosive view of the effects of "progress" on a typical American city would have had difficulty finding an audience in *any* era (even if the film seems remarkably prescient today), there is no doubt that Welles's timing in bringing *Ambersons* to the screen during the early days of America's involvement in the war was highly unfortunate. The *New York Times* spoke for its public: "In a world brimful of momentous drama beggaring serious screen treatment, it does seem that Mr. Welles is imposing when he asks moviegoers to become emotionally disturbed over the decline of such minor-league American aristocracy as the Ambersons represented in the late Eighteen Seventies."

Aside from some frame enlargements that were preserved by Welles himself, and a few snippets in the film's trailer, the missing footage of *The Magnificent Ambersons* no longer exists, having been junked long ago by RKO. Kane's loss of Rosebud was no sadder than this. Welles in later life talked of shooting two new reels to make the ending coherent, using the surviving actors in their old age, but it was not to be.

Bogdanovich tells a moving story of Welles being cajoled to watch *Ambersons* on television in the early 1970s. At first watching from a doorway, Welles "casually made his way across the room and sat on the very edge of a sofa, and looked at the TV intently, but with a kind of desperation combined with a terrible anxiety." After a while, it became apparent that he had tears in his eyes. Bogdanovich adds, "About a year later—we were in Paris—I asked Orson about that evening. I said I supposed it had been painful for him to watch the movie in its butchered form. 'No,' he said, 'it wasn't that—not at all. *That* just makes me angry. Don't you see? It was because it's the past—it's over..."'

For us, thankfully, Orson Welles's past is not over. We still have eighty-eight minutes of *The Magnificent Ambersons* (most of it his). And while watching this wonderful movie, we can follow Wordsworth's prescription about the past and

> ...grieve not, rather find
> Strength in what remains behind.

5: Picking Up the Pieces:
Journey Into Fear, It's All True, The Stranger

Journey Into Fear

In the new contract he signed with RKO after the release of
Citizen Kane, Welles was allowed to direct a relatively ex-
pensive film in which he would not appear, *The Magnificent
Ambersons,* in return for producing a bread-and-butter picture he would not direct but in which he and his stock
company of Mercury actors would appear. That film was
Journey Into Fear, a war thriller set in the Near East, based
on the novel by Eric Ambler. Thrown together with little
preparation, it began shooting under Norman Foster's direction in January 1942, during the final weeks of shooting on
Ambersons. The reason it was rushed into production was
that Welles wanted to discharge his obligation to RKO for a
third picture before he left for South America. With an
often tongue-in-cheek screenplay by Joseph Cotten (who
played the lead role) and Welles (uncredited), *Journey Into
Fear* was intended as a *divertissement,* a semi-serious relaxa-
tion from the demands of Welles's more personal projects,
but it wound up being merely inconsequential.

Playing the first of his costume villains, a glowering Turkish police chief named Colonel Haki, Welles filmed his scenes
mostly at night, after spending the day directing *Ambersons*
(sometimes in full Haki regalia), a hectic situation that no
doubt contributed to the offhand, almost sloppy air that mars
Journey Into Fear. Everett Sloane said that "we did all Orson's
scenes first and he directed them, then Norman did the rest of
it. I think it retains much of Orson's original conception of the

picture." Welles tended to downplay his contribution, however: "For the first five sequences I was on the set and decided angles; from then on, I often said where to put the camera, described the framings, made light tests. . . . I designed the
film but can't properly be called the director."

The story resembles those of several later Welles films. Cotten plays a naive American engineer, Howard Graham, who is
dragged off by the Nazis to prevent him from arming Turkish
ships. Like Michael O'Hara in *The Lady from Shanghai*, Welles's
archetypal "innocent," and Joseph K. in *The Trial*, Graham
stumbles foolishly into more and more danger while trying to
understand why he is being pursued. Welles's Colonel Haki is
in a sinister position of power similar to that of the Advocate
in *The Trial*, and Graham resembles K. in his impeccably busi-
ness-like appearance and in his self-conscious jesting about a
grim situation. The incomprehension of Graham's wife (Ruth
Warrick) is agreeably humorous, and the film is all but stolen
by a greasy, silent, baby-faced villain played by Welles's business manager, Jack Moss, who looks almost exactly like one of
the executioners in *The Trial*. If it doesn't hold together as entertainment or have any special thematic compulsion, *Journey
Into Fear* serves at least as a very rough draft for some of
Welles's later films.

One of the modest virtues of *Journey Into Fear* is that it
doesn't take its absurd situation too seriously. When the villain
sits across the table from Graham and starts to gobble his dinner menacingly, Graham furtively tosses some salt over his
shoulder. Some of the fey humor of the script is more tedious
than charming, however, and Cotten's characterization of Graham becomes distractingly blasé. The net result is a thriller
that isn't thrilling, a second-rate imitation of Hitchcock. Whatever urgency Graham's predicament may be presumed to possess is submerged by the power of set-pieces—a murder during the blackout of a magic act (a good idea indifferently
directed) and a gun duel on a window ledge during a blind-
ing rainstorm. Moderately atmospheric, sprinkled with Wellesian camera flourishes, the film is given its most enjoyable
moments by the performances of such character actors as
Moss, Sloane, Agnes Moorehead, Frank Readick, Eustace

Wyatt, and Edgar Barrier, who skillfully handle the unsettling about-faces demanded by Ambler's plot.

Welles is less successful in his role as Colonel Haki, a man reputed to have a voracious appetite for liquor, intrigue, and bloodshed. The makeup for the character was modeled on Joseph Stalin, and Welles acts Haki with the swaggering hauteur and contemptuous humor of a Broadway actor slumming in a traveling stock company. He seems unable to make up his mind whether the character is supposed to be sinister or amusing, and the result is a caricature, like many of the acting roles he would assume in other directors' films throughout his subsequent career.

After the *Ambersons* debacle, RKO heavily reworked *Journey Into Fear* in Welles's absence before releasing it in August 1942. As Welles told Bogdanovich, "It was the opposite of an action picture, since it was based on the kind of thing that Ambler does so well, which is inaction, antiheroics, and all that. And they just took out everything that made it interesting except the action—trying desperately to turn it into an action-B—and made quite a lot of nothing out of it." Welles threatened to sue but agreed to shoot a brief new ending scene, recut the last reel, and add a narration by Cotten. The final revised version, which runs a bare sixty-nine minutes, was released inauspiciously in February 1943. This misguided attempt by Welles to be a "commercial" producer no doubt was made less distinctive by studio meddling, but the fact that it looks like such a hodgepodge cannot be blamed entirely on the studio. Because of the hybrid nature of the direction, in which Foster was nominally in charge but Welles tried to make little "improvements" here and there, *Journey Into Fear* lacked a firm hand at the tiller. It proved only that Welles could not function effectively when his heart was not really in his work.

It's All True

For Welles aficionados, the triumphant release of the documentary *It's All True: Based on an Unfinished Film by Orson Welles* (1993) was literally a dream come true. I thought I would never see more than fragments of the legendary lost film Welles shot in South America in 1942 for RKO and the U.S. State Department's Coordinator of Inter-American Affairs (Nelson Rockefeller). To be able to see a (nearly) complete reconstruction of one of the three segments of It's All True—Four Men on a Raft, an unexpectedly haunting piece of poetic naturalism—enlarges our conception of Welles, and reminds us that, if he had been able to complete his many unfinished projects, his filmography would be much more diverse than the sum of the films he completed before his death in 1985. As Jonathan Rosenbaum wrote in his Summer 1986 Sight and Sound article "The Invisible Orson Welles," a catalogue of those uncompleted films, "Even the fragmentary evidence already becoming available suggests a different Welles from the one we have become accustomed to calling our own, and clearly this is as it should be: was there ever a film in his career that didn't confound our expectations?"

Much of the writing on the calamitous production of It's All True had centered on Welles's filming of Rio de Janeiro's carnival—the segment of the film that was to have been called The Story of Samba—and on the fatal accident that marred the filming of Four Men on a Raft. The comparatively low-key, and successful, filming of the rest of Four Men on a Raft, in the fishing village of Fortaleza and along the Brazilian coast, had gone largely unreported. But the resourceful makers of the documentary—longtime Welles associate Richard Wilson and devoted cinéastes Myron Meisel and Bill Krohn—have managed to reconstruct that segment from about 140,000 feet of surviving It's All True footage, most of it discovered in a Paramount vault in the early 1980s by studio executive Fred Chandler. In addition to production footage and interviews with Welles and others involved in the filming, the documentary includes tantalizing fragments of The Story of Samba, with both black-and-white and richly variegated Technicolor footage of the Rio Carnival (only 5,000 feet of Technicolor material survived, including some footage of samba dancers shot in a studio). There is also one lushly photographed sequence in black-and-white from the other uncompleted segment, My Friend Bonito (directed in Mexico by Norman Foster), Robert

Flaherty's story of a young boy whose pet bull is spared from the *corrida*.

The enormously complicated political, financial, and artistic issues surrounding the production of *It's All True* and RKO's decision to abort the film are dealt with somewhat incompletely in the documentary, which barely alludes to the controversy over whether Welles himself should share any of the culpability. Starkly disparate accounts of the filming are given in the biographies of Welles by his leading detractor Charles Higham, who blames Welles almost entirely for the debacle, painting him as egregiously undisciplined; by his leading acolyte Barbara Leaming, who places most of the blame on RKO for being duplicitous and unsympathetic to Welles's artistic vision, but suggests that Welles spent too much of his time womanizing; and by Frank Brady, who departs from his generally sympathetic treatment of Welles's career to find much of the director's conduct in Brazil reckless and artistically unfocused, even as he finds RKO's conduct reprehensible.

However, like Welles's own account in the posthumously published *This Is Orson Welles*, the *It's All True* documentary passionately argues that he struggled heroically to make a truthful portrait of Brazil in the face of fierce opposition from both the new regime at RKO and the right-wing Brazilian government. Richard Wilson's 1970 *Sight and Sound* article on the production deals more fully than the documentary does with some of these issues, and further important research was published in 1989 in the scholarly journal *Persistence of Vision* by Robert Stam and Catherine Benamou (who was associate producer and senior research executive on the documentary). The available evidence strongly suggests that although Welles's battles with RKO over time and money ostensibly led to the studio scuttling the film, political considerations were the conclusive factor, due to what Rosenbaum calls Welles's "radical pro-black stance, including the fact that he enjoyed the company and collaboration of blacks, as well as his insistence on featuring non-whites as the pivotal characters in both the film's Brazilian episodes."

Stam's well-documented study, "Orson Welles, Brazil, and the Power of Blackness," argues that "in the case of *It's All*

True, the general indictment of Welles's personality—projected as irresponsible, arrogant, power-hungry, narcissistic—is accompanied by a distinct cultural dimension. A kind of isomorphism links the censure of Welles and the implicit critique of a Brazilian culture at that time (and to some extent still today) very much misunderstood and undervalued. A common hostility embraces both Welles and certain features of Brazilian culture, a hostility subtended, I would suggest, by the implicit racial conventions of enthnocentric discourse. The Rio de Janeiro segment of *It's All True,* for example, was intended to [be] an enthusiastic hommage to the gregarious spirit and protean energy of Rio's carnival, yet a striking feature of the critical discourse is a pervasive, almost visceral, anti-carnivalism. A metonymical 'contamination' links Welles's personality and his carnival subject; the bill of particulars against Welles echoes the perennial accusations against carnival itself—debauched, dissipated, dissolute. The 'tragedy' of Welles's 'fall' must entail a tragic flaw, and that flaw has a name: carnival and its attendant vices."

Perhaps the most important revelation that emerges from the documentary, and the aspect of *It's All True* most pertinent to this study of Welles's work, is what a key transitional film this clearly was not only in his Hollywood fortunes but in his artistic evolution. Working with mostly non-actors on Brazilian locations, with his Hollywood studio career already largely in ruins, Welles (as the documentary aptly puts it) "invented a new style to fit this new kind of filmmaking." Relying more on highly fragmented montage than on long takes and camera movement, freely transforming actual settings into imaginary landscapes, and molding performances from an unusual assortment of people with varied acting skills, it was a style he would pursue for much of the rest of his career. Looser and more improvisatory than his early work in Hollywood, the style was derived both from financial necessity and from Welles's restless spirit of creative experimentation, as he pursued what Truffaut called "his position as an avant-garde director."

Like the documentaries of Robert Flaherty, to which it is much indebted, *Four Men on a Raft* is not an actual record of an unfolding event, but the poetic reconstruction of actuality. Welles recreates the epic journey in 1941 of four Brazilian fishermen (known as *jangadeiros,* since they travelled on a raft, or *jangada*) to protest inequitable economic conditions in their profession and in their remote village on the northeastern coast of Brazil. The *jangadeiros* became national heroes in the course of their journey, which led to some reforms but, as the documentary indicates, did little in the long run to change the lot of their impoverished village and others like it. Welles had angered the Brazilian authorities (and RKO) by filming the wretched conditions in Rio's *favelas,* or hillside shantytowns, for *The Story of Samba,* and his subsequent reenactment of the journey of the *jangadeiros* called unwelcome attention to the superficiality of dictator Getúlio Vargas's commitment to genuine reform. What a tragic irony it was, therefore, when on May 19, 1942, during Welles's reenactment of the *jangadeiros'* arrival in Rio's Guanabara Bay, the leader of the group—Manuel Olimpio Meira, known as Jacaré ("Alligator")—was killed when a wave capsized their raft and he was swept overboard.

Although RKO already had decided to terminate the production, Welles managed to persuade the studio that the anguish Brazilians were suffering over the accident would be compounded by failure to complete the cinematic tribute to the *jangadeiros'* achievement. He had wanted to make *Four Men on a Raft* in Technicolor (some stunning color footage of the arrival in Rio survives in the documentary), but RKO allowed Welles only 45,000 feet of black-and-white 35mm film, a rock-bottom allotment of $10,000, and a crew of five to film with a single camera (without sound) for five weeks in Fortaleza and along the coast. Belying his largely unjustified reputation for extravagance, Welles lovingly and economically crafted the wordless narrative (which runs 48 minutes in the reconstruction) with the enthusiastic participation of the surviving *jangadeiros* and the rest of the villagers. Although the reenactment of the actual voyage is somewhat anticlimactic, hampered by inadequate resources that made the footage seem disjointed and artificial, *Four Men on a Raft* is, as Welles remembered the filming process, "an extraordinary experience."

Grande Othelo, the celebrated Brazilian singer who appeared in *The Story of Samba*, recalled that in making *It's All True*, Welles "came to love not only Brazil, but all of humanity, through the mixture of races he saw here." That theme, which was central to the entire film, was also expressed by Welles in his declaration in a subsequent radio broadcast: "It occurs to me that, since men in the world have to live with one another and get along somehow, they might learn a great deal about tolerance and quiet decency from the Brazilians, who have the blood of all men."

Unlike other Welles films, *Four Men on a Raft* deals not with men of power, but with the ordinary people oppressed by men of power. In writing of *The Trial*, Welles's adaptation of Kafka's novel about a totalitarian state, Truffaut commented that "Welles, who is so much at ease filming power, pride and dominion, maybe isn't equipped to show their opposites: weakness, humility, submission." But while some filmmakers might have fallen into the trap of depicting the Brazilian poor as weak, humble, and submissive, Welles does the opposite in choosing to tell the story of the heroic defiance of the *jangadeiros*. Their humble station is a matter of circumstances, not of temperament, for Welles depicts them as motivated by a simple, unaffected pride; their actions demand not pity but respect. Rather than revealing the secret fragility of the strong, as most Welles films do, *Four Men on a Raft* reveals the secret strength of the weak, the strength that comes from communal resistance to injustice. Welles's treatment of the subject is imbued with the romantic view of the peasantry common to leftist documentaries of the period, as can be seen not only in George Fanto's opulent lighting but also in Welles's frequent employment (for once not ironic) of the heroic low-angle perspective. Yet the director's passionate embrace of the people of Fortaleza and his direct identification with their political protest keeps *Four Men on a Raft* from being sentimental or condescending.

Nor is the film simply a piece of leftist agitprop, for in his close attention to the physicality of the rituals and rhythms of daily life in the fishing village—the building of the raft, the catching of fish, the women's seaside lacemaking, and the courtship, wedding, and funeral of a young fisherman—Welles painted the kind of timeless portrait of a primitive society that Flaherty created in *Nanook of the North* and *Man of Aran*, Murnau in *Tabu*, and Eisenstein in the similarly unfinished *Que Viva Mexico!*. The influence of all of those films is strong in *Four Men on a Raft* (as is the pervasive influence of John Ford, Welles's favorite director), yet Welles's idiosyncratic style is also unmistakably present in the intricately baroque compositions, with their elaborate chiaroscuro of rippling light and shade, the dynamism of their extreme foreground-background tensions, and their always fresh and unexpected vantage points.

One planned element that is lacking in *Four Men on a Raft* is narration. Welles wanted to use the *jangadeiros'* voices as a chorus, and he no doubt would have added some of his own commentary. No such aural material survives, but the documentary provides enough context for the story to make it understandable through the visuals alone, and the non-verbal approach lends the film a rare purity. A more serious problem in the restoration of *Four Men on a Raft* is the somewhat indulgent editing by Ed Marx, who seems to have fallen so in love with Welles's imagery that he occasionally allows the film to become languid and dilatory. Welles once said that the test of a good director is whether he is willing to throw out his most beautiful shots, and though this particular story demanded a somewhat more measured and lingering rhythm than was characteristic of Welles's work in general, it's hard to avoid the feeling that he would have imposed a more rigorous tempo here and there, cutting some shots more succinctly and generally assembling the film in a less conventional manner. "They often speak of Orson Welles as a poet; I see him rather as a musician," Truffaut once commented. "His Falstaff film *Chimes at Midnight* is the film which most resembles an opera. Orson Welles's work is prose which becomes music on the cutting bench. His films are shot by an exhibitionist and edited by a censor."

Welles himself cautioned RKO that the carnival footage he was sending back from Rio could not be properly appreciated until he had a chance to edit and score it; the unorthodox structure of *It's All True*, like the essay-film format of his late film *F for Fake*, would have been crafted largely on the cutting bench. But the fact that one segment of *It's All True* survives and that at least some of Welles's intentions shine through the ruination of this legendary project is nothing short of miraculous, enabling us to begin reevaluating his entire career trajectory from this previously missing step. The long road from Fortaleza leads through the beaches of Acapulco and the crowded streets of San Francisco's Chinatown (*The Lady from Shanghai*), follows the byzantine byways of Morocco and Italy (*Othello*), traverses the dusty paths of Spain and Mexico by horse and donkey (*Don Quixote*), races giddily through a bizarre mélange of European sites (*Mr. Arkadin, The Trial*), and finally, at the end of this most circuitous route, arrives back in the crumbling soundstages of Hollywood (*The Other Side of the Wind*). Perhaps some day, somehow, all the lost footage shot by Orson Welles will see the light of day, and the entire shape of his vision will be revealed. But until then the last word should remain with one of the villagers of Fortaleza interviewed in the *It's All True* documentary. José (Bafou) Pereira da Silva, son of the *jangadeiro* Manuel (Preto) Pereira da Silva, expresses a bittersweet sentiment with which everyone who was ever involved with an unfinished Welles film can readily identify:

"My father said: 'My son, after I die this film may improve your life.' And that's what we are waiting for. You know, a fisherman never leaves an inheritance. This film is the only inheritance the four raftsmen left us."

The Stranger

André Bazin speaks of *The Stranger* as a "parody" of a Welles film, and the remark is judicious. The story offers the elements of a good film—an ex-Nazi teaching at a prep school in a small Connecticut town is hunted down by a war crimes investigator—but much of *The Stranger* (1946) teeters ludicrously into melodramatic hokum. Not only is the film hamstrung by corny dialogue and implausible character relationships (partly due to recutting by the producers), but it revolves around an impossibly hammy performance by Welles that just about singlehandedly destroys the story's tenuous credibility.

Some of the black-comic exaggeration in the director's treatment of the ex-Nazi, Franz Kindler (a k a Charles Rankin), seems to have been intentional. At one point, making a public telephone call from the town drugstore, the supposedly cunning and secretive architect of the "Final Solution" distractedly doodles a swastika on a notepad hanging next to the phone and whistles what sounds like "Deutschland über Alles." And in the outlandishly spectacular finale, the Nazi falls from a church tower after being impaled on the sword of a clockwork angel, a scene the director later described as "Pure Dick Tracy . . . a straight comic-book finish." These elements oddly clash with the supposed seriousness of the theme, undercutting Welles's sometimes cogent but frequently heavy-handed attempt to warn the American public about the postwar resurgence of neo-Nazism, a subject he also stressed in his newspaper columns and radio broadcasts of the period.

Although Welles made uncredited contributions to the screenplay by Anthony Veiller and John Huston (who also was uncredited), his directorial freedom was limited, a situation he accepted for pragmatic reasons. When offered his first chance to direct a movie following the collapse of his deal with RKO, Welles accepted *The Stranger,* as he said at the time, "to prove to the industry that I could direct a standard Hollywood picture, on time and on budget, just like anyone else." Unfortunately, he succeeded all too well in those goals; but despite its conventionality, *The Stranger* failed to make him any more bankable in Hollywood.

Under more auspicious circumstances, Welles might have approached *The Stranger* with greater ambition, for it follows the general thematic pattern of his films: the guilty secret, the nemesis/investigator, the scenes of unmasking, the chastened "innocents," and the protagonist's "tragic fall." Sections of the film, moreover, are excitingly directed on the visual level, especially the baroque opening pursuit of Meinike, another escaped Nazi, in South America (much longer in Welles's original cut), and the murder of Meinike by Kindler at the end of a breathtaking, four-minute tracking shot as they walk through the Connecticut woods. The intricate, metaphoric use of shadows by Welles and cinematographer Russell Metty, the sinuous moving camera shots, and the unobtrusively long takes are often astonishingly subtle in their creation of a mood of guilty foreboding. Some of the performances are memorable, particularly those of Konstantine Shayne as the demented, Bible-reading Meinike and Billy House as Potter, the comical, checkers-playing drugstore man who serves as the film's Shakespearean chorus. *The Stranger* is not quite as bad a film as I claimed in the first edition of this book—its intermittent visual authority becomes more apparent on repeated viewings—but it still is a disappointing piece of work.

Admitting that *The Stranger* was "the worst of my films," Welles said, "It is absolutely of no interest to me. I did not make it with cynicism, however. I did my best with it. . . . The best stuff in the picture was a . . . big chase in South America, with a whole series of very wild, dreamlike events that worried [producer Sam] Spiegel and [executive producer William] Goetz, so they took them out, but I think it was a mistake. The picture would have been much more interesting visually with them in; it was really the only chance to be interesting visually in the story."

Still, it's possible that, even with the other constraints imposed on the director, *The Stranger* could have been greatly enriched if Welles had not been cast by the producers as Kindler, but instead had taken the other key male role, the war crimes investigator, Wilson, played by Edward G. Robinson. (Welles had an even more intriguing casting idea for the investigator—Agnes Moorehead—but Goetz wouldn't hear of it.) Robinson's character has an intriguing ambivalence which isn't fully realized in the overly sanctimonious performance: to trap the Nazi, Wilson is willing to make a pawn of the life of just about anyone, a callous dimension that Welles surely could have insinuated into the role more sharply if he had played it.

After the film's intricate cat-and-mouse setup, the film becomes progressively less interesting as Kindler's relationship with his initially unsuspecting American wife, Mary Longstreet (Loretta Young), gradually takes center stage. The pointless proliferation of closeups as the film heads towards its climax is ample evidence that Welles was losing his grip on how to treat the story. Any drama inherent in Mary's gradual awakening to her husband's past is destroyed, despite Young's workmanlike performance, by Welles's manic face-pulling and sinister muttering. The hero's "secret" becomes a ludicrous joke at the expense of the rest of the world, for it is impossible to conceive of the character passing undetected by anyone, let alone the woman who married him. As critic Walter Kerr wrote, Loretta Young and Edward G. Robinson "were confronted with the spectacle of Mr. Welles, as a disguised Nazi spy, walking through the film with an expression on his face which would have brought out the entire staff of Bellevue in an instant, and how they were able to keep *their* faces straight, I shall never know."

For the film to have made sense on a narrative level, Kindler should have been played with sufficient superficial charm to convince the audience that not only the guileless Mary, but also the other townspeople, supposedly shrewd Yankees, could have fallen for his act without suspecting his inward corruption. As it is, Mary seems unbelievably naive, even criminally so after Kindler confesses to her that he murdered Meinike and she willingly, out of misguided love mingled with masochism, accepts his false explanation for the deed. The shooting script indicates that Welles intended to delve more deeply into the aberrant psychology of a woman of whom it could be said, as Graham Greene wrote of Pyle in *The Quiet American*, "Innocence is a kind of insanity." Because of the commercial imperatives of Young's star *persona*, however, such considerations are only furtively present in the otherwise conventionally melodramatic scenes of the woman's wide-eyed terror as she slowly awakens to her husband's past.

While playing Kindler, Welles might have been well advised to follow the advice the Nazi gives his wife, that they adopt a manner of "perfect naturalness at all times." But that clearly was beyond his capabilities as an actor. The only real force Welles brings to his characterization is the palpable feeling of guilt and self-revulsion emanating from his haunted eyes and from the occasional gagging delivery of his lines, such as his admission to his wife, "Murder can be a chain, Mary—one link following another until it circles your neck." In this rare glimmer of tragic lucidity, Kindler resembles the protagonist of another Welles film, Macbeth, who murdered his way to the crown and came to the awful realization that

> I am in blood
> Stepp'd in so far that, should I wade no more,
> Returning were as tedious as go o'er.

Could anyone seriously defend the totality of Welles's performance in *The Stranger*? Surprisingly, Michael Anderegg attempts to do so in his 1989 essay "Orson Welles as Performer," in which he argues: "Welles's Kindler is so transparent a villain, so clearly not what the all-American inhabitants of Harper, Connecticut, think him to be, that America's complacency and naiveté becomes a dominant issue in the film. Welles performs in such a way that no member of the film audience could possibly make the error his fiancée and others make. Almost as if afraid of allowing the evil of Nazism to appear even momentarily attractive, Welles refuses to act out the charm and plausibility that other characters presumably see in Franz Kindler. . . . Throughout *The Stranger*, Welles delivers even the most innocent-sounding lines with the guilty subtext clearly indicated, continually providing commentary in tandem with representation."

Anderegg's ingenious argument perhaps represents the best elucidation of Welles's intentions in playing Franz Kindler. Such an approach to the character might have been provocative indeed if the film's overall style had only been more expressionistic, more in the vein of *Touch of Evil* or *The Trial*. But Welles's direction was pulled in the opposite direction by his unfortunate need to make a film that would be acceptable by the stylistic norms of 1946 Hollywood; the elimination of the "very wild, dreamlike events" in South America further undercut the film's potential. As a result, the relatively naturalistic style of the release version leads the viewer to expect a dramatization of what Hannah Arendt, in writing later of Kindler's real-life counterpart Adolf Eichmann, would describe as "the banality of evil"—a phrase that does not fit Welles's characteristic attempt to make a Shakespearean villain of Franz Kindler.

6: *The Lady from Shanghai*

After several meandering years, Welles at last hit his stride again with *The Lady from Shanghai*. There is a new freedom of visual style, a willingness to relax, to accommodate *longueurs* and exhilarating bits of simple fun. In no other film, not even *Citizen Kane*, do we share with Welles such a spontaneous delight in the exercise of his gifts. The story is handled in a most cavalier fashion; indeed, it took me eight viewings to detach myself enough to figure out the plot. If it had not been for some of the darker underlying ironies and twists of convention, *The Lady from Shanghai* might have been a popular success. Welles destroys a number of highly romantic myths in the denouement, but he satisfies many of our expectations along the way.

Howard Hawks's *The Big Sleep*, with an even more bewildering narrative, was an enormous success in 1946, the year *Shanghai* was made, and in that postwar *film noir* era, the public might have been willing to accept the novelty of seeing Rita Hayworth as a murderess. However, Columbia was so horrified at what Welles had done to her image, and at his bizarre approach to storytelling, that it held up the film's release for two years. Columbia took the editing out of Welles's hands, made him shoot romantic closeups of Hayworth and other new scenes to order, severely truncated a surrealistic sequence set in the crazy house of an empty amusement park, and added a deliriously corny and crushingly heavy-handed musical score of which the director complained, "If the lab had scratched initials and phone numbers all over the negative, I couldn't be unhappier with the results."

Released on the bottom half of a double bill in May 1948, *The Lady from Shanghai* lost a fortune and further marked Welles as anathema in Hollywood. For all its detrimental effect on his credit with the studios, though, Welles's devil-may-care attitude towards the plot is one of the foremost pleasures of the film. If we do not feel the great compression and exactness of execution that mark *Kane* and *Ambersons* as masterpieces, we can see in the film's unforced pleasantness its superiority to a more pretentious work such as *The Trial*, not only as entertainment but also as a complex and effective expression of Welles's most deeply felt themes. As Robin Wood remarks of Hitchcock's *North by Northwest:* "A light entertainment can have depth, subtlety, finesse, it can embody mature moral values; indeed, it seems to me that it *must*. . . . The tongue-in-cheek element on plot level has the function of directing our attention to other levels."

Comparison with Hitchcock is inevitable, and as a thriller Welles's film has the same elements of irrationality and moral irony that confound critics who see Hitchcock as a mere manipulator of plot crises. In dealing with *The Lady from Shanghai,* the critic has a less onerous task in demonstrating the artist's seriousness, since Welles deals explicitly with themes which Hitchcock treats by implication—i.e., moral conflict within the law (which we see in *North by Northwest* as the government's callous use of a female agent for sexual blackmail, but here as the revengeful trickery of a crippled lawyer), and transference of guilt (implicit in the total lack of justification for Cary Grant's abduction, and surreally explicit here in Grisby's plan to make O'Hara confess to a murder he did not commit).

Part of what makes Welles's film so unsettling is the ironic tension between the moral issues and the characters' apparent lack of interest in them. K.'s whole life in *The Trial* is changed by his investigation into the principles behind his case, and Quinlan in *Touch of Evil* spends most of his time rectifying the moral inadequacy of the law; but in *The Lady from Shanghai* O'Hara treats his legal predicament as only an unpleasant adventure he must get through so he can move on to a more important concern—Elsa Bannister, the lawyer's wife. Unfortunately, as he discovers, she is the instigator of the whole complex murder plot, and the issues encroach heavily on his fate despite his avoidance of them. At the end he has been forced to formulate a philosophical position similar to the tragic understanding Welles's other heroes achieve, but of a less definitive nature. It is less a conclusion than a beginning, a coming to terms with the world.

The Lady from Shanghai is essentially a comedy, although, as Welles said of *Chimes at Midnight*, it is a "somber comedy." In *Chimes*, Welles focuses on another innocent adventurer, but the qualities of resilience, openheartedness, and humor that allowed the young O'Hara to survive his disillusionment become the downfall of Falstaff, a tragic hero whose candor, like Othello's trustfulness, is his point of vulnerability. Michael O'Hara is a young Irish sailor (rather whimsically incarnated by Welles) who has been "travelling around the world too much to find out anything about it"—Bannister's words and a fair statement of the dangers of moral blindness and idealistic gullibility which all of Welles's heroes face. Like the ignoble Van Stratten in *Mr. Arkadin*, he will try anything once, but unlike Van Stratten, he is not out merely for money. He killed a man once, but it was for the Republicans in the Spanish Civil War, a salve for his self-esteem until Bannister's associate George Grisby (a breathtakingly funny and unnerving performance by Glenn Anders) tells him that killing during a war must not be murder. O'Hara's naivete is as touching as it is farcical; he seems to be drawn to the most unsavory, cunning characters as if by a universal design of which he is blithely unaware. He meets the beautiful Elsa and saves her from a mugging in Central Park, and with jaunty humility (which allows him to disclaim any moral identity), tells us, "I start out in this story a little like a hero—which I most certainly am not."

Soon after that Elsa contrives to have her husband, Arthur Bannister (memorably played by Everett Sloane) hire O'Hara as bosun of their yacht for a lengthy "pleasure" cruise. At this point Grisby arrives to offer O'Hara a strange proposition, and the film becomes madly confusing. Harry Cohn, the head of Columbia Pictures, reportedly shouted when he saw the rough cut, "I'll give a thousand dollars to anyone who can explain the story to me!" Lucidity is not one of the film's virtues; an explication of the plot might help. Grisby will give O'Hara $5,000 to confess to killing him, so that he can disappear to a South Sea island, taking along the insurance money his wife will collect for him. Since there will be no body, O'Hara will not be convicted, but since there will be a confession, Grisby will be legally dead. Grisby will then spend his declining years far from the nuclear holocaust that he knows is coming. O'Hara goes along with the scheme uncomprehendingly, hoping to use the $5,000 to lure Elsa from her husband (the height of naiveté). On the night of the fake murder, Grisby shoots a divorce detective who has been hired by Bannister and who has discovered the truth of the plot. Just after Grisby has vanished, the dying detective tells O'Hara that he has been framed, and that Grisby, with Elsa's help, is going to kill Bannister for his money and let Michael take the fall. O'Hara dashes to Bannister's office to prevent the murder, but is greeted by a horde of cops who find the confession in his pocket, and by Elsa and Bannister—and Grisby's corpse.

At this point O'Hara muses, "either me or the rest of the whole world is absolutely insane"—the subtle temptation that also encourages Joseph K. to surrender. Bannister, who has never lost a case, defends O'Hara in a bitterly comic courtroom sequence, but intends to see him convicted. Just before the verdict is given, O'Hara manages to escape from the courthouse by feigning a suicide attempt and posing as a jury member from another trial. He wanders into a theater in Chinatown, followed by Elsa; her servants arrive and hustle him into the amusement park's crazy house. After falling through a vertiginous series of traps and chutes that is a kind of apocalyptic vision of the chaos awaiting his surrender, he winds up in the hall of mirrors, where he is confronted with the endless reflections of his temptress's face. Bannister arrives and tells her that he has explained everything in a note to the district attorney (Elsa killed Grisby because he had lost his head and shot the detective). The husband and wife shoot each other, the mirrors shattering all around them as O'Hara watches. She crawls out of the room, telling O'Hara that he shouldn't try to fight the evil of the world. He leaves her to die. As he walks off into the gray early morning, towards the sea, he tells us, "I went to call the cops but I knew she'd be dead before they got there—I'd be free. Bannister's note to the D.A. fixed it, I'd be innocent officially. But that's a big word, 'innocent'—stupid's more like it. Well—everybody is somebody's fool. The only way to stay out of trouble is to grow old, so I guess I'll concentrate on that. Maybe I'll live so long that I'll forget her—maybe I'll die trying."

Welles explains the plot to us while he is wandering through the crazy house, and it is impossible to pay attention to what he is saying. The only thing we can be sure of (unless we have analyzed the plot in repose) is that Elsa was the cause of it all, Bannister her reluctant protector, and O'Hara the intended victim. Grisby remains an absolute befuddlement. If we can't quite understand what makes him so afraid of the bomb (a common fear but improbable for him, since he seems as invulnerable as Iago until that marvellous moment when his corpse is wheeled past the astonished O'Hara, and the film pirouettes from irrationality into madness), neither can we see a plausible explanation—but for poetic compulsion—for the insouciant humor with which he dupes O'Hara. If the actor had not given such a brilliant, concrete, amusing performance—if the role had been played straight—Grisby might be too abstracted to shake us as much as he does. He would be as repellently sententious as the Advocate in *The Trial*. It is because of his three-dimensionality, paradoxically, that Grisby becomes a poetic force, a Fury wholly dedicated to exposing chaos and evil to the innocent O'Hara.

Bannister's nihilism repels O'Hara, but Elsa offers a subtler temptation—the lure of romantic fatalism. "Everything's bad, Michael," she tells him as they dance. "Everything. You can't escape it or fight it. You've got to get along with it, deal with it, make terms." Surrender is the ultimate evil, the ultimate indignity, in Welles's world, and what Elsa formulates, Bannister and Grisby demonstrate. As in the ending of *The Trial*, the bomb is the character's all-serving excuse for irresponsibility. Michelangelo Antonioni's celebrated statement that "Under the bomb everyone is a hero, and under the bomb no one is a hero" finds its reply in O'Hara's accusation of Elsa: "You mean we can't win? Then we can't lose either. Only if we quit." Welles places his heroes *in extremis* to force them to define themselves, to make them fight or give up. He refuses to blame the universe at large for the failings of the human race, realizing that such a feeling is sentimental at best and suicidal at worst. He surrounds the hero with people who have given in to irresponsibility or self-indulgent hysteria. Elsa needs security so desperately that she has succumbed to Bannister's economic blackmail; murder, self-destruction, is her only way out. We can only pity Bannister's acknowledgment of impotence. Grisby has the dignity of a psychotic who rules his own world with its own laws—like Quinlan in his abuse of legal technicalities, but unlike Quinlan in that his purposes are purely self-serving and self-denying. Grisby does not have tragic stature because there is no moral urgency to his actions. If he still attains Shakespearean comic proportions, it is because he revels in his (avowed) despair to such a degree that we would gladly follow him, were it not for Welles's insistence on man's ability to transcend the folly around him.

It is significant that Welles should give to a beautiful woman, his former wife, the most precise formulation of his ultimate sin. Welles names the Bannister yacht "The Circe," and has Elsa lure the spellbound O'Hara from the depths of the ship by singing a song called "Please Don't Kiss Me"; this sequence was added at the demand of Harry Cohn, but Welles slyly turned it into a dark parody of Hollywood romantic convention. O'Hara's tale of the blood-maddened sharks eating at their own flesh, the exotic haze of Chinatown, the surreal crazy house with its signs reading "Stand up or Give up" and the dragon's jaws which swallow O'Hara, the furtive love-making before writhing sea-monsters in an aquarium, and the symbolic intercutting of the river picnic (Elsa with flamingo and snake, O'Hara with parrots, Grisby with crocodile) continually reinforce the romantic fascination of the lady's siren-like lure of the young sailor adrift in a world of sudden, bewildering dangers. The temptation offered by women in Welles's male-dominated, romantically disillusioned world is that of passivity, of sentimental and distracting reassurance, of a sheltering from reality which can become crippling. Mrs.

Kane's sled, Isabel's selfless devotion, Desdemona's purity, Raina's innocence, Doll Tearsheet's "flattering busses"—all these are touching evocations of a vanished past to which the hero may return for a vision of the alternative to the mania of power, but from which he must divorce himself lest he use its simplicity obsessively, blindly, as a talisman against evil.

O'Hara takes refuge from the malevolence of Bannister and Grisby in his image of Elsa, refusing to see that her complicity with evil has made her unspoiled loveliness all the more deadly for its dissimulation. She could truly say, "I am not what I am." At the end, the romanticist leaves his ideal to die—one of the most harrowing scenes Welles has given us, and the signal of that somber disquiet which will forever follow his mature heroes. When he returns to the man of good will twenty years later, that man is old, gross, and moribund. His gaiety is haunted by melancholy, and his youthful spirit is a mockery of himself.

Welles as the escaped Nazi war criminal Franz Kindler (a k a Charles Rankin) in *The Stranger* (1946), with Loretta Young as his wife. (*RKO/Turner*)

At dinner with his wife's unsuspecting family, Kindler is observed at close range by his nemesis, Inspector Wilson (Edward G. Robinson).

Rita Hayworth as the exotic and troubled Elsa Bannister in *The Lady from Shanghai* (1948). (*Columbia*)

The love scene in the aquarium: Welles's Irish sailor Michael O'Hara with Elsa and various sea monsters.

The bizarre George Grisby (Glenn Anders, right foreground) on a cruise with O'Hara and Elsa's crippled husband, Arthur Bannister (Everett Sloane, left).

O'Hara confronts the destruction of his romantic illusions: the hall of mirrors in the final sequence of *The Lady from Shanghai*.

The prelude to the baroque shootout in the hall of mirrors.

Arthur Bannister about to shoot the woman he loves.

Welles in the title role of his experimental film version of Shakespeare's *Macbeth* for Republic Pictures (1948). (*Republic/The Museum of Modern Art/Film Stills Archive*)

Macbeth as man of action.

Lady Macbeth (Jeanette Nolan) planting the seeds of murder.

The witches in *Macbeth*.

The madness of unbearable guilt: Welles as Macbeth.

Welles, costumed for the title role, directing Suzanne Cloutier as Desdemona in his 1952 film of Shakespeare's *Othello*. (*Castle Hill*)

The opening sequence: Othello's funeral.

Othello and Desdemona: the murder sequence.

The cage fatefully overhanging Iago (Micheál MacLiammóir).

Iago in his cage.

Welles as the mysterious, flamboyantly theatrical tycoon Gregory Arkadin in *Mr. Arkadin* (1955), also known as *Confidential Report*. (*Warner Bros./Dan Talbot*)

The fable about the scorpion and the frog, as told by Gregory Arkadin.

One of Welles's favorite character actors, Akim Tamiroff, as the dying Jacob Zouk, desperately waiting for his goose liver in *Mr. Arkadin*.

The magnificent Katina Paxinou as Sophie, Arkadin's long-ago lover, who cherishes her memories of his secrets.

Welles hosting his 1958 television film *The Fountain of Youth*, based on a story by John Collier. (*Welles Enterprises/Desilu/Paramount/Joseph L. Bridges, Jr.*)

Joi Lansing and Rick Jason as the youth-obsessed lovers, with the phony eternal-youth potion on the mantelpiece between them in *The Fountain of Youth*. (*Joseph L. Bridges, Jr.*)

Touch of Evil (1958): a violent disruption for the honeymoon of Mike and Susan Vargas (Charlton Heston and Janet Leigh).

"We're trying to strap you to the electric chair, boy": Welles as Captain Hank Quinlan in *Touch of Evil*, with murder suspect Manolo Sanchez (Victor Millan) and lawmen Menzies (Joseph Calleia) and Vargas.

Dennis Weaver as the sex-crazed motel "Night Man," menaced by the black-jacketed Grande gang.

Uncle Joe Grande (Akim Tamiroff) sealing a corrupt bargain with Hank Quinlan.

"Your future is all used up": Marlene Dietrich's Tanya, bearer of Hank Quinlan's fortune.

The dying Hank Quinlan in the final sequence of *Touch of Evil*, the last film Welles directed for a Hollywood studio.

7: Welles and Shakespeare: *Macbeth* and *Othello*

Back in the days of the Mercury Theatre, one of the actors in Welles's Shakespearean production *Five Kings* asked another when they would start rehearsing *Henry IV.* "Oh, when Orson's finished writing it," the second actor replied. The feeling that Welles hurled himself against Shakespeare merely to gratify himself with the sound of the collision was as common as it was misleading. This assumption arose in part from the boisterous, uneven quality of some of Welles's adaptations and from the bravura aspects of his style, but it failed to take into account the common source of both the imperfections and the achievements. Shakespeare was Welles's first dramatic love, and whenever he wanted to find himself artistically he returned to Shakespeare's plays. In them he found not only themes compatible with his own and characters large enough to justify his most grandiose conceptions but also a standard against which he could measure his own egotism, a theatrical ideal that challenged him to reconcile his subjective obsessions with the demands of universality.

Welles refused to dramatize *Crime and Punishment,* explaining that he found himself in complete agreement with Dostoevsky and would not be content just to illustrate the book. In Shakespeare, however, he found a superior power whose dramas were capable of broadening, not merely confirming, his own ideas. When he adapted Shakespeare he was able to enlarge his conception of the hero without, as in *Mr. Arkadin,* limiting his social perspective in the process. "Shakespeare is the staff of life," he declared, and it is clear that Welles saw Shakespeare as his artistic conscience, the consummate example of the fusion of a personal vision with the full complexity of human nature. If, like Shakespeare, Welles refuses to judge his characters and never violates his conception of character to make an ideological point, he also, like Shakespeare, at every point makes clear the precise moral structure under which his characters live. In Shakespeare also he is able to find an appropriate setting for his kingly characters to inhabit. Just as John Ford leaves the unheroic present for the American frontier, Welles finds in medieval castles and battlefields a setting congenial to true grandeur of spirit. In *Citizen Kane,* he is able to create a fittingly heroic universe for his hero to rule, but in *Mr. Arkadin* and *The Trial* the moral smallness of the heroes collides with Welles's attempts to conjure up an egocentric universe. The Shakespearean form, however, minimizes such dangers by allowing Welles to allocate to Macbeth, Othello, and Falstaff a degree of social power which would be difficult to justify in a less feudal world.

As the lengthy gestation of *Chimes at Midnight* demonstrates, a Welles adaptation of Shakespeare was not an *ad hoc* project but the result of a lifetime of scholarship and creative experiment. As Welles told it, his mother read him Lamb's *Tales from Shakespeare* when he was two, and when he discovered that they were not the real thing but had been watered down for children, he demanded that she read him the plays themselves. She gave him his first book, *A Midsummer Night's Dream,* for his third birthday, and he quickly began to assemble the complete works of Shakespeare in his library. He attended productions of the plays from an early age, and directed his own adaptations of Shakespeare (as well as his own plays) in his puppet theater for his family, supplying all the voices himself. He played Falstaff at the Todd School, and his other Shakespearean roles there included Marc Antony and Cassius, in his own production of *Julius Caesar,* and Richard III, in *Winter of Our Discontent,* his own amalgamation of *Richard III* and *Henry VI.* At the age of nine, Welles had played King Lear in a condensed version in his backyard; he went on to play Lear on radio in 1946, on television in 1953 (in a production staged by Peter Brook, now available on videotape), and in his own stage production in 1956, and in the final years of his life he still was trying to raise money for a film version of the play.

As a young man, Welles approached his master with boundless ego. He staged an all-black production of *Macbeth* in Harlem, turning the witches into voodoo doctors and changing the locale to Haiti; he played *Caesar* in modern dress as an allegory of fascism; and, most spectacularly, he combined eight of Shakespeare's history plays into the monstrous spectacle *Five Kings,* which sealed the doom of the Mercury Theatre. His three Shakespearean features, *Macbeth* (1948), *Othello* (1952), and *Chimes at Midnight* (1966), were progressively more faithful to the letter of Shakespeare but, paradoxically, less and less faithful to the spirit as he acquired more grace and confidence in uniting Shakespeare's vision to his own.[1] If Welles, in his later years, no longer pulled a stunt like the voodoo *Macbeth,* he took a larger, subtler liberty in changing the emphasis of the Falstaff-Hal story from the moral awakening of the ideal king to the willful destruction of innocence by a young man newly conscious of power. Welles's theme was there in the text all the time, of course, and the kingship theme is as subsidiary to Welles as it is paramount to Shakespeare. In *Chimes of Midnight,* we no longer feel the damaging pull between one moral system and another, as we do, for example, in his *Othello,* in which the director's fascination with the villainy of Iago (Micheál MacLiammóir) often seems to thrust his own comparatively uninteresting performance in the title role into the background. What Welles had conquered by the time he made *Chimes* was the diffusion of emphasis and statement, so that he no longer tried to tell the entire history of England from 1377 to 1485, but concentrated instead on the moral drama behind the story of a single king. The

[1]In addition to the features and his 1933 film of his Todd School stage production of *Twelfth Night,* Welles filmed a forty-minute condensed version of *The Merchant of Venice,* in which he played Shylock, for his uncompleted CBS-TV special *Orson's Bag* (1968-70); excerpts can be seen in Oja Kodar's 1995 compilation film of little-seen or previously unreleased Welles footage, *Orson Welles: The One-Man Band.* A four-minute section of Welles's 1936 black *Macbeth* stage production for the Federal Theatre in Harlem was captured on film in a documentary, *We Work Again,* showing how the Works Progress Administration found jobs for black artists during the Depression.

audience of *Chimes at Midnight* is scarcely aware of the extensive textual revision and rearranging that Welles has unobtrusively performed on the plays; for *Five Kings* that was one of the central fascinations.

If Welles changes Shakespeare's emphasis to ally it more closely to his own, his intention is not to distort, attack, or ignore the text, but to make it come alive on screen. "I use Shakespeare's words and characters to make motion pictures," he once said. "They are variations on his themes. . . . Without presuming to compare myself to Verdi, I think he gives me my best justification. The opera *Otello* is certainly not *Othello* the play. It certainly could not have been written without Shakespeare, but it is first and foremost an opera. *Othello* the movie, I hope, is first and foremost a motion picture."

Macbeth

After *The Stranger* and *The Lady from Shanghai* had failed to reignite his Hollywood career, Welles came up with an ingenious plan to show how he could work cheaply and efficiently and still make a film of artistic distinction. He proposed filming *Macbeth* with sparse settings and all the acting and camerawork rehearsed in advance. His friend Charles K. Feldman, the agent and producer, persuaded Republic Pictures, the much-maligned but occasionally adventurous quickie studio, to back the offbeat Shakespearean project with a B-movie budget of under $900,000. For rehearsal Welles took his cast to the Utah Centennial Festival in Salt Lake City and performed the play for three days in May 1947. He then went to Hollywood, rehearsed his cast for two more weeks, and in June and July, using a prerecorded soundtrack as he had intended to do for *The Magnificent Ambersons*, filmed *Macbeth* almost entirely on Republic soundstages, in only 23 days of shooting.

Macbeth has highly theatrical, unabashedly non-naturalistic sets, using cardboard rocks for the courtyard of the primitive Scottish castle and Republic's standing set of a salt mine (familiar from countless B-Westerns) for parts of the castle's interior. In a move that would prove contentious, Welles had the entire cast speak their lines in a rolling Scottish burr. "Why shouldn't all the Scotsmen in *Macbeth* sound like Scotsmen?" he asked Bogdanovich. "The Scottish lilt and color is so right for all that gooseflesh and grue. If I could make the picture in heaven, I'd make it with a Scottish burr all over again." He also felt that for a mass audience unaccustomed to Shakespeare, "it's easier to understand with Scotch accents, because that speech is clearer, purer, more incisive. It's just a great excuse for people who don't understand Shakespeare anyway to blame it on the burr." But Republic fell at odds with Welles during the lengthy editing process, and before the film was released, it persuaded him to cut twenty-one minutes from the original running time of a hundred and seven minutes. Despite Welles's stylistic audacity and resourcefulness in turning his limited resources into a virtue, *Macbeth*'s unconventional approach evoked derision from American critics when it opened in a few markets in October 1948, following its inauspicious European debut out of competition at that September's Venice Film Festival. Republic decided that the soundtrack was a hindrance and ordered the dialogue redubbed in a less Scottish, more Americanized accent. Welles reluctantly complied, and while he was abroad his associate Richard Wilson supervised the redubbing of about sixty-five percent of the dialogue. The resulting mishmash, a ruin of the film Welles originally intended, was a failure after its release in 1950.

Jean Cocteau, whose own hallucinatory fantasy films have much in common with Welles's approach to *Macbeth*, was the film's most eloquent defender. After Welles showed him the film in a little cinema in Venice, Cocteau called it "a *film maudit*, in the noble sense of the word. . . . Orson Welles's *Macbeth* leaves the spectator deaf and blind, and I can well believe that the people who like it (and I am proud to be one) are few and far between. . . . Clad in animal skins like motorists at the turn of the century, horns and cardboard crowns on their heads, his actors haunt the corridors of some dreamlike subway, an abandoned coal mine, and ruined cellars oozing with water. Not a single shot is left to chance. The camera is always placed just where destiny itself would observe its victims.

Sometimes we wonder in what period this nightmare is unfolding, and when, for the first time, we see Lady Macbeth, before the camera moves back to situate her, it is almost a woman in modern dress that we are seeing, reclining on a fur-covered divan beside the teelphone.

"In the role of Macbeth, Orson Welles proves himself to be a remarkable tragedian, and if the Scottish accent imitated by Americans may be unbearable to English ears, I confess that it did not disturb me and that it would not have disturbed me even if I had a perfect command of English, since we have no reason not to expect that strange monsters express themselves in a monstrous language in which the words of Shakespeare nevertheless remain his words."

My own initial reaction to *Macbeth*, as expressed in the first edition of this book (1972), was largely negative. Basing my judgment on the redubbed and truncated 1950 version, the only one then known to exist, I wrote that the film was handicapped by "extreme budgetary restrictions and a resulting crudeness of tone (which in some ways, however, helps to create the necessary atmosphere of monolithic superstition, though it hinders Welles in smoothly integrating his concept of Macbeth's character with Shakespeare's). . . . The scene of Duncan's arrival in *Macbeth*, for example, cannot, for all its details of pagan drummers and horrific costumes, avoid the distracting appearance of a soundstage with painted backdrop for sky, constructed rocks, and so forth. We are thrown back on our sense of the drama as a theatrical spectacle, and Welles's style is too expressionistic to accomodate such totally unreal surroundings without disturbing the ironic tension he requires between the hero's overweening ego and the constraints of social responsibility. . . .

"The lack of any sense of the hero's moral relationship to society—intensified by the play's supernatural aspects and by the hallucinatory, almost solipsistic nature of Macbeth's ambition, which is too compulsive to admit of rational calculation—turns the drama farther inward than in any Welles film until *The Immortal Story*. We are in a theater of the subconscious. We are led, however, not into Macbeth's superego but into his id. At its most effective, *Macbeth* resembles classic horror films such as *El* and *King Kong* (one of Welles's favorite films), dramas which avoid nuance of character in order to more effectively present the clash of extreme emotions and actions and free us into the world of nightmare. *Macbeth* falters when the camera merely observes the characters giving speeches. The implicit emotional complexity of the words, which the actors (except for Dan O'Herlihy as Macduff) quite simply ignore, serves only to distract us from the directness of the images; in a nightmare we do not pause for contemplation, but are swept along helplessly, uncritically. There is no subtlety in Welles's playing of Macbeth. If his performance, though it is scarcely more than adequate, strikes us as more appropriate than his Othello, which he plays in a similarly transfixed, manic way, it is because the *mise-en-scéne* calculates along such raw, direct lines. Welles employs many long takes, but for budgetary reasons moves his actors much more than he moves his camera; usually we see Macbeth pivoting around in the extreme foreground and the other characters gravitating toward him from the distance. *Macbeth* is marked also by an overwhelming concentration on closeups; again, partly a result of haste and desperation, but also a prime factor in demonstrating the amoral egocentricity of the hero."

What a stunning and unexpected revelation it was in 1980 to see *Macbeth* finally restored to Welles's original version! With the actors and their richly nuanced, Scottish-accented original line readings reunited, the performances (Welles's especially) assumed a new dimension of emotional unity. If Welles's Macbeth still seems too much like a sleepwalker, the performance has far more timber and authority, suggesting more strongly the character's waste of kingly potential; and if Jeanette Nolan's Lady Macbeth still seems limited in her emotional range, her more eloquent tones of anguish in the restored version give her performance the wrenching quality of a stab to the heart. Even more importantly, the film's stylized acting now seems to mesh seamlessly with the stylized settings, the sounds and sights working together to conjure up a nightmarish world of primeval terror. As Truffaut observed, it was in making this "fairy tale" *Macbeth* that Welles "rediscovered freedom, poverty, and his own genius, all intact," and "decided in effect to assume his position as an avant-garde director," a position he would occupy with stubborn integrity for the rest of his life.

Macbeth, in its restored version, fully exemplifies the goal Welles once enunciated in discussing his attempts to bring Shakespeare to the screen: "These are people who have more life in them than any human being ever had. But you can't simply dress up and *be* them, you have to make a world for them. . . . In [Laurence Olivier's 1944 film version of] *Henry V*, for example, you see the people riding out of the castle, and suddenly they are on a golf course somewhere charging each other. You can't escape it, they have entered another world. . . . What I am trying to do is to see the outside, real world through the same eyes as the inside, fabricated one. To create a kind of unity."

What had once appeared "crude" and "distracting" in Welles's *Macbeth* to a much younger critic somewhat uncomfortable (like most American critics) with expressionistic, nonnaturalistic filmmaking no longer seems the product of "haste and desperation" but a triumphant artistic decision. The restoration of excised footage contributes greatly to the film's credibility of texture and to its newfound impression of hypnotic intensity, particularly the restoration of the complete ten-minute take in which Welles, with overwhelming virtuosity and emotional force, stages the events before, during, and after the murder of Duncan.

Welles's *Macbeth* is even more nightmarish than his overtly nightmarish film of *The Trial*, because we do not watch the events unfolding from an ironic distance. We are thrust willy-nilly into a welter of fear and chaos, a vertiginous dance with death, evoked most viscerally in the scene of Duncan's death and the equally chilling seven-minute take of Macduff being told about the murder of his wife and child. The visual strategy in both scenes involves relatively little camera movement, but constant reframing carried out by intricately choreographed movements of characters from the extreme distance through the extreme foreground. The first scene conveys a sickening feeling of being pulled headlong into a dizzying frenzy of murderous abandon, and the second sucks the viewer inexorably into the deadening numbness of grief and revenge.

Welles's Macbeth is the center of a whirlwind of destructive activity evoking not so much a struggle of the will for dominance as a struggle of the mind for consciousness. By surrendering to his worst impulses, prodded by the ruthlessly ambitious and far more decisive Lady Macbeth, he succumbs to a loss of sanity and moral equilibrium. What appalls Macbeth, A. C. Bradley has commented, "is always the image of his own guilty heart or bloody deed, or some image which derives from them its terror or gloom. These, when they arise, hold him spellbound and possess him wholly, like a hypnotic trance which is at the same time the ecstasy of a poet. . . . His imagination is . . . something usually deeper and higher than his conscious thoughts; and if he had obeyed it he would have been safe." The witches in Shakespeare merely prophesy to Macbeth—there is nothing in the play, Bradley points out, that enables us to consider them the masters of his destiny—and their suggestions rouse forces of violence he has long held in submission, directing them to what society considers the legitimate ends of warfare rather than toward illegitimate ambition. Welles makes of the witches something entirely different. In the opening sequence, which in almost every Welles film is the indication of "original sin" and the establishment of an ironic, godlike parenthesis to the hero's actions, the hands of the witches are seen molding a clay figure in their boiling pot, shaping it into the likeness of a child and placing a crown on its head. The witches carry pronged druidical staffs, and stand on a hill when Macbeth first meets them. The last shot of the film shows them standing with their staffs in the fog swirling around Macbeth's castle, which is strikingly reminiscent of the castle in *Kane*.

Welles also creates a new character, a tall, forbidding priest in long braids who leads Duncan and his court in an incantation (actually a common Catholic prayer) to renounce Satan "and the other evil spirits who roam about the world seeking the destruction of souls." The final appearance of the "voodoo" Macbeth comes at the moment when Macduff swings his sword at Macbeth's neck. Welles cuts to the clay figure—its head is cut off, the tiny crown falls to the ground; and Macduff hurls Macbeth's head from the promontory. The feeling is of an inchoate society vacillating dangerously between paganism and a rudimentary Christian ethic. Macbeth is torn between these contradictions without being able to articulate them beyond his realization that

> ... this Duncan
> Hath borne his faculties so meek, hath been
> So clear in his great office, that his virtues
> Will plead like angels, trumpet-tongued, against
> The deep damnation of his taking-off ...

Duncan is thus the prototype of the Christian king, of whom Welles will have more to say in *Chimes at Midnight*, but he is so only in Macbeth's conscience; even less than in Shakespeare do we feel any sense of Duncan's power and nobility. Duncan does nothing in the film but preside over the renunciation of Satan and the peremptory execution of Macbeth's vanquished captive that immediately precedes it; his progress to court is preceded by a swarm of dogs and pigs. Macbeth kisses his lady with gibbeted corpses dangling in the background. Such a society can only encourage Macbeth's ambition.

Shakespeare would not make the witches agents of fate because his conception of character is closely allied to the notion of a great and inviolable order of nature, which Macbeth perceives (though dimly) in his soliloquies. Welles's concerns are with the conscience of the hero as a force reflecting on itself to the exclusion of society. No matter how venal the Welles hero, his struggle is paramount because there is no one else of equal stature; and, unlike in Shakespeare, the hero makes no recognition (until the moment of his destruction) of an order greater than himself. If the witches are to Shakespeare's Macbeth only a catalyst to his ambition, to Welles they are the very agents of Macbeth's destruction, the forces that have formed him and he has not found the strength to surmount.

When Duncan arrives at the castle, Lady Macbeth warns her husband that his face "is as a book where men may read strange matters." That is abundantly true not only of Welles's dazed, horror-stricken performance, but also of the director's more subtly expressionistic use of settings to express the characters' innermost states of mind. His *Macbeth* is more a work of visual (and verbal) poetry than of drama. When Macbeth hears of his wife's suicide and gives the "Tomorrow, and tomorrow, and tomorrow" speech, Welles shows us not the anguished face of a moral partner but great rolling banks of fog—as if her death is not a vision of the folly of mortal pride but the sublime temptation of a dreamlike merging into the shadows of a dim, unformed existence. "Torn between heaven and hell," Welles's *Macbeth*, in the words of André Bazin, offers "a prehistory of the conscience at the birth of time and sin, when sky and earth, water and fire, good and evil, still aren't distinctly separate.... Kane's drama is transposed onto the most elevated plane of ethics and poetry in the case of Macbeth, who wallows in his crimes, but in whom we nevertheless sense a mysterious spark of innocence and something like the possibility of grace and salvation."

Othello

"Strange sense of Eternity in relation to film of *Othello*" is an entry in the amusing diary which Welles's Iago, his old friend Micheál MacLiammóir, kept of the filming and published as *Put Money in Thy Purse*. None of the projects in Welles's checkered career, even the legendary *Don Quixote*, better attests to his persistence in the face of monumental difficulties. The filming of *Othello* took the better part of four years, with Welles taking time out to raise money by acting in Henry King's *Prince of Foxes* and Henry Hathaway's *The Black Rose*, which he regarded as jokes, and in Carol Reed's classic *The Third Man*. No space here to detail Welles's endless search for a Desdemona or his frantic attempts to cut corners and continually reassemble the cast from everywhere in Europe; once, for example, he spirited equipment from the set of *The Black Rose*, under cover of darkness, and hurriedly shot scenes for *Othello* while nobody was looking. MacLiammóir saw the cast as members of a "chic but highly neurotic lumber camp."

By necessity, Welles's visual strategy in *Othello* is exactly opposite to that of his *Macbeth:* lacking the money to build the elaborate sets planned by art designer Alexander Trauner, aside from the doge's palace, Welles instead utilized the interiors and exteriors of existing buildings and other settings in Italy, Morocco, and on the island of Torcello. At one point, when the promised costumes didn't arrive, Welles filmed the scene of the attempted murder of Cassio in a fishmarket he transformed into a Turkish bath, dressing most of the characters in towels and creating an unforgettable scene. Welles often linked several disparate locations together through ingenious, fast-paced editing, giving the film an intoxicating freedom in evoking the mood of Renaissance Venice. The film's often spectacular cinematography—credited to five cameramen, but clearly the result of the director's unified vision—transforms all these actual locales into states of mind, as *Macbeth* did with its purely fabricated materials. We see this perhaps most clearly in the scene on the parapet in which Iago goads Othello's jealousy. The photography is that of an eerie, slightly unreal twilight. Othello wears a massive white robe, light from the left casting a hazy aura on his profile; he strides back and forth, driving Iago closer and closer to the edge of the precipice, below which, from a dizzying height, we see waves smashing. The direction and lighting convey, in a vivid and unforced manner, the metaphor of the tragic fall, dramatizing the dangerous forces unleashed in Othello by Iago's reckless prodding of his emotions. A superb instance of seeing "the outside, real world through the same eyes as the inside, fabricated one," this creative transformation of actuality, the integration of character and poetry with visual rhythm into a truly Shakespearean *mise-en-scéne*, would be carried to even greater heights by Welles in his use of Spanish locations to recreate medieval England in *Chimes at Midnight*.

Welles's heroism in completing *Othello* under such daunting circumstances makes criticism of the result seem almost churlish, but the fact remains that *Othello* as a story stubbornly resists much of Welles's moral framework, and his style, never more floridly expressionistic, is for the most part unsuited for a character conflict that depends so much on psychologically subtle, introspective development. *Macbeth* succeeds in its stylization largely because of Macbeth's comparatively simpler, more elemental conflict—Lady Macbeth's evil is relatively single-minded and direct, compared to the devious treachery of Iago. Welles places great weight on Iago in the early, formative scenes of *Othello*, showing Othello only in brief scenes of courting and military pomp; but when Othello's passion finally takes hold of him, Welles almost wholly excludes Iago from the action. Iago is primarily a catalyst in Shakespeare, too, but the emphasis in Shakespeare is less on the acting-out of Othello's passion than on the development of it. Welles would like the film to be about the tension between dormancy and power in Othello, it seems—he omits much of the intricacy of Iago's schemes, tending instead to cross-cut from Iago watching to Othello doing—but, with the deliberations scanted, the film teeters wildly into unrestrained grand opera.

Welles revels in what he tries to exorcise, much like Ingmar Bergman in his unbearably claustrophobic *Hour of the Wolf*, another story of the impingement of mind into matter. Instead of making us share in madness by carefully displacing ordinary human emotions into an irrational context, as Bergman does in *The Shame* and Welles in *The Lady from Shanghai*, *Othello* presents a mere spectacle of frenzy and disintegration, fascinating as spectacle but alienating as drama. *Othello* seems to be a veritable celebration of Welles's obsessions; we hunger for a spark of sanity. And Manny Farber's comment on Liv Ullmann in *Hour of the Wolf*—"like a sharp knife going through old cheese"—could be applied to Suzanne Cloutier's Desdemona, a clear, forceful characterization as revivifying as a breath of nascent oxygen.

I hesitate to apply the word "decadent" to any of Welles's work, because his style usually has compelling reasons for pushing past the limits of naturalism, but in comparison with a powerful (if confusing) narrative such as *The Lady from Shanghai*, *Othello* is self-absorbed and rhetorically diffuse—decadent indeed. Like Othello, Michael O'Hara in *Shanghai* is of a "free and open nature," and naively subject to the machinations of a superior, envious, and self-destructive intellect. But in that dark comedy, we take a detached, morally qualified view of O'Hara's difficulties while at the same time sharing in his emotional compulsions. Welles's Othello might invite our derision, so anesthetized he seems next to the clear-willed Iago, but Welles's wooden and largely unconvincing performance will not allow us to see anything but tragic nobility behind the character's actions.

"I frankly don't think that I am particularly good as Othello," Welles said in 1950, "but even so I firmly believe that this will be a remarkable film." The last romantic lead Welles attempted in his film career, Welles's Othello has the outward trappings of majesty, virility, and boldness, but it lacks the emotional highs and lows demanded by the text. The performance lacks humor, and its monotonous tone soon becomes wearisome. It is far less passionate than the images, and even more than in *Macbeth*, the camera has to supply the feeling. Eric Bentley, writing about *Othello*, aptly commented of Welles, "[H]e never acts, he is photographed." The film suffers grievously from sound recording problems, as well as from the difficulties of shooting in many disparate locales and continually reassembling cast members from all over Europe; those production handicaps necessitated a great deal of evasive and overly frenetic camerawork and editing. The camera seldom stops jumping around to let us look at people's faces and listen to Shakespeare's words (many of which also sound muffled), and several key speeches are staged in long shot, with the characters' backs frequently turned to the camera, making it hard to empathize with Othello at dramatically indispensable moments.[2]

[2]The 1992 "restoration" of the film released by Castle Hill Productions misguidedly attempted to smoothe over some of the film's synchronization problems by electronically altering dialogue. To quote Michael Dawson, co-producer of the "restoration": "The sections out of sync[h] were digitally processed so that syllables and vowels could literally be expanded or compressed to match lip movement." In a further attempt to bring the film in line with contemporary technical expectations, the film's musical score was rerecorded, and its sound effects were replaced. But Welles was always willing to sacrifice synchronization for a line reading, not the other way around; the richness and complexity of the film's original scoring (by Francesco Lavagnino and Alberto Barberis) has been needlessly diminished; and Welles's original sound design (technically imperfect though it may have been) is unheard. All

Granted that Othello is the most difficult part Shakespeare ever wrote, according to Laurence Olivier, who played Othello on film as a flamboyant, swaggering, almost ludicrous innocent (Welles unkindly remarked that Olivier's Othello reminded him of Sammy Davis, Jr.); still, Welles's admiration for Othello as the only character capable of action in a world of impotent observers dangerously circumvents any kind of qualification to his actions. When Desdemona is killed, we are shocked and horrified, but we are shocked at the enormity of the gesture, not by its injustice. As Othello, Welles conveys little real feeling aside from anger; the speech to the senate about his wooing of Desdemona is delivered in a flat manner which suggests that her attraction to him was inevitable— there is little of the sense of wonder which Olivier so simply conveys. Gone, too, is Othello's childlike "My wife! My wife! What wife? I have no wife," after the murder. Desdemona is merely an unfortunate victim, and her death is not so much a reproach to Othello's folly as a confirmation of his unreflected ability to act.

It is strange, too, to see Welles playing the "innocent" in a drama of power and entrapment; this was the only time in his film work, aside from *Shanghai*, in which he assumed that role. In his *Macbeth*, Lady Macbeth is almost irrelevant dramatically; she finds little resistance to the violent working-out of his ambition, once the weird sisters have spoken to him. But in *Othello*, Welles misguidedly plays the dupe. No doubt it would have been impossible for him to ask another actor to spend four years in the central role (and at such a low salary), but Welles seemed to find the character strangely irresistible, also playing Othello on the London stage under Olivier's aus-

in all, despite the visual splendor of the photography in the new release prints (made from the negative of the 1955 U.S. release version), the "restoration" of the film is a shameful travesty of film history. It's symptomatic of the deceitfulness involved that the film was advertised as "Orson Welles' Lost Masterpiece," for even though the U.S. release version had not been available for many years, Welles's *Othello* had never been "lost." See Jonathan Rosenbaum's insightful essay "*Othello* Goes Hollywood" (originally published in 1992 in the *Chicago Reader*) in his 1995 book *Placing Movies*. In 1995 the Criterion Collection released a laserdisc edition of the film, using a print of the 1955 U.S. release version.

pices in 1951, while the film was still in production. Perhaps at this point in his career, cut loose from the hostile moorings of Hollywood and adrift in the uncharted waters of the postwar European cinema, Welles felt both a sense of victimization in his career and an urgent need to explore the freer, more adventurous side of his character; among his unrealized projects of the time was a film of *The Odyssey*. It is no accident, then, that Othello loses much of his tragic stature and that Iago becomes the most interesting character, if not the central character, in the drama as Welles films it.

Welles and MacLiammóir decided that sexual impotence would be the motive for Iago, and MacLiammóir gives a marvellous performance, using the effeminate Roderigo as his lackey (oddly, Welles himself dubs in Roderigo's voice) and lowering his eyes darkly when he sees Desdemona throw herself into Othello's arms. This emphasis is consistent with Welles's basic themes. The malign cripple Bannister uses O'Hara and his own wife in a similarly masochistic scheme, sexual impotence serving as another metaphor for a twisted moral sense and the pathos of the character defining his lack of moral stature. Our first sight of Iago after the prologue is as he stands in the back of a church watching Othello's wedding, and his muttered imprecation "I hate the Moor" immediately assumes connotations of both jealousy and of sacrilege. Welles makes much throughout of Othello's easy martial power, his implacable worldly confidence; phallic cannon blasts occur buoyantly as he kisses Desdemona and when he enters her bedchamber, and ironically after he shouts "Cuckold me!" and when Iago says that he will use Cassio against Othello.

The full extent of Welles's fascination with Iago is revealed at the very onset, when Iago is dragged past the funeral procession of Othello and Desdemona and thrown into a cage, thence to be suspended and to ponder the depths of his malignity. The cage appears throughout the film—hanging outside the nuptial chamber!—and the emphasis given to it, like the emphasis on Iago at the beginning, is a reflection of his control of Othello at the expense of his own life. Welles usually reserves such metaphors for his hero. Even in *The Lady from Shanghai,* Bannister is introduced well after O'Hara, after we have been well prepared to see O'Hara as the central figure. But the beginning of *Othello* establishes a dual hierarchy which is never quite resolved. The first thing we see in the film is the face of Othello, eyes closed, upside down. Slowly, almost imperceptibly, the image begins to move. We are eerily dissociated from any sense of time or space, and it is only when Welles cuts to a medium shot of a procession that we understand that Othello is dead and is being carried by pallbearers.

Welles used this startling image at two other key moments in his films, and always in moments of acute powerlessness: we also see O'Hara's face upside down and resolving into focus at the start of the crazy-house sequence, and Joseph K.'s face upside down, eyes closed and resolving into focus as he awakes at the beginning of *The Trial.* (Similarly, in Fred Zinnemann's film *A Man for All Seasons,* the face of Welles's Cardinal Wolsey is last seen upside down as he is dying, naked to his enemies.) Several times in *Othello,* when Othello first succumbs to the throes of jealousy and when he reels around after stabbing himself, Welles creates an hallucinatory centrifugal motion by panning rapidly around with Othello from an extremely low angle, making the whole world seem to be swimming around behind his madly moving figure. These images convey an overwhelming sense of vertigo, of a world without a governing principle. The surrender to chaos is at the center of this film. Suicide, an act Welles explicitly condemns in *The Trial,* is the only course open for a character as morally impotent as Othello, whose nobility is solely in the grandeur of his self-destruction.

If Welles was temperamentally wrong to play (and probably to direct) Othello—as he was temperamentally right for Falstaff, Brutus, and Lear—this does not preclude his *Othello* from having many moments of spellbinding purity and grace: the inexorable repetition of the movement of Desdemona's veiled cortége; the camera's breathless rush toward Desdemona as she watches Othello address the senate; the mysterious shot of two mechanical bellringers sounding after Iago says "I am not what I am"; the slow movement of Othello's hand down Desdemona's dress toward the rosary in her hand as he accuses her of infidelity; the chilling shot in which the camera moves away from Iago and his shadow follows Othello; the radiant appearance of Desdemona on her husband's return from sea, banners and heralds of his victory in shadow all around her; and the silent, astonished writhing of her face as Othello smothers her in the handkerchief. If the film as a whole is severely flawed, these moments are indeed as hauntingly beautiful as their antecedents in Shakespeare's verse.

8: *Mr. Arkadin*

And now I'm going to tell you about a scorpion. This
scorpion wanted to cross a river, so he asked the frog
to carry him. "No," said the frog. "No, thank you. If I
let you on my back you may sting me, and the sting
of a scorpion is death." "Now where," asked the scorpion, "is the logic of that? For scorpions always try to
be logical. If I sting you, you will die—I will drown."
So the frog was convinced and allowed the scorpion
on his back, but just in the middle of the river he felt
a terrible pain and realized that after all the scorpion
had stung him. "Logic!" cried the dying frog, as he
started under, bearing the scorpion down with him.
"There is no logic in this!" "I know," said the scorpion,
"but I can't help it—it's my character." Let's drink to
character!

—Orson Welles in *Mr. Arkadin*

If *The Stranger* is self-parody, albeit unconscious, *Mr. Arkadin*,
based on an original story by Welles, is something more dangerous and more interesting. Like Sternberg's *The Devil Is a
Woman* or Ford's *Donovan's Reef*, *Mr. Arkadin* is a film in which
the director pushes his style past its limits, treating his most
personal themes self-consciously, with a measure of irony, and
in a manner not pretending to physical or psychological realism. The result of such stylization, if successful, is a refine-
ment of the artist's themes to a high pitch of intensity, an in-

toxicating liberation. The given story is kept purposefully simple so as not to hinder the free expression of character and motif. The pitfalls of such excess are obvious, though for Sternberg and Ford the problem is less acute because on a basic level the concerns of the director and the general audience coincide. Ford's audience can respond to Lee Marvin playing with toy trains without having to see in it a comic treatment of the primitive anarchism of Liberty Valance; Sternberg's audience can respond to the charms of Marlene Dietrich. But Welles pretends to no such level of common response, and in this we may see the essential failure of *Mr. Arkadin*.[1]

Thematically, Welles is returning to *Citizen Kane* from a more disillusioned viewpoint. Gregory Arkadin is a legendary vizier of finance who lives in a fairytale castle, shepherding his daughter's waning innocence while brooding over the ruined lives he has left in his wake. (Welles based the character, like Colonel Haki in *Journey Into Fear*, on Joseph Stalin.) A young American named Guy Van Stratten comes to Arkadin in search of possible fortune and is hired to reconstruct the fragments of his shadowed past, much as Thompson delves into Kane's life—but with the crucial difference that Arkadin is still alive, lending to the research a disturbing air of godlike detachment. Van Stratten finds out too much and frightens the old man by threatening to tell his daughter about the origin of her father's

[1]It should be noted that Welles felt *Mr. Arkadin* was "destroyed" after the editing was taken out of his hands. While the film's oblique, elliptical narrative style befits its cryptic and peripatetic protagonist, the reediting may be partly to blame for the film's tendency to become *excessively* oblique and elliptical. For a tentative exploration of variant texts of the film and the radio play by Welles upon which it was based ("Greek Meets Greek," an episode of *The Adventures of Harry Lime*), see Jonathan Rosenbaum's article "The Seven Arkadins," Film Comment, January/February 1992. The first released version of the film, a Spanish-language version which opened in Madrid in March 1955, had different actors playing some of the characters; the differences between two subsequently released English-language versions (one titled *Confidential Report*) are relatively minor, but Welles said that fourteen minutes of footage had been eliminated from his (unseen) version and that the film was restructured against his wishes. However, much about the making of *Mr. Arkadin* remains obscure, and further research needs to be done before the director's original intent can be fully understood. Another source of confusion is the novel of *Mr. Arkadin* (1955), which, although credited to Welles, is in fact a novelization ghostwritten by critic Maurice Bessy.

fortune (white slavery). Arkadin flies to silence Van Stratten, but Van Stratten persuades Raina to tell her father, "It's too late." Not realizing that she still does not know the whole truth, but is only pretending in order to save her unscrupulous boyfriend, Arkadin jumps from his airplane. Thompson's realization was that the life of even a legendary man is too complex to be rationalized away, but Van Stratten's conclusion is more cynical: he finds that simply by threatening to confront legend with truth, he can destroy the meaning of both.

To Welles, Van Stratten is "The worst man in the story. He has no substance, no human substance. He's a shallow hustler." We do not need the wretched performance of Robert Arden to see that Van Stratten is, in the words of a French critic, an "uninteresting adventurer." Arguing, on the other hand, that Arden has been blamed unfairly for embodying Van Stratten's weaknesses, Jonathan Rosenbaum goes on to assert that "Arkadin and Van Stratten are presented as moral equivalents—older and younger versions of the same unscrupulous lout." While that may be an accurate reading of Welles's intent, such an equivalency in fact does not exist in the film, because of the relative degree of tragic stature Welles cannot help seeing in Arkadin. Raina Arkadin's stoical acceptance of her father's life and death suggests his wasted potential, despite his brutality and self-annihilation. Her equanimity, her sanity, her stance outside of judgment (well played by Paola Mori, who subsequently became Welles's wife) indicates that Raina's love for Arkadin is more mature than Isabel's for George or Desdemona's for Othello. "He was capable of anything," Raina says simply, without sentimentality but with a kind of quiet awe and respect. The plight of the Welles hero seems more terrible when we reflect that his struggle for dignity is no longer a vital concern for those around him. It is a lonely self-examination in an arena peopled with impassive spectators. There is no Thompson to be chastened by the example; Raina accepts her father's actions as inevitable.

But it would be futile, and misleading, to discuss *Mr. Arkadin* in terms of "believable" characters and situations. Indeed, Arkadin's sole purpose is to obliterate the truth about himself and to vanish into the shadow of legend. We are back to the stylization of *Macbeth*, to the melodrama of *The Stranger* without the pretext of naturalism. Arkadin's face is false to an unmistakable degree, to the point at which it must be assumed that Welles intended it to be seen as a disguise. Welles's nose has never before looked so fabricated, his costumes never so bizarre. He sports a variety of masks, and at one point dresses as Santa Claus! In several scenes we are permitted to see the backing which secures his wig, mustache, and beard to his head.

Although it requires an overwhelming degree of willing suspension of disbelief on the part of the viewer, the theatricality of Arkadin's person is not a gaffe on Welles's part but the expression of the fear closest to his soul. Arkadin has no more desire to live when he believes he can no longer hide the truth about himself from the one person he cares for, Raina. Welles's youthful idealism was reflected in Kane's attempt to preserve the spirit of his past by entombing himself, Pharaoh-like, with the relics of a happier existence. Arkadin, however, pleads that he has no memory prior to a snowy night in the winter of 1927 when he found himself in Zurich with two hundred thousand Swiss francs in his wallet. "The great secret of my life," he tells Van Stratten, is that "I do not know who I am." That this is an outright lie may be clear to the viewer, but it is not to the hapless Van Stratten. Arkadin hires Van Stratten to discover the last remaining traces of his prior existence so that he can systematically obliterate them. He then plans to obliterate Van Stratten, by now the embodiment of his past, but failing to do so, must destroy himself. Lucidity is the ultimate crisis in Welles's universe. His heroes not only deceive others, but they either believe their own lies or act as if they do, and they destroy themselves at the moment when they can no longer hide their self-deception. Myth-making and iconoclasm are the two essential, irreconcilable poles of Welles's personality. A crucial passage of dialogue sums up Arkadin's reasoning:

Arkadin: You are a dangerous man to be seen with.

Van Stratten: Yeah—I guess that's the way you had it planned all along.

Arkadin: I knew what I wanted—that's the difference between us. In this world there are those who give and those who ask, those who do not care to give, and those who do not dare to ask. You dared, but you were never quite sure what you were asking for. Now there's nothing more you can hope to beg from me, Van Stratten. Not money—certainly not my daughter. Not even your life.

In keeping with the egocentricity that is Arkadin's sole *raison d'être*, the place he inhabits is no place in particular. The camera ranges all over the world, but what it sees is unreal. We see Arkadin standing immobile in the cabin of a wildly gyrating boat, but the boat has no destination. He gives a masked ball, but for no purpose other than to hide his face from Van Stratten until the hour of unmasking. This is reminiscent of a chillingly ironic scene in Chaplin's *The Idle Class*. The tramp wanders into a costume ball and is accepted by the partygoers because they think that he is masquerading as a tramp. The joke is on them. Arkadin, as mockingly solipsistic as Chaplin's tramp, merges silently with the crowd, cannily luring them into acknowledging that they too are hiding the secret of their natures. The crowd has no equivalent understanding. Arkadin is a mystery to Van Stratten not for moral or aesthetic reasons—as Kane is to Thompson—but because the key to the mystery is simply the key to money (and, eventually, to Van Stratten's self-preservation). Sex or love does not enter into Van Stratten's relationship with Raina; she is only a key to the key. A procession of religious *penitenti* outside the castle makes no more impression on him than the profane chaos of the party. Simple words of his narration whisk him here and there in a *rondo* of pointless frenzy.

Welles prefaces *Mr. Arkadin* with a text explicitly stating his theme, which is also a central theme of his work as a whole: "A certain great and powerful king once asked a poet, 'What can I give you of all that I have?' He wisely replied, 'Any-

thing, sir . . . except your secret.'" The problem with the film is
that it treats this theme at the expense not only of character
and dramatic logic but also of specific interest. Van Stratten
can be accepted as a one-dimensional foil and Arkadin as a
philosophical proposition if we consider *Mr. Arkadin* a reflec-
tive commentary by Welles on the pattern of his career, but it
is difficult to accept *Mr. Arkadin* as an integral, coherent work.
The Old Man and the Sea enables us to see with extraordinary
clarity the elements of wish-fulfillment and ego-projection underlying all of Hemingway's work, but the basic anecdote of
the story has been diluted by overemphasis, so that the story
is submerged by the symbolic weight of its component parts.
Mr. Arkadin is similarly self-indulgent.

In freeing himself of the burdens of naturalism, Welles also
dissipated much of his underlying theme, so that we have no
interest in Van Stratten and little respect for Arkadin. Though
Welles demands of us that we find in the sinister Arkadin a
vestige of passion and nobility of purpose, the character is too
abstracted to move us in a *particular* sense, as we are moved
by Macbeth or Othello. Welles has said of *Mr. Arkadin* that
"the point of the story is to show that a man who declares
himself in the face of the world, I am as I am, take it or leave
it, that this man has a sort of tragic dignity. It is a question of
dignity, of verve, of courage, but it doesn't justify him. . . .
Arkadin created himself in a corrupted world; he doesn't try
to better that world, he is a prisoner of it." Unfortunately, as
with Joseph K. in *The Trial*, we are forced to *will* Arkadin our
understanding and sympathy, and the effort breaks the back of
the work. When Welles tells us at the outset that Arkadin's
suicide "was very nearly responsible for the fall of at least one
European government," we register this as a given fact but
feel no conviction of the social power we see in Kane.

It seems that Welles needs a realistic context in which to
place his supermen. A superman without recognizable human
beings under his control is not a superman but an eccentric.
When Susan leaves Kane, he falls into the position of helpless
dependency she had filled only a moment earlier, and the contrast is shattering. But when Arkadin falls from Raina's existence, we can only mirror her expression of futile regret. The

price he pays for his self-dramatization is only that of losing an audience. We may feel that we have witnessed an extraordinary gesture, but it is a sentimental gesture. Arkadin destroys himself to prove that he has no reason to live. Welles's other heroes have a reason to take others with them as they die, but Arkadin is merely an exhibitionist.

9. The Fountain of Youth

First Person Singular was the singularly apt subtitle of Orson Welles's radio series *The Mercury Theatre on the Air*. Although he signed off each of his programs with the words "Obediently yours," Welles was about as self-effacing as a drunken butler, intruding himself into the plots of everything from *Heart of Darkness* to Commander Edward Ellsberg's *Hell on Ice*. He continued to refine the first-person narrative technique in radio and, eventually, in films and television.

In an original radio drama he broadcast shortly before the premiere of *Citizen Kane*, a fable about fascism in small-town America entitled *His Honor, The Mayor*, there is a brief scene in which the beleaguered mayor sits down to a hearty breakfast. This prompts a long rumination from Welles beginning, "Take my word for it, when responsibilities get to be almost unendurable, a man on a diet takes to his sugars and starches as an addict retreats to his opium-pipe, or a drunkard to his bottle." Welles used this interlocutory technique heavily in the early scenes of his radio shows. Only after the issues were thoroughly defined would he withdraw and let his characters work out a solution to the problems he had outlined: "As I told you, this story hasn't any moral or any message of mine tied to it. It's *about* morals and messages though, and I was serious when I said I hoped you'd draw your own conclusions." The commentary not only enabled Welles to streamline complex narrative lines, but also gave a wholly personal cast to the way he forced the audience's attention onto his own presence in the drama. As a show progressed, his omniscience and omnipresence would make him seem godlike, and the characters functions of his own thoughts and desires, even if he refused to judge them.

Welles's films reflect the influence of radio in their narrated prologues, which often provide a poetic or literal synopsis of the story, and in the director's dual presence as protagonist and commentator. But because of the cinema's heightened complexity, Welles had to invent ingenious new means of storytelling to approximate the confidential intimacy which was so effortlessly possible in the one-dimensional world of radio. He said he loved "innocent" forms of entertainment, such as magic, Westerns, and the early horror films, because they take the audience back to the beginnings of storytelling . . . back to the bard strumming his lyre and murmuring in the darkness of the cave. This may also explain his nostalgia for radio, which persisted decades past its death as a dramatic instrument.

In 1956, Welles made a television pilot film for Desilu, *The Fountain of Youth,* based on John Collier's short story "Youth from Vienna." It was to inaugurate a series of short story adaptations he would host, narrate, and direct, much like his old *First Person Singular* broadcasts on radio. The second program was to have been based on Collier's "Green Thoughts." At the end of the pilot Welles describes "Green Thoughts" as "a sort of spook story with a seasoning of giggles," which is also an apt summation of *The Fountain of Youth.* Welles explained his plan for the series in a 1982 interview with Bill Krohn for *Cahiers du Cinéma:* "I was going to be the permanent star—not as a host like Ronnie Reagan coming on at the beginning and end of *Death Valley Days,* or like Hitchcock, but woven all the way through the show, and it's a style I'd like to go back to. I was very fond of it, that way of doing it. It was based entirely on back projection, there was no scenery. We just took the props from the prop department and put them behind the screen, and a few little things in front."

Needless to say, *The Fountain of Youth* was considered eccentric, and Welles never found backing for the series. Given a single showing on NBC-TV in September 1958, the pilot won a Peabody Award for creative achievement and then disappeared into the oblivion of the vaults, not surfacing again until 1969, when it played theatrically during a Welles retrospective at Hollywood's Los Feliz Theater (it has since been released on videotape).

When I discussed *The Fountain of Youth* with Welles in 1970, he described it as "a film conceived for the box." In that it differs from his 1968 film *The Immortal Story*, which was shown on French television simultaneously with its theatrical premiere; despite its stage-like spareness and compression, *The Immortal Story* is a story film conceived for the large screen, with all the pretense of showing real people involved in a real drama. But *The Fountain of Youth*, with its mixture of bold stylization, puckish humor, and bardic intimacy, draws on Welles's "radio side." He is on screen, in Mephistophelean evening dress, longer than any of the putative principals, often stepping in front of the camera while the scene behind him blurs or fades away; he speaks the characters' unspoken thoughts, interprets their motives, warns of impending events, and occasionally even speaks their lines while they move their mouths like puppets. The most nostalgic touch comes at the very end, when Welles signs off, "Till then, I remain—as always—obediently yours . . . ," as the screen darkens around his darkly smiling profile.

Form follows function in *The Fountain of Youth*, for the theme of the piece is narcissism. The Collier story is a whimsical takeoff on the Faust theme; it is about an endocrinologist, Humphrey Baxter, who develops an eternal youth potion and uses it to tamper with the affections of a naive young actress, Caroline Coates. Like Collier, Welles relegates the Faust business to a red herring (the potion turns out to be a fraud, nothing but water and salt, which the scientist has been using as a kind of truth serum), in order to reduce our metaphysical speculations to a baser, more human, level. Welles had the distinct advantage over Collier of working in a visual medium. None of his other films has made such extensive use of mirrors, for instance, and the sheer physical data of the characters' faces and bodies (e.g., the pneumatic bliss of watching Joi Lansing waddle through the role of Caroline) speak volumes. In fact, it is problematic who should be considered the protagonist of the tale: Caroline, who has Humphrey in her spell, or Welles himself, who has both of them in *his* spell.

I opt for Welles, on the evidence of one splendidly theatrical moment. It occurs after a gossip columnist burbles into a radio microphone about Caroline and Alan Brodie (Rick Jason), her tennis-player Valentino, and we see a rococo fountain cascading against a lowering sky. Welles begins talking about the legendary fountain of youth and the myth of Narcissus. Suddenly he is before the camera, telling us *sotto voce*, "It was his own expression he fell for . . . and he fell in." The camera holds on Welles for a long moment, with vague shadowy forms moving in the studio behind him, as he contemplates that statement with a bemused expression. It's as if he's saying: "*Here's* Narcissus, ladies and gentlemen. My name is Orson Welles. You will shortly be watching several varieties of human being fall under the spell of vanity, but don't be smugly superior, for it is your obedient servant who is playing out his obsessions so that you, on the other side of the lens, will see them in yourselves. Who knows what evil lurks in the hearts of men? The mirror knows."

The early sequences are suffused with that offhand indulgence toward human weakness which Welles often uses to implicate the audience in the characters' dilemma. The prologue of *The Magnificent Ambersons*, for instance, introduces the family's snobbery in a humorous light (young George snapping his whip at the inviting butt of a street laborer, Isabel curling her nose at Gene Morgan's horrid automobile). The nostalgia Welles shares with his characters is a melancholic glance back at a time of moral innocence. He lets us indulge in the pleasures of irresponsibility before we have to face its consequences. In *The Fountain of Youth*, as in *Ambersons*, he dwells on the romantic quaintness of vanished artifacts and customs to keep us aware of their evanescence. The story is prefaced by a shot of a magic lantern flashing into the camera; the characters are introduced with stills; honky-tonk music on the soundtrack whisks us back to the 1920s. In this context, Humphrey's dabbling with the sources of life seems, at first, an invigorating rebellion against his own encroaching decay, a Lawrentian howl against the stuffiness of the laboratory.

The play in which he spots Caroline is titled *Destiny's Tot,* but destiny is the farthest thing from his mind: what we actually see of the play is Caroline lasciviously posed against a barnyard backdrop to an undertone of orgasmic clapping. Stunned by the spectacle, the scientist removes his social mirror—takes off his glasses—in a gesture that will be echoed at the end, when he confronts Caroline with the truth about his deception. Humphrey (Dan Tobin) is not the effortlessly passionate young scientist of the Collier story, but a tweedy middle-aged remnant of the Victorian era uncomfortably stranded, like Gene Morgan, amidst the technological brutalities of the new century. Just as Gene's automobile quickly evolves from a romantic fancy into a soul-devouring monster, Humphrey's potion begins as an offshoot of his fascination with Caroline but soon leads to cool talk about how the potion is obtained in an "extremely delicate operation which unfortunately is fatal to the animal we get it from. It's quite a common animal . . . man." The brittleness of Humphrey's dream is beautifully captured in the fast montage of stills Welles uses to depict the couple's first kiss.

Befitting the medieval (or is it futuristic?) nature of Humphrey's experiments, his laboratory is an eerily unreal chamber with outsized jars and bottles looming behind him like the odd shapes moving behind Welles in the studio/laboratory he inhabits. To cinch the connection, the director has placed one incongruous object in the laboratory—a bulky old-fashioned radio with a giant shell for a speaker. Like other Wellesian Faust figures (Bannister in *The Lady from Shanghai*, Arkadin, Quinlan in *Touch of Evil*, Mr. Clay in *The Immortal Story*), Humphrey tests his powers by constructing a fable with living chracters. Removed, by his romanticism, from the world of ordinary people, he tries to twist reality to fit the shape of his own ego. The irony in *The Fountain of Youth* is that the man who pulls the strings is also attached to an invisible set of strings. When Humphrey divulges his secret to Caroline and Alan in the laboratory, Welles mocks the "secret" by supplying the first lines for each character. During the scene the camera moves repeatedly in and out on the vial as it changes hands, giving it an almost palpable power of involuntary attraction.

A clock ticks with hallucinatory slowness throughout the scene, and Caroline and Alan exchange glazed, zombie-like looks as Humphrey facetiously "marries" them by joining their hands around the vial.

"Time, which was the cause of all this trouble, went on," Welles murmurs in one of the subsequent scenes, barely suppressing an unholy smile at the thought of Caroline and Alan examining each other for wrinkles and arguing over who should drink the potion. Caroline is Youth, and youth is impermanence, and what is it that Humphrey wants if not to immortalize the moment? The grotesqueness of an older man, a man of superior intellect, pursuing a young floozie evokes all the destructive illogic of the romantic impulse. Caroline is the *reductio ad absurdum* of romance, all surface and show. Humphrey doesn't want her for herself, but for what she represents. She is a token of everything missing in his life, beginning with sex, which is nothing if not a struggle to escape into a timeless state of perfect irresponsibility. The rub is, of course, that the moment of happiness disappears as soon as consciousness returns to savor it. In Welles's fundamentally romantic viewpoint, women stand for everything a man strives after but cannot possess, so they are also the source of his destruction. They are beyond reason, beyond morality, beyond responsibility.

The last section of *The Fountain of Youth* is given over to a series of expressionistically lit, ballet-like gestures in which the two youths act out the consequences of Humphrey's narcissism while he, with scientific detachment, disappears from view. Welles fades in on the vial shining unnaturally out of the darkness, harsh electronic sounds hovering in the air. A hand comes out of the void to put the vial on a mantel, and the light rises to reveal both Caroline and Alan gazing into a mirror—the lens of the camera. The effect is profoundly disturbing, for we are watching them but they are watching *us*. They fade away, again leaving the vial shining in the darkness. Soon we see Caroline standing behind Alan as he gazes into the camera. Welles narrates in a hushed voice, "She watched him in the mirror, and he saw her ... watching him." Suddenly everything but his hand and the vial plunge into darkness, a *coup de théâtre* which defies verbal description except to say that it is the closest equivalent to a shudder ever put on film.

The world turns into a crazy house (compare the last reel of *The Lady from Shanghai*) when Alan, succumbing to the temptation of drinking the vial, refills it with water and bitters to let Caroline do the same. The vial on the mantel, seen through the camera/mirror, dissolves to a shot of an actual mirror, which in turn dissolves to a shot of that mirror seen through another mirror. The master of ceremonies explains off-screen, "Now the emptiness of one's own home at midnight can seem like an injury ... " The emptiness of mirrors reflecting upon themselves with no one, but the audience, looking into them: the emptiness of a mind disintegrating. Our mind.

The next shot, as extraordinary as anything Welles ever conjured up with his camera, shows Caroline standing in silhouette before a huge mirror. The mirror mocks its function, for it does not reflect anything at all; instead it is filled with a frozen view of her own face, grinning. The mirror is festooned with a garland of thorns. Welles's voice, portentous and rhythmic as the ticking of the clock in Humphrey's laboratory, intones, "She could feel and almost hear the remorseless erasures of time," as she runs her hands over the mirror. A clock begins ticking, and the face in the glass begins to metamorphose. Like the Picture of Dorian Gray, the mirror reveals the hidden emptiness of death. Layer after layer of luxuriant flesh dissolves relentllessly down to the skull. She screams, cymbals crash, and our mirror, the screen, is engulfed with hers in utter darkness. A still shows Caroline drinking the potion—time has stopped—before Humphrey tells her that it has all been a trick.

An even deeper influence on *The Fountain of Youth* than radio, perhaps, was magic. While putting on *The Mercury Wonder Show*, in which he sawed Rita Hayworth and Marlene Dietrich in half, "Orson the Magnificent" declared, "I discovered at the age of six that almost everything in this world was phony, worked with mirrors. Since then, I've always wanted to be a magician."

10: *Touch of Evil*

In 1957, largely through the intervention of Charlton Heston, Welles was given the chance to direct his first Hollywood feature in ten years. He originally had been approached by producer Albert Zugsmith to play the heavy in a Universal-International crime thriller based on the novel *Badge of Evil* by Whit Masterson (a pseudonym for Robert A. Wade and H. Billy Miller). According to Zugsmith, Welles also expressed interest in directing the film. But when Heston was offered the starring role, he was told only that Welles would be in the cast, and he replied, "You know, Orson Welles is a pretty good director. Did it ever occur to you to have him direct it?"

The studio had misgivings, due to Welles's longstanding and largely unmerited reputation for profligacy, but it perhaps figured that he couldn't go too far out of bounds with the material he was given. Welles accepted with alacrity, demanding only to write his own screenplay, since he found the studio's scenario (by Paul Monash) "ridiculous." However, as John Stubbs demonstrated in his 1985 study of the evolution of the project (included in Terry Comito's 1991 book about the film), Welles did use some elements from Monash's script, and although he claimed he did not read the novel before making the film, he incorporated some elements that Monash had not used from the novel. Nevertheless, as Heston put it, Welles "took what was a very routine police story, the kind they do on television, on *Hill Street Blues* or something, and rewrote the whole thing in a couple of weeks, and gave it what distinction it had. That was entirely his."

Shooting the film in the bizarre atmosphere of Venice, California, which stood in for the hellish Mexican border town of Los Robles, Welles peopled it with a cast which, as Pauline Kael remarks, is "assembled as perversely as in a nightmare": Marlene Dietrich as a cigar-smoking Mexican madam, Dennis Weaver as a sex-mad motel clerk (one of the film's intriguing prefigurations of *Psycho*), Zsa Zsa Gabor as the manager of a strip joint, Joseph Cotten as a coroner, Akim Tamiroff as a smalltime hoodlum, Mercedes McCambridge as the leader of a leather-jacket gang. Plus Heston as a straight-laced Mexican narcotics official, Janet Leigh as his naive, frustrated American wife, and Welles himself as the corrupt American police detective, Captain Hank Quinlan. Grossly overweight (Welles padded himself for the part), jowly, and sweaty, Quinlan looks like a grotesque, malignant toad, an impression accentuated by Welles's distorting use of extreme wide-angle lenses and low camera angles.

Nonplussed by the film, the studio took the editing out of Welles's hands after it saw his preliminary cut, and barred him from the lot. While the film was reworked in an attempt to make its unconventional narrative style more linear, studio director Harry Keller was called in to shoot some bland and clichéd connecting footage. The studio previewed a version running one hundred and eight minutes, but trimmed it by fifteen minutes before the film's release in February 1958. The title was changed to *Touch of Evil*—"what a silly title," Welles remarked at the time, although he later conceded that it "sounds all right."

André Bazin congratulated Welles for making a film capable of pleasing both drive-in audiences and serious *cinéastes*, but despite the favorable response in Europe (where it won a best-picture award at the film festival of the 1958 Brussels World's Fair), *Touch of Evil* had little opportunity to please either audience in the United States. Unceremoniously dumped on the market on the bottom half of double bills, it was scorned by most reviewers as little more than the lurid B-picture promised by the advertising ("This was her wedding night," the trailer leered over shots of a terrified Janet Leigh being menaced in the motel. "Where was the man she had

married? Who were these hoodlums?"). Although it marked
the end of Welles's Hollywood directing career, *Touch of Evil*
has grown steadily in reputation over the years, advancing
from cult status in the 1960s to be recognized widely today as
a classic of the American cinema. As Andrew Sarris has written, "*Touch of Evil* is a movie which makes you rethink what
a movie should be."

In the early 1970s, Robert Epstein of UCLA discovered a
print of the hundred-and-eight-minute version of *Touch of Evil*,
which was subsequently reissued by Universal. My 1975 interview with Epstein about the discovery, published in *Daily Variety*, incorrectly indicated that this version corresponds closely
to Welles's cut; although I corrected that mistaken impression
in a 1976 letter to *Sight and Sound*, it continues to be widely
believed. The longer version in fact is not the director's cut
but the studio preview version, which, although it contains
several previously unseen scenes and additional parts of
scenes directed by Welles, also contains even more footage interpolated by Harry Keller than did the 1958 release version.
Welles's extreme displeasure with the studio's cutting and
sound mixing of the longer version is evident from his fifty-
eight-page memo on the subject to studio president Edward
Muhl, parts of which were published in the Fall 1992 issue of
Film Quarterly. Still, the fifteen minutes of previously unseen
footage, described in minute detail in Comito's book, helps
clarify some important plot points and adds vital dimensions
to our understanding of the characters, even if Welles might
have tightened up the somewhat labored comedy of the car
chase involving Tamiroff's Uncle Joe Grandi and Quinlan's
deputy, Pete Menzies (Joseph Calleia). While it can be argued
that the shorter version has the virtue of moving the story
along more efficiently, if less coherently, the added layers of
thematic density in the longer version more closely approach
Welles's original schema for the film, even if he was not allowed to bring it fully to fruition.

Touch of Evil is a richer, more personal, and (a vital point)
more entertaining film than *The Trial*, which is a less deeply
felt, more studiedly allegorical treatment of the abuse of the
law. In *The Trial*, as he had done previously in the parodistic

Lady from Shanghai, Welles concentrates on a seemingly innocent man trapped by an inhuman legal system; the complexities of the system at first seem merely irrational and finally are seen to be the logical extension of the contradictions of character. In *Touch of Evil,* on the other hand, Captain Quinlan deftly uses official power for personal and corrupt purposes, like Kane with his newspapers and Arkadin with his financial empire. The emphasis shifts from the "innocent" who outwits the law to the man destroyed by his own overreaching, like Bannister in *The Lady from Shanghai.*

The emphasis again returns to the "innocent" in *The Trial,* but the humor of Welles's adaptation of Kafka is so dark, so abstracted, that we find it too hard to see ourselves in Joseph K. Welles denies us the conventional sympathy which his pathetic situation might offer by making Anthony Perkins's K. smug, self-righteous, and cruel, and we are turned back on our intellectual understanding of his position. Quinlan is a much more accessible character. His emotions are closer to the surface, though Welles never indulges in sentimentality. Where Quinlan differs from K. is that we easily ratify the validity of his emotions, even while we condemn his actions; with K., we must transfer our concerns to an abstract concept of personal responsibility. If repeated viewings of *The Trial* tend to diminish our pleasure in it (it is a film I admire, but don't particularly enjoy), *Touch of Evil* gains in fascination, each viewing revealing new levels of irony, moral complexity, and wit. Quinlan is the most sympathetic Welles hero until Falstaff, but his actions are the most odious of any Welles hero's. The enormity of the gulf between Quinlan's intentions and his actions helps Welles make one of his most lucid philosophical presentations.

Quinlan's wife was long ago murdered by a man who got off free because Quinlan, then a rookie cop, could not prove the case. Though "in some mud hole in Belgium the good Lord done the job for me, in 1917," Quinlan has become obsessed by this palpable demonstration of the inadequacy of the law. If a murderer can escape because of lack of evidence, he reasons, why not plant evidence to be sure of capturing the right man? Quinlan's idea is a perfect illustration of Raskolnikov's dictum in *Crime and Punishment:* "The 'extraordinary' man has the right . . .

in himself . . . to permit his conscience to overstep certain obstacles, but only in the event that his ideas (which may sometimes be salutary for all mankind) require it for their fulfilment. If it is necessary for one of these extraordinary people for the fulfilment of his ideas to march over corpses, or wade through blood, then in my opinion, he may in all conscience authorize himself to wade through blood—in proportion, however, to his idea and the degree of its importance—mark that."

His badge allows Quinlan to make corpses of the men he arrests (the change of title from *Badge of Evil* to *Touch of Evil* deemphasizes the film's critique of the abuse of police power, making it more universalized), and Quinlan justifies his actions by believing that he has never framed anyone who wasn't guilty. Until the chance arrival of an outsider, Heston's upstanding and self-righteous Ramon Miguel Vargas, Quinlan's methods have never upset anybody. But Vargas discovers that Quinlan has planted evidence implicating a Mexican shoe clerk, Manolo Sanchez (Victor Millan), in the murder of a local bigwig, and is appalled. We too are appalled, because we see only the false evidence and share Vargas's sympathy for an apparently innocent man. In the last moments of the film we are told that the shoe clerk has confessed: Quinlan was "right" after all. But this is a red herring, for the moral issue Welles is exploring does not revolve around Sanchez's guilt or innocence. On a plot level, as the longer version of the film makes more evident, any confession wrung out of a suspect by Quinlan and his department is highly dubious, given their habitual use of third-degree interrogation methods. But the larger issue is the difference between law and lynch-law. As the witnesses of his death put it, Quinlan was a great detective, but a lousy cop.

A conventional moralist would have loaded the issue by leaving no doubt of the clerk's innocence, but Welles forces us to maintain an ironic position. Quinlan's *game leg* tells him that the man is guilty! How outrageous, we agree with Vargas—but if we feel that the man's confession reverses Quinlan's guilt we have missed the point entirely. In the extraordinary interrogation scenes, a series of three uninterrupted, intensely claustrophobic takes in a single apartment (the first, which lasts five minutes and twenty-three seconds, involves more than sixty camera movements),[1] Welles deviously involves us in Quinlan's machinations. Sanchez is silly, smug, absurd ("the very best shoe clerk the store ever had," he tells us). Quinlan is brutal, unreasoning, and easily able to intimidate the suspect. The Mexican is obviously being persecuted, Quinlan is an obvious bully. But Sanchez offends us by being a fool, and Quinlan makes us admire his godlike insouciance. It is typical of Welles that the people who are right are the people we don't like, and the people who are wrong have admirable qualities—Quinlan is not only a great detective, with brilliant intuitions, but he is consumed with a passion (however twisted) for what he considers to be justice. Welles is a rhetorician who forces us to acknowledge that issues exist apart from their proponents. Or, more precisely, he separates an issue from its proponent in order to free us from sentimental identification, to let us see the issue itself more clearly. If we are to agree with Sanchez that he is being persecuted, we must do this not through facile sympathy with a noble figure of defiance; we must sympathize with a clown. And if we are to condemn Quinlan's actions, we must condemn the actions of a man we see to be adept and brimming with recognizable human emotion. The parable about the scorpion and the drowning frog becomes clear. The logic is in principle, not in character.

Welles sets Quinlan off with a beautiful array of counterposing characters. Quinlan's mad passion is understood only by his deputy, Menzies. Menzies hears Quinlan's confession in the bar, a confession of motives he has heard many times before. He accepts it while still continuing to prod Quinlan about his methods. But when Quinlan commits murder in a demented attempt to frame Vargas's wife, Menzies realizes that he must make Quinlan admit the truth about himself. Like Leland in *Citizen Kane*, Menzies is committed to love and friendship at the cost of his own integrity, until his feelings of betrayal by his friend lead him, in turn, to betray that friend.

---

[1]Welles told me that while "Everyone talks about the opening shot" in *Touch of Evil*, he considered the first interrogation scene "the greatest use of the moving camera in the history of cinema."

Joseph Calleia's mournful tremulousness and accumulating anger work in powerful counterpoint in his deeply moving performance, building up to the key exchange (which appears only in the longer version) when Vargas expresses disgust to Menzies over their use of a bugging device to nail Quinlan, and the anguished Menzies replies, "How do you think I feel about it? Hank is the best friend I've ever had. . . . I am what I am because of him."

"Quinlan is the god of Menzies," Welles has commented. "And, because Menzies worships him, the real theme of the scenario is treason, the terrible impulsion that Menzies has to betray his friend." Menzies has debased himself by playing Quinlan's accomplice—he has surrendered his own moral identity—and when Quinlan's quest for "justice" finally drives him to the very act which had provoked the quest, Menzies realizes with terrible clarity the insanity of his own actions. Welles crystallizes all the tensions of the relationship in a powerful "syllogism" of images: Quinlan long ago saved Menzies's life by stopping a bullet meant for him, causing his game leg and necessitating his use of a cane (this is explained by Menzies in the longer version, but was implied in the shorter version); Quinlan tacitly admits his guilt by leaving the cane next to the murdered man's body, convincing Menzies to confront him; and, finally, when Quinlan has shot Menzies, only to be himself shot by Menzies, he says, "Pete . . . that's the second bullet I stopped for you." The assistant district attorney, Schwartz (Mort Mills), and Marlene Dietrich's Tanya sum up the tragic friendship of Quinlan and Menzies as they look at Quinlan's body:

> *Schwartz:* You really liked him, didn't you?
> *Tanya:*   The cop did. The one who killed him. He loved him.

Vargas, whom Welles described as "my mouthpiece" in *Touch of Evil,* is the holder of liberal ideas; he speaks up for the principles of law; he is played by a man who embodies stoic incorruptibility and sincerity. But his posture is stiff, humorless, and self-righteous. When he stands up to Quinlan, we know that we are in the presence of a prig. He is colorless next to Quinlan. We admire his tenacity in ferreting out proof of Quinlan's treachery, but we cannot help enjoying Quinlan's candor: as he tells Sanchez, "There's an old lady on Main Street last night picked up a shoe. The shoe had a foot in it. We're going to make you pay for that mess." If we are going to side with Vargas, we do so fully aware that he has no comprehension of the twisted passion for justice which underlies Quinlan's illegal behavior.

Welles makes a subtle implication in the celebrated opening shot, a magnificent unbroken travelling movement (lasting three minutes and eighteen seconds) which combines the planting of a bomb in a car and its journey through border customs with the passage of Vargas and his wife behind it. If Welles had not filmed the dual journeys in one continuous shot, he would have lost the tension of inevitability, the feeling that what the couple is doing (crossing a border, a metaphor to be re-echoed throughout the film) is inextricable from what is happening to the car. If Welles had cut back and forth from the couple to the car, he would have implied either a parallelism or a contrast. Instead he suspends any kind of moral statement until the couple kiss—and he cuts to the car exploding. An image for the violent disruption of their relationship, clearly, but, even more strongly, a linkage of actions which implies a cause-and-effect relationship. In some unknown way, Welles is saying, something about this couple contains the seeds of violence and murder. Their complacent blundering into danger, and her unconscious racism toward her husband's people, are gradually linked by Welles with the pervasive taint of corruption on both sides of the border and with the barely repressed undercurrent of violent racial and sexual hostilities.

We feel unsure of Vargas, despite his moral authority, because of his stiff, moronic treatment of his wife, who is ingenuously, absurdly dependent on him. He interrupts their honeymoon to handle the case and packs her off to a motel in the middle of nowhere which proves to be run by the Grandi family, the scurviest group of misfits this side of *Los Olvidados*. Whatever respect we have for Vargas as a spokesman for a higher order of justice is steadily undermined by his disregard for his wife's safety. Only after she is drugged, (almost) gang-raped, and tied to a bed with a corpse hanging over her head does he realize that he has been derelict in his responsibilities to her. The debasement of the marriage parallels the assaults made on Vargas's complacent assumption that the law is above human meddling. The order that Vargas believes in and represents is artificial, bloodless. After his wife is kidnapped, he abruptly redefines himself: "I'm no cop now, I'm a husband." For him, character is logical.

Welles evokes Quinlan's idealistic beginnings in his encounters with Dietrich's Tanya, who knew him in his better days but now fails to recognize him at first because of his paunch and general decrepitude. The brittle evanescence of Sternberg hovers over the scenes in which Quinlan takes refuge from violence in Tanya's brothel, listening to her playerless pianola. Tanya is totally, unabashedly corrupt. She does not even care to romanticize her function. When the dazed Quinlan asks her if she has been reading the cards, she puffs on her cigar and says that she has been doing the accounts. Still, she is able to tell him, when he demands his fortune, "Your future is all used up." The brothel scenes have a soft chiaroscuro about them that is in total contrast to the wild, monstrous shadows and violent camera movements of the rest of the film; Tanya's brothel is a place of rest, of comedy, of dreams. Even Quinlan seems to realize that her solace is professional and disinterested. "You're a mess, honey," she tells Quinlan, advising him to "lay off those candy bars." He grunts, admitting, "Well, it's either the candy or the hooch. I must say I wish it was your chili I was gettin' fat on." She is unimpressed. "Better be careful. It may be too hot for you."

For all her cynicism, we can see in Tanya the spirit of Mrs. Kane, the evocation of an existence simple in its compassion and unencumbered by any contact with the harshness of reality. But, like Mrs. Kane, Tanya cannot offer the hero the consolation of permanence (and it is significant that the heroes' female companions in *Touch of Evil, The Trial, Chimes at Midnight* and *The Immortal Story* are all prostitutes). Mrs. Kane sent Charles to his fortune because she wanted him away from his father. Her tragic choice was between one kind of damnation and another, more solitary kind, and she decided

to let him damn himself rather than smother him in illusory
security (a lesson Isabel Amberson learned only at the cost of
her own life). By now, however, the woman from the past has
no compunction in releasing the hero to his fate. Quinlan,
with his power ebbing away, becomes pathetically vulnerable
in her presence, but still Tanya will not give him a spurious
fortune. Nor does she suffer, like Mrs. Kane; she merely observes and understands. Tanya arrives just as Quinlan falls to
his death, betrayed by his passions and killed by his only
friend. Her comment is laconic: "He was some kind of a man.
What does it matter what you say about people?" No judgment is called for at the scene of Quinlan's death. He has
summed up his contradictions in his actions.

Welles examines the price of illegitimate power, however
pure its motive. Vargas tells Quinlan with great conviction, a
conviction we share, "A policeman's job is only easy in a police state. That's the whole *point*, captain. Who is the boss, the
cop or the law?" But for Quinlan, who lives by his emotions,
an abstraction like "police state" is of no importance. He has
chosen to disregard the consequences of following his nature,
and accepts the result with the dignity of a tragic hero, even
as he tumbles backward into the slime of a polluted canal after trying to wash Menzies' blood from his hand (an allusion
to *Macbeth*). The hideous darkness and orgiastic rhythm of
Touch of Evil describes perfectly the destruction Quinlan has
wrought on the world around him. The Welles hero has progressed far beyond Kane and Arkadin in self-realization. Kane
clung to the glass ball, the image of his past; Arkadin vainly
invoked the name of his daughter. Quinlan dies in a world so
foul that his malignity almost seems, because of its unsparing
candor, to be a virtue. In that "almost" lies the disturbing
moral tale Welles has chosen to tell.

11: *The Trial*

I couldn't put my name to a work that implies man's ultimate surrender. Being on the side of man, I had to show him in his final hour undefeated.

—Orson Welles

Of all Welles's films, *The Trial* is the most difficult to watch. The unrelieved grimness of its moral tone and the heaviness of its humor begin to exhaust even a sympathetic audience long before the end; perhaps Welles was correct when he said once that a good film could be made from Kafka's novel but that he was not the man to do it. Still, *The Trial* is clearly all of a piece. Welles has effectively adapted Kafka's narrative to the demands of his own moral universe. The critical question is not whether Welles has "faithfully" adapted the book, but to what degree Welles's profoundly personal style can afford to accommodate the characters and meanings of a writer almost totally dissimilar in style and temperament.

The problem does not arise in discussing Welles's adaptation of Booth Tarkington's *The Magnificent Ambersons* or Isak Dinesen's *The Immortal Story*. In those films there is no irreconcilable tension between material and realization but only a beneficent contribution, a broadening of Welles's scope. *Mr. Arkadin*, which Welles based on his own original story, might have benefited from the detachment demanded by one author's adaptation of another. Some proponents of the *auteur* theory have, however, placed an unfortunate emphasis on the importance of "tension" in directorial style. The argument that the significance of a work arises from the tension between the given material and the director's attitude towards it would imply, if carried to its extreme, that the richest work would result from a total disparity between material and style. Few theorists, obviously, would carry the argument that far, but it is dangerous to treat such tension as an end in itself, rather than as a factor contributing to the totality of the work. Left to himself, Welles would probably not have supplied the intricate journalistic satire of *Citizen Kane* or the mystical overtones of *The Immortal Story*, but his worldview shows no strain in accommodating such attitudes. The problem when considering a director's sources is not so much to point out what the director has rejected—a peripheral concern in the case of a successful work—but what he has accepted and has thus made his own.

Kafka's work is essentially comic. His heroes are driven from tranquillity by an inexplicably malevolent force that has fallen upon them totally at random; it is a dark parody of the doctrine of original sin. There is punishment and guilt but no corresponding cause. The "sin" is assumed as a prior condition of existence. Kafka's heroes are faceless; they have no power, no stature (but for some ironic bureaucratic authority), and ultimately no dignity. They are not tragic but comic and pathetic. K. realizes at the end of *The Trial* that he is dying "like a dog." What is tragic in Kafka is existence in general, the kind of inexorable logic that begins in the commonest actions and proceeds through an endless maze of controvertings of the ordinary, ending in the inevitable death of the hero. K. submits to the knife, unable even to kill himself, which would imply an acknowledgment of responsibility. "The responsibility for this last failure of his," the narrator comments, "lay with him who had not left him the remnant of strength necessary for the deed." We are told that Kafka would laugh to himself while reading parts of *The Trial* to his friends. If this strikes us as curious, we should consider that the godlike narrator of *The Trial* is his own tragedian. The desolation of Kafka's world is the result of a prior act of will on the part of its creator, who is not God, certainly, but Kafka. The powerless beings under his control are acting out the drama of his own overweening pride. It is Kafka who has not left K. the remnant of strength necessary to act of his own volition. It is Kafka who denies meaning to his characters' lives and refuses to consider the possibility of a higher order. Pity his characters—for their impotence, which they are tempted to regard with guilt, is but a comic statement of their creator's preordination of defeat as the universal principle.

This, of course, is the exact inverse of Welles's position. He holds his heroes to a code of justice and condemns their violation of its principles, not their ignorance of principle. He forces his heroes to choose between responsible self-determination and godlike arrogance. "All the characters I've played are various forms of Faust," he has stated. "I hate all forms of Faust, because I believe it's impossible for man to be great without admitting there is something greater than himself—either the law or God or art—but there must be something greater than man. I have sympathy for those characters—humanly but not morally." Given this seemingly irreconcilable conflict between Kafka's material and Welles's philosophical attitude, we can expect an extreme dialectical tension between the characters' actions and the director's view of them. If we must continue to talk of Welles and Kafka—as we do not need to talk of Welles and Tarkington, but may refer only to Welles—it is because the story proceeds not so much by emotional intensification as through rhetorical interplay. What Welles has done in taking *The Trial* as his basis is to treat the Kafka theme of preordained defeat as a constant challenge to the stability of his own moral order.

Welles's egocentric visual style is at a pole from Kafka's method of presentation. Of all filmmakers, Alfred Hitchcock is the closest to Kafka. His style has the same lucidity and syntactical logic, the same orderliness and simplicity mocking the chaos of the world situation, though with an accompanying tragic sense perhaps attributable to his skeptical Catholicism. *The Wrong Man*, the admirable "rough draft" for *North by Northwest* drawn from an actual incident of an arrest similar to that in *The Trial*, lacks the giddy humor of Hitchcock's later film but could well serve as a step-by-step illustration of how to film the nightmarish aspect of Kafka's world. Kafka's method is to describe each of his settings in terms of naturalistic time and space, and then to introduce an illogical system of character relationships which makes the seeming logic of time and space a parody of a stable world order. Welles completely distorts time and space here, juxtaposing patently disparate locales and cutting on K.'s movement out of and into each of these otherwise unrelated settings, making the universe totally a function of K.'s actions. The denouement conveys a spatial idea that Welles had planned to express in more schematic fashion before he was given a gigantic abandoned railway station as his principal set. "The production, as I had sketched it," he explained, "comprised sets that gradually disappear. The number of realistic elements [was] to become fewer and fewer and the public would become aware of it, to the point where the scene would be reduced to free space, as if everything had dissolved." In the final images, the baroque shapes of *The Trial's* space-time continuum are abstracted into a thin line between bare earth and gray sky, and the struggle of Joseph K. does indeed become the center of the universe.

To understand the full complexity of Welles's point of view here, we must assess the exact nature of his rhetoric. A crucial point is his dual presence both as director and in the person of the Advocate (Welles also dubbed in no fewer than eleven other character voices, making himself seem omnipresent and godlike). The Advocate assumes a more important function than in the novel, in which he serves mainly to distract K. farther and farther from the possibility of effectively resolving his case. Welles's demonic playing makes the Advocate not a distraction but the very embodiment of the temptation against which K. must struggle. This is confirmed by the Advocate's reappearance in the cathedral at the end, taking over the interrogatory function Kafka assigned to a priest. In the monstrous immobility—one can almost say lack of spiritual identity—to which the Advocate has given himself over, and in the totally subservient position of his client Block (who acts "like a dog"), K. can see clearly the implications of despair. Like Kurtz in *Heart of Darkness*, Welles's Advocate presents the hero with a vision of chaos that makes possible the hero's moral victory.

Few other films have been offered in rhetorical exchange with another work; among the examples are *Rio Bravo* to *High Noon* and *Le Mépris* to *The Odyssey*. Welles does not assume that his audience has read Kafka's novel; such an assumption would place the work in the realm of criticism rather than of artistic expression, and Welles is no polemicist. Instead, he is careful to keep us constantly aware of a philosophical position inimical to his own. We can see this most clearly in the cathedral scene, which has the Advocate reciting Kafka's parable of the law—the tale of a man who waits his entire life before a great door, which is closed without a word from behind it—and K., making a climactic assertion of personal responsibility, interrupting him to speak for Welles's position. The ensuing interchange, written almost entirely by Welles, crystallizes the conflict in K.'s mind and precipitates his immediate destruction. In the light of the focal point it occupies in the drama, it deserves quoting in full:

Advocate: Some commentators have pointed out that the man came to the door of his own free will.

K.: And we're supposed to swallow all that? It's all true?

Advocate: You needn't accept everything as true—only what's necessary.

K.: God, what a miserable conclusion. It turns lying into a universal principle.

Advocate: Attempting to defy the court by such an obviously mad gesture—you hope to plead insanity? You've laid some foundation for that claim by appearing to believe yourself the victim of some kind of conspiracy.

K.: That's a symptom of lunacy, isn't it?

Advocate: Delusions of persecution . . .

K.: Delusions?

Advocate: Well?

K.: I don't pretend to be a martyr, no.

Advocate: Not even . . . a victim of society?

K.: I am a member of society.

Advocate: You think you can persuade the court that
you're not responsible by reason of lunacy?

K.:   I think that's what the court wants me to believe. Yes, that's the conspiracy—persuade
us all that the whole world is crazy—
formless, meaningless, absurd! That's the
dirty game. So I've lost my case. What of
it? You—you're losing too. It's all lost.
Lost—so what? Does that sentence the entire universe to lunacy?

Enter a priest.

Priest: Can't you see anything at all?

K.:   Of course. I'm responsible.

Priest: My son—

K.:   I am not your son.

The subtle difference between K.'s position and Welles's is
that Welles endorses K.'s principle—an individual has the
power to prove the existence of an order greater than himself—but does not endorse K.'s subsequent action of arrogant
destructiveness. Society for Welles is a projection of the hero's
conscience; in a profound image he has K.'s executioners
make their final appearance by emerging from behind his
body on the steps of the cathedral. But Welles's K. lets nothing
outlive him. In an ecstatic solipsistic gesture he hurls the executioners' dynamite away from him into an empty landscape.
It explodes in a permutation of blasts culminating in the frozen image of a mushroom cloud, followed only by a godlike
light streaming from a projector as the filmmaker identifies
himself from the fourth dimension. K.'s tragic decision to be
the agent of universal destruction is the ratification of his final
dignity, but it is also the measure of his moral stature. The
desolation of the final landscape of *The Trial* is even more vast
than that of *Touch of Evil.* In the very act of proving that there
is an order to the universe, K. presumes to judge the universe.
It is fitting that he realizes his responsibility for his individual
actions, but when he extends his responsibility to the universe
in general, he oversteps the boundary between man and superman.

K.'s act of defiance redeems the formlessness around him by asserting man's position as master of his destiny, but it creates a new, more deadly chaos—the uncontrolled power of the ego. Kafka reassures us by postulating a sympathetic, good-willed, amorphous hero. If he is defeated, we are at least given the option of considering him an innocent victim. He can be considered guilty only if we consider him an active agent of the destructive system, and Kafka conveys this only in the comic sense of a rat intuitively knowing his way to the end of the maze. In Welles's terms, K. is guilty first of all because he has allowed himself to function as part of a system destructive of free will. We understand this through Anthony Perkins's skillful playing of K. as a self-righteous bureaucrat foolishly reveling in his status as assistant manager of his department, with attendant power to punish subordinates. The final irony, though, is that K., in Welles's words, "is not guilty as accused, but he is guilty all the same." His guilt, in the final analysis, is the sin of pride. It is significant of Welles's darkening attitude that the hitherto helpless K., on realizing his moral power, should immediately use it to a more evil effect than even Macbeth or Arkadin could manage. Macbeth's actions resulted in the overthrow of a dynasty, Arkadin's nearly resulted in the fall of several European governments; but the petty, self-pitying, naive, childish K. has it in him to destroy the universe.

"Your Honor, I've become obsessed with this deep feeling of hate and anger": Welles in one of his finest screen roles for another director, the Clarence Darrow–like defense lawyer Jonathan Wilk in Richard Fleischer's *Compulsion* (1959). (*Twentieth Century-Fox*)

Welles as the barbarian Burundai in *The Tartars* (1962), one of the many ridiculous roles he took in potboilers to help finance his own stubbornly independent filmmaking career. (*MGM*)

Welles wanted to direct the film version of Joseph Heller's antiwar satire *Catch-22*, but settled for the role of General Dreedle, opposite Alan Arkin's Yossarian in Mike Nichols's disappointing 1970 film. (*Paramount*)

Anthony Perkins as the anxious, guilt-ridden bureaucrat Joseph K. in Welles's 1962 film version of Franz Kafka's *The Trial*. (*Paris-Europa Productions/Hisa Films/FI-C-IT/Globus-Dubrava*)

Welles as the sinister figure of the Advocate in *The Trial*, with Romy Schneider as his mistress Leni.

The tyranny of the legal system, as seen in the Advocate's towering visual relationship to Joseph K.

The strange sexual tensions of the Advocate's ménage: Leni with their live-in client Block (Akim Tamiroff).

Leni displaying her webbed fingers to Joseph K.

K. pursuing Suzanne Flon's crippled Miss Pittl in the eerie European landscape of *The Trial*.

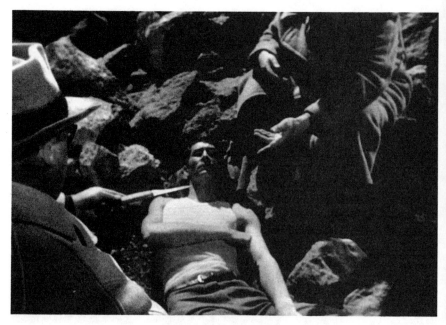

The death of Joseph K.

Welles's masterpiece, *Chimes at Midnight* (1966): the tavern scene with Welles as Sir John Falstaff and Keith Baxter as Prince Hal. (*Internacional Films Española/Alpine Productions*)

Male friendship in *Chimes at Midnight*: Falstaff with Hal and Poins (Tony Beckley).

Two Shakespearean comic grotesques, the tongue-tied Silence (Walter Chiari) and the garrulous Justice Shallow (Alan Webb).

Prelude to the Battle of Shrewsbury.

In the midst of the battle.

Prince Hal at Shrewsbury, eulogizing the fallen Hotspur (off-screen).

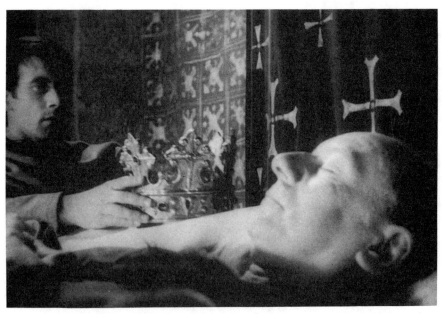

Hal and his father, the moribund King Henry IV (John Gielgud).

Tavern raillery turns to cruelty: Poins, Doll Tearsheet (Jeanne Moreau), and Hal with the supine Falstaff.

"We have heard the chimes at midnight": Falstaff reminisces by the fire with his old friend Justice Shallow.

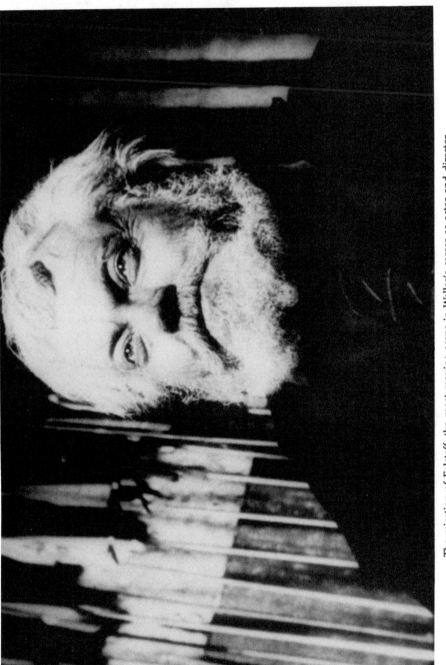

The rejection of Falstaff: the most moving scene in Welles's career as actor and director.

Welles as Mr. Clay, the cold-hearted Macao merchant in his 1968 film of Isak Dinesen's *The Immortal Story*. (ORTF/Albina Films)

Mr. Clay's carriage pursued through the streets by Paul, the penniless sailor (Norman Eshley).

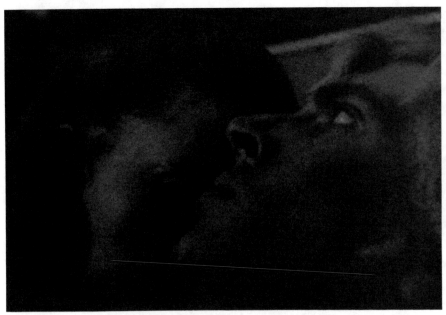

Mr. Clay's puppets, Virginie (Jeanne Moreau) and Paul.

A new level of eroticism flowered in Welles's work during the late 1960s: Jeanne Moreau as Virginie in *The Immortal Story*.

"I have heard it before, long ago . . . but where?": Roger Coggio as Mr. Clay's clerk, Elishama Levinsky, listening to the seashell in the final shot of *The Immortal Story*.

Welles around the late 1960s.

12: *Chimes at Midnight*

Chimes at Midnight is Welles's masterpiece, the fullest, most completely realized expression of everything he had been working toward since *Citizen Kane,* which itself was more an end than a beginning. The younger Welles was obsessed with the problem of construction, and solved it perfectly with a style that locked the apparently powerful hero into an ironic vise of which he was almost totally unaware. We could not be farther from the characters, and perhaps this distancing, however suited to the telling of a story of futile omnipotence, reflected a young man's tentative first take on old age and legend: faced with the problems of defining Charles Foster Kane and of defining himself artistically, Welles contrived a style to prove that definition is illusory. In *Chimes at Midnight,* Welles has fused his own viewpoint and that of his hero into a direct communication of emotion. His style, though every bit as deliberate and controlled as in *Kane,* no longer demands our attention for itself. There is nothing here to correspond with *Kane's* mirror trickery; there *is* a battle sequence that is one of the greatest achievements in action direction in the history of the cinema, and which moreover is constructed in a highly orchestrated rhetorical pattern, but it presents itself to the audience not as an artistic demonstration but as an overwhelming physical experience.

I think that in *Chimes at Midnight,* Welles finds himself where Beethoven found himself when he replaced musical instruments with voices in the Ninth Symphony: he has broken the bounds of his tools (the camera and the cutting bench) and has given everything over to human instruments (his actors).

When told that no one could possibly sing some of the notes he had written, Beethoven replied that it was no concern of his. Welles is more pragmatic—since he himself must make the actors correspond to his purposes—but there is the same rhapsodic exhilaration in his submersion into faces and voices. As Pierre Duboeuf has put it, "He broods with a disquiet like Rembrandt's over his own face, and it is not inconsequential that he finds there other attunements, accents less brilliant but more human, which he substitutes for the dazzling flashes of the past." We feel, as we do to some degree in *The Magnificent Ambersons*, that Welles is rejecting the mask of self-conscious stylization in order to find himself in a relaxed, sensual spontaneity. A crucial difference, however, is that Welles hid himself behind the camera in *Ambersons*, revealing himself through his attitude towards other people, and here he looms before us buoyantly fat, literally and figuratively much more himself than he had ever been before.

And, appropriately, the story he is telling is the story of a man who (prodigious liar though he may pretend to be) cannot help being entirely candid in his emotions; a man whose complete lack of emotional pretense, when confronted with the world's demands of responsibility and self-denial, becomes the very cause of his destruction. During production, Welles explained his intentions: "*Chimes* should be very plain on the visual level because above all it is a very real human story. . . . The Falstaff story is the best in Shakespeare—not the best play, but the best story. . . . Everything of importance in the film should be found on the faces; on these faces that whole universe I was speaking of should be found. I imagine that it will be the film of my life in terms of closeups. . . . A story like *Chimes* demands them, because the moment we step back and separate ourselves from the faces, we see the people in period costumes and many actors in the foreground. The closer we are to the face, the more universal it becomes. *Chimes* is a somber comedy, the story of the betrayal of friendship."

After the film was completed, he observed, "*The Ambersons* and *Chimes at Midnight* represent more than anything else what I would like to do in films . . . what I am trying to discover now in films is not technical surprises or shocks, but a more complete unity of forms, of shapes. That's what I'm reaching for, what I hope is true. If it is, then I'm reaching maturity as an artist. If it isn't true, then I'm in decadence, you know?"

The reader of these descriptions should not suppose that *Chimes* is as fluid and deceptively nonchalant as a Renoir film; far from it. When Welles talked about a "plain" style, he meant that the camera is at the service of the actors, and not vice versa (as in *The Trial*, for instance). When a director matures, his work becomes more lucid, more direct, allowing room for deeper audience response; as Truffaut put it, what is in front of the camera becomes more important. And "direct," in the complex rhetorical world of Welles's films, means not that the issues are simplified, but that their presentation is— we feel them with more intensity and passion. Compare the climax of *Kane*, in which Kane slaps Susan, to the muted climax of *Chimes at Midnight*, in which the newly crowned King Henry V (the former Prince Hal) banishes Falstaff and the old man murmurs, "Master Shallow, I owe you a thousand pound." The scene in *Kane* is exciting and moving, but its theatricality tends to widen the gulf between Kane's emotions and our comprehension of them. If *Citizen Kane* has a flaw, it is in its relative dispassion—a scheme in which we are so far removed from the hero that we may easily watch his struggle with mere fascination. *Kane* is perhaps too mathematical in conception; the true hero, it is not unfitting to say, is not Kane but Welles himself. But in *Chimes* there is finally no distance between Welles and Falstaff; a simple exchange of closeups between Hal and Falstaff conveys emotions infinitely deeper than does Kane's explosive action. It is the difference between the expression of an emotion and the sharing of an emotion.

Welles's liberties with the text in *Chimes at Midnight*, extensive though they are, generally escape our notice, not only because he has so smoothly transformed Shakespeare's concerns into his own but also because his concentration on Falstaff enables him to achieve a dramatic focus which Shakespeare's historical concerns tend at times to dilute. The story is taken from *1 Henry IV* and *2 Henry IV*, with bits from *Henry V, The Merry Wives of Windsor*, and *Richard II*, and a narration from

Holinshed's *Chronicles*. Shakespeare seems to have intended Falstaff as a relatively simple comic counterpoint to the King-Prince-Hotspur story in the first part of *Henry IV* (as the rather awkward alternation of historical and comic scenes would suggest) and only gradually discovered that Falstaff was so profound a character that he all but overshadowed the drama of kingship. Not only the greater length given to Falstaff's scenes but the immeasurably more fluid structure of the second part—in which the imbalance threatened by Falstaff's preeminence becomes qualified by the crisis in his relationship with the Prince—attest to Shakespeare's fully ripened understanding of Falstaff's meaning. We have of course been prepared for the rejection of Falstaff by the great tavern scene in the first part, but in the second, Falstaff takes on a graver aspect, not only in Hal's eyes as a threat to his princely dignity but in his own as well. Images of age, disease, and death suddenly proliferate, and the gay denunciations of honor give way to sober, more closely reasoned (and more witty) inward reflection. Shakespeare also creates four new companions for Falstaff—Pistol, Doll Tearsheet, Shallow, and Silence—as if to compensate for Hal's growing absorption into himself. "In the first part of the play," Welles comments, "the Hotspur subplot keeps the business of the triangle between the King, his son, and Falstaff (who is a sort of foster father) from dominating. But in my film, which is made to tell, essentially, the story of that triangle, there are bound to be values which can't exist as it is played in the original. It's really quite a different drama."

We can see in Welles's decision to make Hal a subordinate figure to Falstaff not only an extremely ironic attitude toward the idea of the "Christian king" (a concept as alien to Welles as it is central to Shakespeare and, in a modern guise, to John Ford, from whom Welles borrows greatly in this film), but also a more definite emphasis on the essential *goodness* of Falstaff's character, the tragic nobility of even those attributes—his disregard of health and social discretion—which inevitably will destroy him. The act of banishment by Shakespeare's Hal is not a tragic decision; it is the seal of moral maturity, the "noble change" he proclaims to the "incredulous world." Shakespeare is at pains in *Henry V* to present the war he will wage on France as the God-given and ancestrally determined right of empire. On our first sight of Hal after the ceremony of coronation, he proclaims the war and a sentry cries, "No king of England, if not king of France!" The new king's motivation is not blind egotism but rather a shrewd, if callous, political opportunism. The waging of war on France is a direct result of his father's dying advice to "busy giddy minds with foreign quarrels." In Welles's more critical view of Hal, this action seems a repudiation of the lessons in generosity that Falstaff tried to teach him. Throughout the film, Hal is as truly a tragic figure as is his father, who had wrested his kingdom illegitimately from Richard and was then doomed to face unceasing rebellion.

Hal comes intc his crown legitimately, by right of birth, and in Shakespeare's terms is thus rightfully able to purpose the building of an empire. But for Welles (for Shakespeare too, but to a lesser degree of emphasis), Hal has lost the better part of himself in his rejection of Falstaff and all he stands for. The banishment is inevitable if he is to acquiesce to his position of power, but the price of the world dominion he will achieve is the subjection of his own moral nature, as Welles makes clear in his first action after the banishment. Hal's final words to Falstaff have a meaning entirely opposite to their meaning in the play: "Being awaked, I do despise my dream.... Presume not that I am the thing I was.... I have turned away my former self." And his last words in the film show how much he has deluded himself: "We consider it was excess of wine that set him on." Welles holds on the new king's pose of bemused reflection for several long seconds, and in the next shot shows us Poins eating an apple (the end of innocence) and Falstaff's coffin.

For Shakespeare, Falstaff is essentially a comic figure because, while innocent of worldly ambition other than to live heartily and to be Hal's companion, he is destructive of kingly power, and must be sacrificed without question to the demands of a greater order. For Welles, the greater order is *Falstaff*, and Hal sacrifices both Falstaff and himself in the submission to his own will. Hal is as destructive of innocence as Falstaff is of kingship. And Welles gives us a strong sense of a curious moral trait of Falstaff's which several Shakespearean commentators have pointed out: though essentially innocent, he seeks out the very force that will destroy him. In this we can see a quality in Falstaff which precludes calling him a merely comic figure. If we can call *Chimes at Midnight* the tragedy of Falstaff (and we can, even though he makes moral decisions only by instinct), it is tragedy perhaps more in the Aristotelian than in the Shakespearean sense of the term. Welles's description of Falstaff is profound: "What is difficult about Falstaff, I believe, is that he is the greatest conception of a good man, the most completely good man, in all drama. His faults are so small and he makes tremendous jokes out of little faults. But his goodness is like bread, like wine.... And that was why I lost the comedy. The more I played it, the more I felt that I was playing Shakespeare's good, pure man."

We do not see in Falstaff an essentially noble man of extraordinary gifts who destroys himself through a grave flaw in his nature which is also the source of his nobility; we see in him something rather more subtle and less absolute—a man of extraordinary gifts which destroy him because he fails to acknowledge their irreconcilable conflict with the nature of the world. His moral blindness (which is to say his childlike emotional candor, an attribute he is sometimes apt to use as a ploy) is his only real flaw. Much as Othello was blind to the existence of the kind of power Iago possessed, Falstaff is blind to the possibility that Hal could reject his gift of absolute love. A. C. Bradley remarks of Othello that we share his "triumphant scorn for the fetters of the flesh and the littleness of all the lives that must survive him." Falstaff, we can say, has a triumphant acceptance of the absoluteness of the flesh and a spontaneous respect for all the lives around him.

The likeness of Hal to Iago is more than casual. Just as his father has been careful to cover the illegitimacy of his kingship with actions that assert his legitimacy—the vanquishing of internal rebellion—Hal schools himself in hypocrisy. From the first, Welles makes clear that Hal's merry-making with Falstaff is fraudulent, both a distraction from his impending moral crisis and a testing of his ability to withstand the temptations of instinct. Iago's "I am not what I am" finds many

echoes in Hal, from his first soliloquy ("... herein will I imi-
tate the sun, / Who doth permit the base contagious clouds /
To smother up his beauty from the world"), delivered with
Falstaff musing vaguely in the background, to his final "Presume not that I am the thing I was," which leaves Falstaff des-
titute and uncomprehending. A great deal of the film's pathos
and irony comes from the reversal of old and young men's
roles. Falstaff's innocence is a sublimely defiant gesture on
Welles's part. Playing a role he first took on as a young man,
he now, having grown into the part, makes Falstaff's constant
protestations of youth an accusation not only of Hal's unnatu-
ral suppression of youth but of death itself. Much more than
in Shakespeare, the spectacle of an old man shepherding the
revels of a saturnine young man strikes us as a bitter defiance
of age and the logic of destiny. Falstaff seeks out Hal because
Hal is the least capable, due to his princehood, of casting off
responsibilities and the promise of power, and when this ultimate test of his goodness fails, Falstaff fails with it. The heroism lies in the disparity between the greatness of the purpose
and the inadequacy of the means.

When a tragic hero is destroyed, Bradley remarks, the pri-
mary impression is of *waste*. Waste is our feeling when
Welles, at the end, shows Falstaff's huge coffin being wheeled
slowly across a barren landscape with only a quiescent castle
breaking the line of the horizon, the narrator telling us of Hal,
"a majesty was he that both lived and died a pattern in
princehood, a lodestar in honor, and famous to the world al-
way." We know that what the narrator is saying is literally
true (it was written of the historical Henry V, who had Sir
John Oldcastle, Falstaff's prototype, executed for treason), but
we cannot help sense the tragic irony as we see the remnants
of Hal's humanity being carted away. His expressions and carriage during the banishment speech convey that mingled
grandeur and grief-stricken horror that came so naturally to
his father after a lifetime of scheming, and when he turns
away from Falstaff into a tableau of banners and shields, he
becomes a smaller and smaller figure vanishing into the endlessly repetitive corridors of history. If we never sympathize
fully with Hal, if we feel, as Welles does, that there is some-

thing "beady-eyed and self-regarding" about him even after he becomes king, we never cease to admire him, even in his tragic folly.

Thanks to Keith Baxter's marvellous performance, Hal is dignified and comprehensible even at his cruellest and most vain. Welles's instincts are acute here, for the unpleasantness of Joseph K. is almost fatal to *The Trial*, and Hal, who quite resembles K. in his self-righteousness, needs a sense of human dignity and compassion to make him a suitable subject of Falstaff's attention and to make him fully aware of what he is rejecting when he banishes Falstaff. Hal fills us with awe in that chilling moment when he turns from Falstaff and whispers to himself, "At the end, try the man," as if reciting a prayer; in his sudden childlike humility when his father appears, wraithlike, and demands his crown; and most of all in his powerful, serene silence after the battle, when he drops his pot of ale and walks mutely off to follow his destiny. Welles creates a mythic finality about Hal when, cutting away from Hotspur resolving to duel him to the death, he shows us a cloud of dust, which rises to reveal Hal standing helmet and shield in hand on the battlefield (an echo of John Ford's introduction of John Wayne in *Stagecoach*, dust rising to show him with rifle in one arm and saddle in the other).

Death hangs over the entire film, and the gaiety seems desperate. Both Hal's foster father and his real father (magnificently played by John Gielgud) are dying, and he is too preoccupied with his own legendary future to be of solace to either. His fun takes odd and vicious forms, as if he were reproaching both himself, for wasting time, and the butts of his humor, for encouraging him. He wants to see Falstaff "sweat to death" running from the Gadshill robbery, wants to expose him as a monstrous liar, wants to "beat him before his whore." One critic has suggested that in the first part of *Henry IV*, Hal is killing his patricidal tendencies (by killing Hotspur, his father's rival), and in the second part is killing his libido, his narcissistic self-adoration (Falstaff, of course), in order to prepare himself for the assumption of kingship. Welles replaces this sense of "penance" with a sense of vertiginous self-destruction. Like his father, like Hotspur, like, indeed, Falstaff,

Hal has sought precisely the course that will destroy him. Hal is frightening because he is so young and yet seems so old. Welles draws a striking parallel in the feelings of Hal and both his "fathers" when he follows the king's speech on sleep with Hal telling Poins, "Before God, I am exceeding weary," and Falstaff murmuring, "S'blood, I'm as melancholy as a gibbed cat or a lugged bear."

Bells ringing in the distance give funereal punctuation to the very first scenes in the film, and motifs of rejection and farewell are dominant throughout. The battle sequence, the cataclysm of destruction at the center of the film, begins in splendid romantic exuberance and ends with agonizingly slow, ponderous clouts from soldiers writhing dully in the mud. Welles edits the battle on the principle of "a blow given, a blow received," and the predominant feeling is of a monumental impasse, of incredible exertion without effect. Falstaff's flesh finally gets the better of him, and he lies helplessly sprawled in bed as Hal and Poins taunt him before Doll Tearsheet, his wit his only reprieve. The king seems chilled and mummified in his huge tomb-like castle. Hal and Hotspur seem almost inert when they duel in their armor shells. But Falstaff! Falstaff runs with a breathtakingly funny agility through the charging troops (a stroke of genius), and weaves his way through an unheeding, mindless tavern full of dancers. But he does not disappear into the aimless masses; he seems doomed to stand out awkwardly from the landscape, like a castle. Everything in the film is on the verge of slowing to a standstill.

But for the battle sequence, *Chimes at Midnight* has none of the violent movements from exhilaration to dejection of Welles's earlier films; its equipoise reflects an achieved serenity. Throughout the film, most bitterly in the strained playacting between Hal and Falstaff in the tavern scene that foreshadows the climax, the awareness of destruction is present even in moments of "respite." Falstaff battles this awareness throughout; his attempts to ignore it provide the comedy. He has none of Kane's guile and worldly ability, and his greatness presents itself as a monstrous jest impossible to ignore but easy to dismiss. He demands nothing but attention, and offers all of himself in return. His egocentricity, like his body, is carried past the ridiculous into the sublime, to the point of melancholia. He fears nothing but death, and reproaches Doll Tearsheet with, "Thou'lt forget me when I am gone."

One of the many things Welles and Falstaff have in common is their theatricality. Falstaff, like Welles, is always *on;* he is a ham, and he loves to put on a show, ordering people around and making himself the center of attention. This "directorial" attribute helps explain why Welles was so much more at ease as Falstaff than he was in his other Shakespearean roles on film—he was better at playing an extroverted manipulator like Falstaff than he was at playing more passive characters like Macbeth or Othello, who are manipulated by others.

The notion of role-playing, of theatricality as a way of dealing with life, is one of the key dramatic (and comic) conceits in Shakespeare's Falstaff plays. Hal has to choose which role he is better suited to play in life, wastrel or king, and Falstaff is the overpowering director who tries to mold Hal's character in his own image. Welles brings out these themes with particular brilliance in his staging of the tavern scene, in which Falstaff and Hal play multiple roles in an emotionally complex psychodrama. "Shall we have a play extempore?" Falstaff suggests with a sly wink. Conducted on a stagelike platform with serving wenches as audience, the scene resembles a kind of prankish Mercury Theatre rehearsal session. Falstaff first takes the role of King Henry IV, wearing a pot for a crown and hilariously imitating Gielgud's voice. He chastises Hal for his wanton behavior—ironically, of course—and then turns the discussion to an unabashed, out-of-character defense of himself. "Him keep with, the rest banish," Falstaff's "king" exhorts Hal. When the tables are turned, however, Hal, playing his father, quickly reveals a vicious contempt for Falstaff, calling him "that old, white-bearded Satan" in tones decidedly uncomic. Falstaff is roused to a buoyant speech in self-defense—the speech of a lifetime for Welles, full of bluster and spirit—but when he concludes, "[B]anish plump Jack, and banish all the world!," Hal chillingly warns, "I do. I will."

Here, in a flash, the ultimate fate of their relationship is made known. The "lie" of the theater uncovers a painful truth.

Undoubtedly the single most moving scene Welles ever acted or directed on screen is Falstaff's rejection by Hal at the coronation ceremony. There is an almost shocking vulnerability in Welles's acting when he bursts through the solemn crowd, scandalizing everyone, and calls out, "My King! My Jove! I speak to thee, my heart!" Hal turns to face him in a menacing low angle, his carriage rigid as a statue's, and delivers the blood-curdling denunciation, "I know thee not, old man. Fall to thy prayers. / How ill white hairs become a fool and jester!" The life seems to drain out of Falstaff before us as, eyes filling and jaw quavering in helpless anguish, he watches the king walk out of his life forever. Those who consider Welles an unemotional actor will find their rebuke here. It may have taken him fifty years to achieve such nakedness and candor, but he reached it nonetheless. *Chimes at Midnight* is Welles's testament.

13: *The Immortal Story*

In *The Lady from Shanghai,* Welles, playing a young sailor, told us that Macao was the wickedest city in the world. He said it with bravado, hoping to impress the young woman who later would try to destroy him. Welles made sport of a naive young man's deadly tendency to be siphoned onto the most malign of characters—a descent into the maelstrom. The powers of evil, the lawyer, his wife, and his partner, set up a drama to ensnare the young sailor. In *The Immortal Story,* Welles uses this fable as the basis of a philosophical inquisition. His source, Isak Dinesen's novella, reads like a *précis* of his themes, and he follows it quite closely, shading in his own rhythms and overtones. His hero, Mr. Clay, a moribund and fabulously wealthy Macao merchant, wants to prove his power by making the archetypal sailor's story—the story of a rich old man who hires a young sailor to impregnate his wife—pass from legend into fact. "I don't like pretense," he muses. "I don't like prophecies. I like facts. . . . People should only record things which have already happened."

The Lady from Shanghai is packed with bewildering action; almost nothing happens in *The Immortal Story.* But for a short chorus of merchants in an early scene and the handful of Chinese who pass through as mute witnesses, the only people in the film are the four principals: Clay, his clerk Levinsky, the young sailor, and Virginie, the woman Levinsky hires to play the part of Clay's wife. A courtyard, two sparse rooms, and Clay's mansion form the whole of the setting, and two tattered sails in the foreground of the opening shot suffice to indicate the existence of the outside world. This is an interior drama, a meditation. The old man is disconcerted when he finds that all three of his puppets also know the sailor's story; this is an omen, a definition of the forces he will have to over-step to carry out his will. He continues undaunted, bursting into the bedchamber, unable to conceal his passion: "Because you move without pain, you think you move at your own will. Not so—you move at my bidding. Two young, strong and lusty jumping-jacks in this old hand of mine!"

Welles is, as he has said, primarily a man of ideas, and each of his films is to some extent a philosophical drama. Aside from *The Fountain of Youth*, *The Immortal Story* is the most the-atrical film in Welles's career. The stage is simple and bare, the props are laid out for our inspection, the issues are stated and reiterated in different keys, and the characters are aware of their roles. A further peculiarity: *The Immortal Story* is a mini-ature, just under an hour long, and it was Welles's first film in color since the Carnival segment of *It's All True*. The color is soft and dreamlike, recalling Fellini's statement that color in movies is "like breathing underwater" because "cinema is movement; color is immobility." *The Immortal Story* is a drama of ideas, linear and intellectually direct. But it is emotionally mysterious, developing a tension between immobility and purpose.

Citizen Kane is about mystery, certainly, but the mystery of *fact*. With its maze-like system of cross-references, it strikes me as essentially evasive, centrifugal (which is not to judge it, only to explain it). Welles assembles all the facts, disproves all of them, and declares his unwillingness to define the hero. We are made to understand the meaning of legend and to wonder at the meaning of fact. We see, hear and feel much about Kane (much more than about Mr. Clay), but we know that we do not understand him. *The Immortal Story* approaches legend from the inside out. It is centripetal—*Kane* in negative. But be-cause the making of legend is itself a subjective process, its meaning determined in the mind of its beholder, *The Immortal Story* seems to me to strike into the heart of the matter. What it loses in breadth it gains in lucidity. It omits all that is pe-ripheral to Clay, and defines him as the doer of an essential deed, which in one stroke ennobles him and renders meaningless his prior existence. This is Welles's *Tempest*. We are taken directly into the mind of the filmmaker, and leave our spectators' seats to witness the pulling of the strings above the stage. Clay's musings coincide with the flow of the director's reasoning; when the mechanics of the story have been set completely in motion, Clay dies and the director withdraws after allowing Levinsky to make a final statement of the theme. The screen dissolves to *white;* darkness would be inappropriate to our lucidity.

In the late work of great directors, the youthful delight in flaunting one's tools and one's splendid flashes of insight gives way to a clear-eyed simplicity which some may mistake for senile fixation. Renoir gives us *Le Petit Théâtre de Jean Renoir,* Ford *The Man Who Shot Liberty Valance,* Lubitsch *Heaven Can Wait,* Hawks *El Dorado,* Dreyer *Gertrud,* Welles *The Immortal Story.* If it comes to Clay in his last moments to dare the impossible—if it comes to Welles to eschew camera movements and bizarre perspectives—it is because he has seen everything happen. As Clay eats a solitary dinner, his face reflected in a last, nostalgic, melancholy series of mirrors, Welles tells us, "It was only natural that things should be as they were, because he had willed them to be so." And yet there is something Clay has not touched, cannot touch, something his machinations call up and cannot dispel. In the extraordinary erotic scenes which lie at the core of the film, Welles shifts suddenly, breathtakingly, to the rapturous intimacy of a hand-held camera as Virginie drifts naked through the bedchamber blowing out the candles in grave preparation for lovemaking (recapturing a scene from *The Scarlet Empress,* one of the many echoes of Sternberg in this delicately masochistic film). The young sailor enters to find her lying nude in the bed, her arms crossed over her breasts as if in mingled shame and self-protection, and during his undressing Welles gives us magnificent closeups of her face, her mouth, her eyes. Despite the frank surrender of Elsa in *The Lady from Shanghai,* there was no nudity, no overt eroticism in that strangely chaste film. But here the tentative, spontaneous attraction between the two is an assertion of defiant tenderness, a mockery of Clay's massive, rotting flesh. No Welles hero, not even Quinlan or Falstaff, is closer to decay than this bitter old man.

In *Chimes at Midnight* and *The Immortal Story*, Welles moved ever closer to the faces of his characters. Earlier in his career, he had avoided, almost feared, closeups, preferring the distancing of rhetoric and the qualification of irony. The faces were masks, and the cool baroque style reflected the desperation of his characters' self-deception. *Mr. Arkadin* is the apogee of this tendency; from that point on, his characters are increasingly willing to admit their duplicity. In *The Immortal Story*, everything happens in the glances passed from one person to another, and in their echoes on the face of the hero. Welles has come full circle from the reporter's futile investigation in *Kane*; the story has worked its way back to its source, the storyteller and his audience. K. found it "a miserable conclusion" that lying should be regarded as a universal principle; Clay, like Falstaff, devotes himself to turning lying into truth. Why then does he die when his drama is consummated? He doesn't die in the novella. The novella's sailor entrusts Levinsky with a precious shell as a parting gift to Virginie; Welles has the sailor give it to Clay himself for deliverance to her, and a sudden closeup of the shell rocking back and forth on the floor of the verandah where Clay sits shows us that the old man has died.

Welles is not, like Chaplin, a solipsist, though his heroes are. At their deaths, the world flies apart from its bearings— signified usually by the wrenching of chronology and by the grandiosity of their death scenes—but Welles's style gives an ironic qualification to their solipsism. The unfortunate Othello and Arkadin commit suicide, but no Welles hero offers himself up as a martyr, as Chaplin does in *Monsieur Verdoux*. The Welles hero dies fighting, and if he takes the world with him at the end, the act makes clear the presumption implicit in his defiance. Welles is a tragedian. He squares his accounts with the world.

The Immortal Story differs from previous Welles films in that its prologue—usually his instrument for invoking a prescience of death—concerns itself with *past*, not future, destruction. A chorus of three merchants, lesser Clays (an invention of Welles's), discuss briefly and pointedly the circumstances under which Clay drove his partner (Virginie's father) to suicide and took over his mansion. Welles's earlier heroes looked to the past for the comforting, if illusory, memories of innocence; Clay reveres the past, but only because it confirms his present position. He has Levinsky read his old account books to him, and scorns the prophecy of Isaiah (". . . in the wilderness shall waters break out") that Levinsky carries with him. Innocence, desire and fecundity have no value for Clay. He contrasts the sailor's ideals with the solidity of gold: "He's young. Eh, Levinsky? He's full of the juices of life. He has blood in him. I suppose he's got tears. He longs, yearns for the things which dissolve people—for friendship, for love . . . And gold, my young sailor, is solid, it's hard, it's proof against dissolution." Clay's realization of the sailor's story is a gesture of contempt toward prophecy, an attempt to turn possibility into the *passé*, but both Levinsky and Virginie prophesy several times that Clay's latest venture will be the cause of his death. Clay believes that it is the future which is dangerous, because it means death, but it is finally the machinery of the past, the sum of his delusions, that leads him to destruction.

The past tense of the prologue warns us that the story will not so much concern a hero's attempts to recapture the past as his attempts to escape it. But where can he escape? The glass ball at the beginning of *Kane*, like the prologue to *Ambersons*, summons up feelings of mystery and romance. The merchants' grim analysis in *The Immortal Story* leaves us in desolation, and it is only at the end that Welles invokes possibility—in the shell, which gives out the sound of the sea, a message from another world. Thus the typical pattern of a Welles film is exactly reversed, and the dropping of the shell has a meaning quite unlike the dropping of the glass ball. When Kane dies, our feeling is of awe and excitement, and the shattering of the ball is thrilling—we share the grandeur of Kane's release. It is only subsequently that we are made aware of the feelings of loss and futility associated with the ball. By the time Clay drops the shell, however, we have faced the fact that he has obliterated all the alternatives to the bleakness of self-serving. Then, when we see the noiselessly swaying, mute shell (we do not see it drop), we realize suddenly, with great force and compression, that there has always been an alternative—the liberating voice of mystery unheeded. The sensation of discovery coincides with the moment of destruction.

Clay dies because his ego, his consciousness, has overwhelmed him. Virginie looks quietly away as Levinsky pronounces his master's epitaph: "It's very hard on people who want things so badly that they can't do without them. If they can't get these things, it's hard. And when they do get them, surely it is very hard." He puts the shell to his ear and listens to the echo of some long-vanished wave. "I have heard it before, long ago . . . but where?" The *futility* of Kane's life is epitomized by the burning of the sled at the end of the film; forgotten *possibility* is Clay's final perception. Half a lifetime lies between the meticulous qualification of *Citizen Kane* and the impassioned simplicity of *The Immortal Story*. The inversion of the emphasis reminds us that Welles's deepest concerns are not with failure but with potentiality.

14. F for Fake

> F for Fake is a very important film because it asks the one question every artist has to face at some time in his career: What is art?
>
> —Jean Renoir

Throughout his career, Welles had a fascination with dramatizing the process of storytelling. His omnipresence as character and string-puller in his works for various media made him the least self-effacing of directors. His delight in flaunting his command of the tools of his craft permeated his narratives, compelling the audience to look beyond the surfaces of events and giving the stories layer upon layer of irony and complexity. In his late work as a filmmaker, Welles took us directly into his workshop, concentrating self-reflexively on the artistic process with a fable about storytelling, The Immortal Story; a film about a film director, the uncompleted *The Other Side of the Wind;* a commentary on one of his own movies, *Filming "Othello";* and a meditation on his own art and the meaning of authorship, F for Fake.

F for Fake (1974) and Filming "Othello" (1978) are free-flowing, idiosyncratic essay films, or, in the felicitous phrase of critic Stuart Byron, "grace-note metafilms." Welles's minimalist approach to filmmaking in those movies involved reworking pre-existing footage in combination with some newly shot material, linked by the filmmaker himself addressing the audience from his cutting bench. Partly an ingenious response to his poverty of means and physical immobility, that methodology was also the culmination of his longstanding concern with breaking the bounds between fiction and documentary. *The War of the Worlds* radio broadcast (science fiction in the form of a simulated news broadcast), *Citizen Kane* (with its parody of a *March of Time* newsreel), and the reconstructed documentary/essay film *It's All True* are some of the early career landmarks pointing forward to *F for Fake*, which, as Jonathan Rosenbaum observes, involves "collapsing, combining and/or juxtaposing fiction and non-fiction in order to facilitate and broaden a filmmaker's grasp on a subject in the interests of truth."

Fittingly for a film in which authorship is a central issue, *F for Fake* is largely composed of reedited footage (including outtakes) from a film by another filmmaker—a television documentary by François Reichenbach about art forger Elmyr de Hory, including commentary by Elmyr's biographer, Clifford Irving. Welles initially bought the footage from Reichenbach as the basis for a planned film of his own on Elmyr, but after Irving was caught forging an "autobiography" of Howard Hughes, Welles discovered a wealth of ironies in the younger man's wry analysis of Elmyr's career as a faker. Irving's mingled admiration and antagonism toward the aging artist also touched a deep chord in Welles, since the love-hate relationship between the two men on screen is closely akin to all the other Wellesian male friendships.

A most engaging rogue, and something of a genius himself, Elmyr elicited boundless admiration from Welles, who says in the film, "Hemingway wrote a great short story about an old bullfighter, called 'The Undefeated.' Well, all the heroes aren't in the bullring—here's our hero." Welles clearly identified closely with Elmyr's precarious financial state and with his ingenious ways of putting off the inevitable disaster; and in 1976, shortly before the film's U.S. release, Welles was thrown into a severe depression when the old forger committed suicide to escape a probable jail sentence. Many prescient references are made in *F for Fake* to Elmyr's fear of imprisonment and death, and Irving makes a comment that could be applied to all of Welles's screen heroes: "He has developed a fiction about his life, and to destroy that fiction would tear down the whole castle that he's built—of his illusions." That is just what Irving does by exposing Elmyr in the filmed interviews, as he also did in *Fake!*, his 1969 biography of Elmyr. Welles makes the Falstaff-Hal comparison explicit by describing Elmyr as "the old emperor of the hoax" and Irving as "the pretender." Welles's attitude toward what he sees as Irving's betrayal of Elmyr also resonates with the director's Arkadin-like hostility toward biographers who sought to expose *his* guilty secrets to the world.

While treating the Hughes-Irving scandal largely in come- dic terms, Welles clearly finds in it further justification for his suspicion of biographers. And even though Hughes's desire for privacy reached pathological dimensions, Welles empa- thizes with the impulse that drove the embittered tycoon— and fellow moviemaker—to retreat from the world (twice in the film Hughes is heard saying, "I only wish I were still in the movie business"). Hughes was living at Las Vegas's Desert Inn when the scandal arose, and Welles (who also lived in Las Vegas in his later years) recognized that Hughes was, like the elderly Kane, a virtual prisoner in his own private kingdom. Looking up at Hughes's hideaway, Welles muses, "What was he doing up there? What were *they* doing to him? If he broke his silence, would it be a—cry for help?"

Appropriately enough, in light of all these Wellesian paral- lels, the other major "faker" exposed in *F for Fake* is Welles himself. Not only does he take mischievous pleasure in fool- ing the audience about the veracity of the episode depicting an erotic encounter between Oja Kodar and Pablo Picasso, he devotes one entire section to confessing his earlier frauds, in- cluding the escapade at Dublin's Gate Theatre, in which, at the age of sixteen, he won a job by passing himself off as a star of the Broadway theater; and his 1938 *The War of the Worlds*, which he evokes in *F for Fake* by means of footage from *Earth vs. the Flying Saucers* and (ironically) a faked simu- lation of his original radio broadcast. Welles also draws a tenuous parallel between Elmyr's art forgeries and his own magicianlike career as a filmmaker. "Up to your old tricks, I see," Oja Kodar comments to Welles after the film's opening hocus-pocus. "Why not?," replies Welles. "I'm a charlatan." However, in a 1983 interview with Mary Blume in the *International Herald Tribune*, Welles commented, "In *F for Fake* I said I was a charlatan and didn't mean it . . . because I didn't want to sound superior to Elmyr, so I emphasized that I was a magician and called it a charlatan, which isn't the same thing. And so I was faking even then. Everything was a lie. There wasn't anything that wasn't." (Can *that* statement be believed?)

François Truffaut told me he was convinced that Welles made *F for Fake* for only one reason: to rebut Pauline Kael's 1971 claim that he tried to steal authorship of the *Citizen Kane* script from Herman J. Mankiewicz. Welles brings his old cronies Joseph Cotten and Richard Wilson on screen to testify that Howard Hughes was the first tycoon considered for filmic treatment by Mercury Productions, before it was decided that a Hearst-like figure would be more suitable as the protagonist of *Citizen Kane*; *F for Fake* includes a parody of the *News on the March* newsreel in *Citizen Kane* (i.e., a parody of a parody), showing how Hughes's career could have been given similar treatment. All of Welles's ruminations in *F for Fake* about the quackery of art experts and the ultimate unimportance of genuine authorship to the value of a work of art are, Truffaut contended, "an attack on Pauline Kael." This seems to me a valid observation. Welles was deeply wounded by Kael's allegations, wondering in a letter to Bogdanovich, "Even if the code of the *duello* weren't defunct—how the hell do you 'call out' a lady critic at dawn?" He did it, in effect, by satirizing Kael in the character of the castrating film critic played by Susan Strasberg in *The Other Side of the Wind* ("a rat of a woman," the script calls her), and by making *F for Fake*.

Welles has more in mind in *F for Fake*, however, than simply correcting the historical record on Kane or engaging in a rhetorical *duello* (however oblique) with Pauline Kael. By showing that Elmyr de Hory's talents as a painter are quite literally indistinguishable from those of the celebrated painters whose work he so brilliantly forged, Welles is questioning not only the credibility of art experts, but also the romantic cult of personality that surrounds modern artists. One of Elmyr's party guests is heard describing the art world as "a huge confidence trick." If the artist's identity cannot be determined with certainty by those regarded as art experts, and if (as the film claims) many of the paintings of great masters hanging in prominent art galleries actually were painted by Elmyr, does it mean that those paintings should be considered less valuable as works of art? Should artistic quality and monetary value be considered indistinguishable? Why is Elmyr de Hory not celebrated for his talent, but regarded as a criminal? Does it really matter, in the end, what signature is inscribed on the work of art, or whether the signature is authentic?

Welles's teasing sleight-of-hand methodology in *F for Fake* includes the extended opening credit sequence, which shows a brush painting the words "François Reichenbach presents," followed by the symbol ? being painted by Welles on the screen of a movieola displaying a Ray Harryhausen image of interplanetary destruction from *Earth vs. the Flying Saucers*. This has led some viewers to wonder whether the actual title of *F for Fake* is ? (*Variety*'s review gave the title as *Question Mark*). Welles's subsequent on-screen identification of *F for Fake* as "a film by Orson Welles" has also been questioned, in light of the fact that so much of it was filmed by Reichenbach. But Welles's extensive and highly personal reediting of the Reichenbach footage, along with his addition of new contextual material, surely makes that question irrelevant. In candidly raising such questions, Welles is demonstrating what he meant by declaring in a 1958 interview with *Cahiers du Cinéma* that "for my style, for my vision of the cinema, editing is not simply one aspect, it's *the* aspect. . . . The only time one is able to exercise control over the film is in the editing."

Welles's growing fascination with the power of editing as his career progressed stemmed in part from the necessity of shooting his films in increasingly fragmentary fashion, often by using doubles, combining disparate locales, and other *trompe l'oeil* techniques. *F for Fake* literally foregrounds these "magical" aspects of the editing process, while assuming much of its meaning from the rearrangement of materials, in such a dazzlingly fragmented style that some sections become a cinematic equivalent of cubism. A particularly marvelous instance of

Wellesian editorial *tour de force* is his elaborately artificial montage of glances between Irving (accusatory, skeptical) and Elmyr (uneasy, evasive) while Irving disputes Elmyr's denial that he ever forged a signature on a painting; Welles creates an entire dramatic scene virtually out of nothing, bringing out meanings that perhaps were latent in the two men's relationship but remained undeveloped until he applied *his* sensibility to the footage. That montage demonstrates what Picasso said in a famous remark quoted by Welles in the film: "Art is a lie that makes us realize the truth." In a darker sense, Welles's increasing recognition of the omnipotence of editing in the filmmaking process also may have reflected his anguish over losing control of his own films, such as *The Magnificent Ambersons, The Lady from Shanghai,* and *Touch of Evil,* to reediting by other hands. The resulting questions of mixed authorship have kept film scholars busy researching and analyzing and authenticating, in a manner not unlike that of the art experts Welles derides in *F for Fake.* As the experts battle it out over the provenance and the intent of paintings or films, the original artists become little more than bemused bystanders.

Welles's attitude toward critics and scholars of his own work was highly ambivalent. On the one hand, he recognized that, as a filmmaker without a mass audience, he needed the attention and acclaim of those experts to keep his career alive. But he also could not help resenting *cinéastes* for the power they held over his destiny as a filmmaker. He not only had to live with negative and distorted views of his life and work, but also with the intense, almost microscopic scrutiny devoted to every aspect of his films by his often proprietary admirers. Such scrutiny can lead to paralyzing self-consciousness, a danger that Welles tried to exorcise by dealing with it head-on in his later work. In *The Other Side of the Wind,* Welles mocks the presumption of film scholars, journalists, and assorted hangers-on by showing them surrounding and harassing the director, Jake Hannaford (John Huston), who simultaneously courts and despises them. Because of his role as a media icon, Hannaford's personality as a man and an artist is in danger of disappearing behind the haze of legend and lies, partly self-generated as a smokescreen to hide his true passions. In *F for Fake,*

Welles depicts Elmyr de Hory as an artist who, in a far more calculated manner than Hannaford, has created a false persona both for survival and as revenge against an art world that would not accept him for his own value. Elmyr's slyly humorous enjoyment of his mendacity is seen as a send-up of the whole distorted system of artistic celebrity in a capitalistic society, but the darker side to the artist's dilemma is reflected in Elmyr's anxiety over his always precarious financial circumstances, and in his fear of incarceration.

Whether or not he truly regarded himself as a "charlatan," Welles shared many of Elmyr's artistic and personal dilemmas, and admired his way of "translating disappointments into a gigantic joke." In speaking of his own career in *F for Fake*, Welles emulates Elmyr's jaunty yet bittersweet tone. Recalling the nationwide panic that resulted from his *War of the Worlds* hoax, Welles mentions that someone who broadcast an imitation of his program in South America went to prison as a result. He adds, "I didn't go to jail—I went to Hollywood." Welles also alludes humorously to *his* habitually precarious financial state by saying in the opening scene, "For my next experiment, ladies and gentlemen, I would appreciate the loan of any small personal object from your pocket..." The obvious shoestring nature of the film, which the viewer is allowed to watch being pieced together by Welles at his cutting bench, further attests to his identification with Elmyr's ingenuity in staving off ruin by creating art from minimal resources.

In the film's whimsical fable about Picasso, Welles depicts a fictional art forger, said to be Oja Kodar's grandfather, whose crime (like Elmyr's) is that of "committing masterpieces." A director who struggled throughout his career to make personal works of art in a commercial medium that usually worked against him, Welles implicitly viewed himself as unjustly accused of the same crime, to which *F for Fake* is his eloquent and defiant plea of *nolo contendere*. With mingled bitterness and admiration, both Elmyr and Welles contrast their impoverishment with the art market's celebration of Picasso's ability to turn even his most casual brushstrokes into gold. A grotesquely mutated distortion of the value of art, that power was made possible by Picasso's near-deification by critics and the general public. That Elmyr is capable of turning out convincing facsimiles of Picasso's style in equally casual fashion underscores the hypocrisy and gullibility of the art market.

The Picasso episode dwells lovingly on Oja Kodar's nude body in repose and rhapsodizes over her semiclothed figure running in slow motion under the lascivious gaze of Picasso, seen in black-and-white stills "watching" her from behind his window shutters. The elderly artist's outburst of potency when confronted with Kodar's ripe figure has direct parallels in Welles's later work. For much of his career, Welles dealt with sexual subjects, if at all, in an oblique and almost puritanical fashion. But under the influence of Kodar, his companion and collaborator from 1962 until his death in 1985, Welles burst forth with an increasingly frank exploration of eroticism (both heterosexual and homosexual) in *The Immortal Story, The Other Side of the Wind,* and *F for Fake,* as well as in his and Kodar's unfilmed screenplay *The Big Brass Ring* and in the nine-minute trailer he made for *F for Fake,* which is composed in large part of nude figure studies of Kodar filmed especially for the trailer. Describing her influence on Welles to Jonathan Rosenbaum, Kodar said of *The Other Side of the Wind,* "When you see the film, you will feel that somebody else worked with him because there are things that he never would have done alone and never did before. He was a very shy man, and erotic stuff was not his thing. And in this film, you will see the erotic stuff. He kept accusing me with his finger: 'It's your fault!' And he was right—it's my fault!"

Although some of the "erotic stuff" of Welles's old age never reached the screen, or has yet to be seen in public, Welles's lushly erotic portraiture of Kodar in *F for Fake* is unembarrassedly, deliriously personal. As boyishly revealing as any student filmmaker flaunting his girlfriend's nudity on screen, Welles makes the audience complicit in his own act of cinematic voyeurism. Using the camera to caress the female form in such a voyeuristic manner may imply a diminished potency on the part of the voyeur, and the extended *cinéma-vérité* sequences of men yearningly watching Oja stroll haughtily through the street in a minidress are a clear visual equivalent of masturbation, particularly the shots of (mostly old) men playing with their hands and fingers as they ogle her. But in identifying himself with the elderly Picasso's "extremely fruitful" resurgence of creative and sexual potency, as well as with the effortless artistic fecundity of Elmyr's old age, Welles goes beyond voyeurism to celebrate his own creative fecundity during what could be called his "Oja period." That this blaze of carnal inspiration came so late in Welles's life makes it all the more poignant, like his depiction of Elmyr in his Ibizan villa at sunset, seeking solace from the handsome young gay companion/admirer of what Welles ironically refers to as the artist's "golden years."

And what about the solace of art? With all the lying and fakery and corruption that surrounds the creation of art in *F for Fake,* what does the word "art" mean to Orson Welles? Oja's grandfather speaks for the filmmaker when he says on his deathbed, "I must believe that art itself is real." That line, in fact, is spoken by Welles himself, playing Oja's grandfather, while Oja takes over the role of Picasso. In the film's most moving sequence, filmed in an apocalyptic dusk outside Chartres cathedral, Welles speaks in his own voice, dropping all pretense and facetiousness to deliver a magnificent soliloquy on the transcendent reality of art. He describes the cathedral as "the premier work of man, perhaps, in the whole Western world—and it's without a signature." With unabashed emotion in his voice, he concludes, "Maybe a man's name doesn't matter all that much." Welles is suggesting that, when considered in that ultimate philosophical sense, an issue such as that of the script credit for *Citizen Kane* fades into insignificance in the bright light of the film itself. As he told Bogdanovich, "Why *not* talk about a team? Who cares if somebody discovers a grip or a propman who says I didn't make *Citizen Kane?* Maybe it's true—what of it? Maybe Houseman wrote it and the grip directed it. What does that matter? What matters is the film."

The man who so often boasted "My name is Orson Welles" was the least anonymous of filmmakers. Not for him the self-effacing craftsmanship of the builders of Chartres. But Chartres, Welles tells us, stands for something greater than the individual: "a celebration to God's glory and to the dignity of man. All that's left, most artists seem to feel these days, is man—naked, poor, forked radish. There aren't any celebrations. Ours, the scientists keep telling us, is a universe which is disposable. You know, it might be just this one anonymous glory, of all things—this rich stone forest, this epic chant, this gaiety, this grand choiring shout of affirmation—which we choose, when all our cities are dust, to stand intact, to mark where we have been, to testify to what we had it in us to accomplish."

Welles's work as a filmmaker, for all its bombast, for all its egoism, has served the same purpose. Like his protagonists, Welles was often tempted by pride and by the trappings of worldly power. But in the final analysis, he was big enough to acknowledge his own limitations, and that is *his* glory.

In kingly robe, Welles directing *The Other Side of the Wind*, his still-unreleased satire of Hollywood (1970–76). (*Gary Graver*)

Welles travesties his own past in one of his many buffoonish appearances on American television: a spoof of his 1938 radio broadcast *The War of the Worlds* on *Laugh-In* (1970). (*NBC-TV*)

In his 1974 essay film *F for Fake*, Welles meditates on his own art and the meaning of authorship. (*SACI/Les Films de l'Astrophore/Janus Film und Fernsehen*)

"The old emperor of the hoax" and "the pretender": art forger Elmyr de Hory (right) with his biographer, Clifford Irving, in documentary footage shot by François Reichenbach and incorporated by Welles into *F for Fake*.

Cinematic illusion in the railway station: the opening sequence of *F for Fake.*

"Up to your old tricks, I see": Magic was not only Welles's lifelong avocation, but also his favorite metaphor for art.

Oja Kodar, Welles's companion and collaborator in his later years, inspired him to explore sexual themes with greater candor in such films as *F for Fake* (pictured) and *The Other Side of the Wind*.

Orson and Oja share an intimate moment on screen in *F for Fake*.

A figure study of Oja Kodar in her role as Picasso's model in *F for Fake*.

The hypnotic eyes of the filmmaker/magician: this frame enlargement from *F for Fake* captures a familiar Wellesian expression.

Welles holding the clapper board for his indispensable cinematographer, Gary Graver, during the making of *The Other Side of the Wind*. (*Gary Graver*)

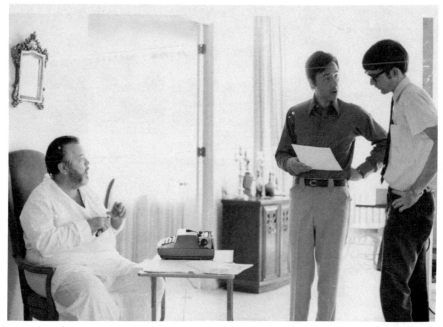

The first day of shooting on *The Other Side of the Wind*, Los Angeles, August 23, 1970: Joseph McBride (as the film historian Mr. Pister) rehearsing with Welles and Peter Bogdanovich. (*Felipe Herba*)

"Rembrandt": Gary Graver in a photograph taken by cast member Felipe Herba in the midst of a scene on the first day of shooting, with Welles watching from the background. (*Felipe Herba*)

Carrying Mr. Pister's omnipresent tape recorder, Joseph McBride watches Welles filming a scene for *The Other Side of the Wind* inside a bus, Los Angeles, 1971; the sign on the bus refers to the central character, legendary movie director Jake Hannaford (played by John Huston).

John Huston, Welles, and Bogdanovich on the set of *The Other Side of the Wind* in Carefree, Arizona (1973). (*Gary Graver*)

Welles in a studio directing Huston with Edmond O'Brien as Pat, Hannaford's first assistant director and a charter member of the "Hannaford Mafia." (*Gary Graver*)

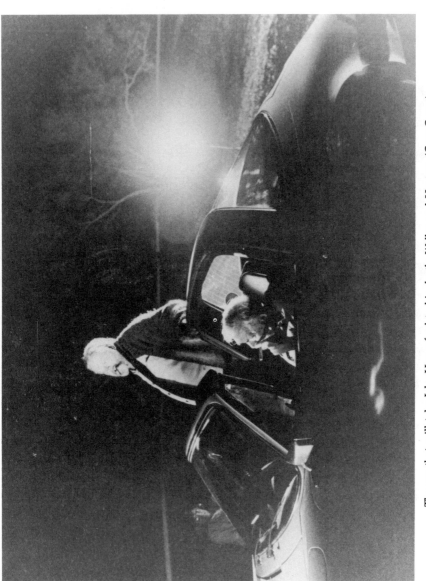

The car that will take Jake Hannaford to his death: Welles and Huston. (*Gary Graver*)

"An attack on machoism": Hannaford in a Hemingwayesque pose. (*Gary Graver*)

Welles's Falstaffian laugh was often heard during the six years of filming on *The Other Side of the Wind*. (*Gary Graver*)

A late portrait of Welles and Oja Kodar, with Welles's poodle Kiki. (*Gary Graver*)

Near the end of his life in 1985, Welles had this test shot taken for his unrealized film of Shakespeare's *King Lear*. (*Gary Graver*)

15: The Other Side of Orson Welles

Ah, but Orson. Mostly, he's a child. . . . You worry
very much when you love Orson, because you never
know where he is. He disappears, you don't know
where he is and it is nearly impossible to find him, because his life is always complicated. . . . And besides,
that huge, strong man, you know that he's very easily
loved, that he's very fragile, but it's very easy to hurt
him . . . so you love him and you want to protect him.
And if he calls you and says, "I need you," then you
say "Orson needs me and it's something important."
His career is so strange because he's capable of such
beautiful things and it's so hard for him now to make
a film that you wouldn't be the little stone that would
stop the machine from going, once he has the chance
to make a film. I think that's why we all do react that
way.

—Jeanne Moreau

I: Meeting Orson Welles (1970)

Welles was always Somewhere in Europe during the four
years I spent writing this book, so I never tried to arrange a
meeting. But in the summer of 1970, when the book was virtually completed, I learned that he was in New York City. By

the time my letter arrived, though, he was gone again. Then he was supposed to come to Chicago, but he didn't. I began to wonder if Orson Welles wasn't really a pseudonym for Howard Hughes. That August I travelled from Madison, Wisconsin, for my first visit to Hollywood (surely the last place Welles would be) to interview John Ford and Jean Renoir, the other two of my three favorite directors. My stay was almost over when I learned from Peter Bogdanovich that Welles was a couple of miles away, appearing on Dean Martin's television show.

So I picked up the phone and called him. He invited me for lunch and mentioned that he was about to start shooting a new film, *The Other Side of the Wind*. Would I like to be in it? Flabbergasted, I said of course, it would be wonderful. He explained that he would be taking a troupe down to Tijuana on Sunday afternoon to film scenes of the hero, an aging movie director, watching the bullfights with some of his young admirers—"test scenes" to help him raise enough money to complete the film. I remembered that Welles had wanted to make a similar story, called *The Sacred Beasts*, several years before. This would be a "permutation" of the earlier script, he said.

After spending an evening discussing the mysteries of Welles's career with Bogdanovich, who was then in the midst of collaborating with him on their interview book *This Is Orson Welles*, I went to Welles's rented house high in the Los Angeles hills. He was typing in the foyer, swathed in a massive white silk dressing-gown that made him look like a polar bear. I was waiting to hear his laugh—that immense, intimidating, chilling laugh so familiar from the screen—but when it came, I was surprised. When Welles laughed, he started slowly, cocking an eye towards his companion, watching his response. When the response was encouraging (how couldn't it have been?), the laugh swelled and began to gather force, like a typhoon, until his features were dissolved into a mask of Falstaffian delight. Still, the laugh was ingratiating, not intimidating, for Welles kept a slight portion of that eye fixed on his companion.

Visitors were offered Wellesian cigars (seven inches long, by my measure) from a box on the piano. When there was hesitation, Welles would insist. Soon there would be four or five miniature Orsons trundling around the house. I lit one and sat down to talk with a man whom, a few hours before, I had known only as a figure of legend. Welles had a good time puncturing my illusions. He poked fun at me for being so absorbed in movies. "I've never been excited by movies *as movies* the way I've been excited by magic or bullfighting or painting," he said. "After all, the world existed for a long time without people going to movies." I said that he had given his life to movies, but I could see that it was the other way around: movies have only served to give him to us.

We talked for a while about the endless vagaries of production and distribution, and then he brought another of my fancies down to earth. I asked him why, in recent years, his movies had less and less of the razzle-dazzle of his youth. Was it a kind of growing serenity? "No, the explanation is simple," he said. "All the great technicians are dead or dying. You can't get the kind of boom operator I had, for example, on *Touch of Evil*. That man, John Russell, is now a lighting cameraman. I have to make do with what I can get."

Watching Welles work the next day, I realized something about him I had known but had never really understood. He genuinely lived for the moment. Though he took great care with each detail of his work, he jumped at every chance to add something new, something unexpected, to his prior conceptions. "Movies should be rough," he told me. I asked if he had been working on the script of *The Other Side of the Wind* when I had walked in. He laughed and said there wasn't any script, the film would be improvised. Seeing my surprise, he said that he had written a script which would have run for nine hours on the screen, but had put it aside because he realized that he was writing a novel. "I'm going to improvise out of everything I know about the characters and the situation," he said. He had a large cardboard box crammed with notes sitting next to his typewriter.

I was restless in my hotel that night. My only previous "acting" experience had been a walk-on in one of my own films which was flubbed because I had misjudged the depth of field and walked so close to the lens that I came out as a blur. I suppose I should have been terrified, but all I could think about was how much fun it was going to be.

Shooting in Tijuana was impossible, I learned the next day, because of some government edict against taking cameras across the border. So we gathered at Welles's house on August 23 to begin filming *The Other Side of the Wind*. The scene was part of a birthday party at which the director-hero, Jake Hannaford, is besieged by the myrmidons of the media. "The joke is that the media are feeding off him," Welles explained, "but they end up feeding off themselves. It's sort of his last summer. That's what it's all about." Welles sat down with Bogdanovich and me and two other young *cinéastes*, Eric Sherman and Felipe Herba, who had also been recruited for the film. Welles brimmed over with amusement as he told us about our roles. Bogdanovich would be a foundation-backed hustler following Hannaford around doing an interview book; I would be a pompous cinema esthete spouting blather from my book about Hannaford; and Sherman and Herba would be a blasé *cinéma vérité* crew ("the Maysles brothers," Welles called them) doing a documentary about the great man. Welles said he did not yet know who would play Hannaford; so our scenes today would be shot with the hero off-screen (which would certainly help point up the isolation of the man from his sycophants).

Welles asked Bogdanovich and me to start throwing him fatuous questions which we could use in the film. Bogdanovich asked if his character should be effeminate, and it was decided that no, he should be excitable, like Jerry Lewis. So he began quacking away like Lewis, and Welles toned the voice down here, broadened it there, parrying the lines back and forth with him. I mentioned a pet theory I had about Ford, how his films since 1939 could be taken as an oblique reflection on the changes in American society, and Welles quizzed me on how I would develop it, warning me to keep it fairly straight. He finally went to the typewriter and we concocted a speech (Welles supplying the final wording): "The main thrust of my argument, you understand, is that during the Thirties Hannaford's predominant motif was the outsider in absurd conflict with society. In the Forties he achieved salvation. In the Fifties . . ." Here Bogdanovich would break in with, "Never mind the Fifties. Open the whisky bottle." Welles roared with delight; so much for the critics!

We spent half an hour thinking up these ridiculous questions. Once, when I suggested asking Hannaford about the work of Dziga Vertov, Welles said, "You're kidding! Who's that?" "Dziga Vertov, the Russian director of the 1920s," I replied. "He made newsreels known as *Kino-Pravda*." Welles had a great time with that one before ruling me out of order. "Come on, now," he said. "You're supposed to be playing a serious character." We did wind up with a Godardian-Vertovian question, though. I would ask Hannaford, while riding in the back seat of his car, "Mr. Hannaford, is the camera eye a reflection of reality, or is reality a reflection of the camera eye? Or is the camera a phallus?" (For the last line I was indebted to Peter Fonda's admiring description of the camera of Roger Vadim, though I didn't let on to Welles what the source was.)

I was beginning to appreciate fully Welles's sense of humor, which was sometimes submerged under the rhetorical cocoon surrounding his characters and usually fails to emerge from an analysis of his films. And when the shooting started, I could see firsthand the delight he took in the physical act of direction. His young crew officially numbered four, but eventually all twelve people present pitched in to help, and almost everybody appeared before the camera, including Welles's houseboy.

It seemed that what Welles was shooting today—brief, fairly simple hand-held shots—was pure caviar to the director. I quickly realized that I couldn't be either good or bad, just myself, because the character I was playing was a fool. Comic relief was the order of the day, and Welles's brio belied the idea that directing comedy is a dour business. It certainly was hard work, though. "Now you appreciate what actors go through," Welles told me when I sighed after the seventh take of one shot went wrong. Since I was the buffoon among buffoons, I was loaded to the teeth with props—a tape recorder, a still camera, a coat over my arm, papers in my shirt pocket, and a gigantic whisky bottle. I apologized for my awkwardness with the props, and Welles said reassuringly that the only actor he ever knew who could handle so many props well was Erich von Stroheim. Adding to my surrealistic appearance was something Bogdanovich had noticed the night I went to his house —I had been without notepaper that day at a screening of Fellini's *Satyricon,* and had scribbled some notes on my wrist in the dark. Welles told me that, in the film, I should have my wrist and arm covered with notes—"Oedipus Complex," "Mother Fixation," and so forth. When the shooting was over, he paternally insisted that I scrub my wrist and arm completely clean, even though I was too tired to lift a bar of soap. (Since the story all takes place on a single day, to keep in continuity throughout the extraordinarily protracted shooting process I had to keep scribbling notes on my wrist for six more years! Mercedes McCambridge, who was also in the cast, advised me, "When you work with Orson, you keep your costume in a box in the attic." More than twenty-five years after we began shooting, I *still* have my costume in a box, in case it might be needed, even if I can't fit into it anymore.)

In twelve hours of shooting that first day, Welles completed twenty-seven shots. It was fascinating to watch him sculpt each shot from the bare bones of dialogue. For example, the pontificating about Hannaford in the different decades of his career was broken into two shots, the second of which required fourteen takes. I began to understand what Welles once said about his direction of actors: "I give them a great deal of freedom and, at the same time, the feeling of precision. It's a strange combination. In other words, physically, and in the way they develop, I demand the precision of ballet. But their way of acting comes directly from their own ideas as much as from mine. When the camera begins to roll, I do not improvise visually. In this realm, everything is prepared. But I work very freely with the actors. I try to make their life pleasant." Setting up the first shot for the scene, Welles chose a stark wall, couch, and table for the background. Because the setting was a party, with cameramen's lights present, the lighting was not to be overly refined. Directing from a thronelike chair at the typewriter table ("because this is an *auteur* film"), Welles took an active part in the lighting, ordering his cameraman, Gary Graver, to forget about an elaborate cross-lighting pattern he had set up when the director wasn't looking. But he did tell Graver to set up a light behind a bedroom door in the background so it would cast a serrated pattern on the floor. "That's the only beautiful thing I want in the shot," he said. Then, turning to Bogdanovich with an arch expression, he muttered, "Von Sternberg . . ." Welles ran quickly and efficiently through the lighting, keeping Graver (whom he called "Rembrandt") constantly on the move.

Bogdanovich and I were rehearsing our lines, and Welles interrupted us to give directions. The scene would begin with an off-screen hand giving Bogdanovich the whisky bottle from camera left, and bits of dialogue were added, to be spoken while I was talking. (Later that day, when the soundman broke into the shooting of another scene to tell Welles that there was overlapping dialogue, the director replied, "We *always* have overlapping dialogue." That was the soundman's last day on the picture.) Bogdanovich was to ignore me disdainfully while I was talking. When I would say "during the Thirties . . . ," he would give me the bottle, taking my tape recorder, and tell me to open the bottle. I would ask, "How?" In the meantime, the houseboy (standing in the background wearing a camera around his neck and munching a chicken breast) would slowly cross in front of us, and Bogdanovich would ask him, "Where's Andy?" The question would go unanswered—the houseboy would act stoned.

Then Bogdanovich would tell me, "There's a cork, isn't there?" and I would look down and find no cork on the bottle. The Maysles brothers, who would be chattering in the background all the while, would now run like hell behind us with their equipment in search of a shot. I would resume my talking, and the Maysles brothers' assistant (actually Graver's assistant) would dash *between* us holding a still camera and a blazing sun-gun, chasing after them. Bogdanovich would then interrupt me ("part Jerry and part Noël Coward," Welles told him) with, "Never mind the Fifties. Open the whisky bottle."

In addition to all this, the tape flew off my recorder when I handed it to Bogdanovich during a run-through, and Welles insisted on keeping the action in the film. So we rehearsed dropping the tape.

Finally, we were ready to go. The first part of the scene—up to the exchange of the bottle and the tape recorder—went fairly quickly. Welles said he would cut to an insert of some kind and return to the same shot of Bogdanovich and me from the knees up. We began to shoot the second part of the scene. Chaos. I would bobble my lines, Bogdanovich would react too slowly, the guy eating the chicken would take too long in getting past us, the Maysles brothers would run through at the wrong time . . . After several takes fell completely flat, all of a sudden one of them worked. But in a rhythm totally different from what Welles had planned. All the cues were different, but it seemed to jell anyway. Welles said he might wind up using the shot, but would appreciate it if we'd try it again, *his* way. Bogdanovich and I started to chatter about ways to improve the shot. Welles ordered quiet. "The *thespians* are causing trouble," he said. "What do you want?" Cowed, we fell silent. "All right, then," he said. "Let's do it again, shall we?" About an hour later, we were done.

The rest of the day was taken up with scenes of the media people assembled in various parts of the house, thrusting equipment forward at Hannaford, and with some hilarious scenes inside and outside a car moving through the streets of Los Angeles and Beverly Hills. Welles told us to leave without him to shoot the scenes inside the car because it would be more interesting if we'd spring the results on him after following his instructions. "I did that with one scene in *Touch of Evil*," he recalled. "Remember that wide-angle shot of the two men driving through the street? There was no soundman, no cameraman, and no director." Where was the camera? I asked. "Strapped to the hood of the car," he said with a triumphant grin.

Relaxing aboard a homebound jet that night, I began to think back on recent events. Four days earlier, Renoir had told me that to learn about directing, I should try a little bit of acting (he meant in an amateur movie). Now I had ceased looking over Welles's shoulder and had begun looking directly into his eyes. My subject had climbed down off the pedestal I had built for him and, curiously, he now seemed larger than ever. As his cameraman said admiringly after the day's shooting, "Welles doesn't play it safe."

II: The Other Side of Orson Welles (1976)

Orson Welles sat Buddha-like in his director's chair, puffing his customary seven-inch cigar, watching the crew of *The Other Side of the Wind* set up a shot for a sequence taking place at a drive-in movie. The actual location work at the drive-in had been done in 1971 in the San Fernando Valley area of Los Angeles, and these matching shots of people in cars were being done four years later, indoors, at a rundown Hollywood studio. The cinematic sleight of hand necessary to make the scene look convincing was typical of the bizarre shooting methods of the film, which takes place in a single night. The film's setting is Hollywood—it deals with an aging movie director, played by John Huston, and his confrontation with the "New Hollywood"—but scenes were filmed as far afield as Connecticut, France, and Spain.

Cinematographer Gary Graver had lit the white backdrop of the Hollywood sound stage so that it would appear black in the scene. Welles watched with bemusement as crew member Lou Race scurried around with a fog machine, spreading billows of white bug spray to help create the illusion of a misty night. The cast held their noses and coughed as the spray rose in fancy curlicues, beautifully backlit by colored filters, until Welles told Race to stop. "We can't film that," he said. "It's far too baroque—even for a Welles film."

The director's booming laugh filled the sound stage as the spray settled down, and the filming resumed. The complex and protracted shooting of *The Other Side of the Wind*, which crew members describe as "the greatest home movie ever made," often strained the patience and endurance of the most loyal people in the company, but no one will deny that it was a unique and exciting experience. By the time shooting was virtually completed in 1976, I had spent six years acting in the film, playing a film critic named Mr. Pister. "The high priest of the cinema," Welles sarcastically dubbed the character.

Welles had been working on the script for the film since the early 1960s, when it was to be called *The Sacred Beasts* and was to take place among jet-setters on the bullfight circuit. During the filming, the plot, dialogue, and cast of characters were in a constant state of revision. The company was only mildly surprised one night in early 1975 when Welles, picking up on a casual remark by one of the extras, suddenly decided to film a musical production number. Money problems were, as usual for Welles, part of the reason for the film's uncompleted state (several producers came and went on the film, which was started with Welles's own money and also was partially financed by the Iranian government), but his longtime associate Paul Stewart, a member of the cast, felt it was Welles's "tremendous need for perfectionism" that made the shooting schedule so extended. Graver told me, "It's really a handmade movie, frame by frame, and nobody makes a movie like that anymore; that's why it's taken so long."

Welles was asked so often when he would finish the film that he became defensive on the subject. In an April 1976 *New York Times* article about "The Film That Orson Welles Has Been Finishing for Six Years," Charles Higham blamed the protracted shooting schedule on Welles's alleged "fear of completion" and asked, "Is the present delay with *The Other Side of the Wind* another illustration of a tragically self-destructive genius?" "Why should I have to answer all of these questions?" Welles was quoted as saying. "I haven't committed a crime. I'm just a poor slob who's trying to make pictures."

Nevertheless, at times he was able to treat the matter with some levity. On one occasion, when the fifteenth take of a complex shot went wrong, Welles got out of his chair and began walking away. Graver, finally solving the technical problems, called out, "I've got it!" But Welles wearily replied, "No, Gary. *God* does not want me to make this shot."

Despite such production headaches, it was clear that Welles thrived on the unorthodox shooting methods he imposed on the film. He frequently expressed unwillingness to work under conventional studio methods, and the problems he had to overcome were, in his view, the stimulus for unorthodox solutions. Nowhere was this more evident than in the shooting of a key scene, late in the film, in which Huston slaps Susan Strasberg, who plays Juliette Rich, a magazine critic modelled more or less on another Welles nemesis, Pauline Kael.

In the scene, Huston becomes fed up with the constant insinuations about his masculinity made by Strasberg's character, and the slap occurs when she accuses him of sadistically destroying his actors. Though the scene had been carefully planned on paper, there were some surprises when it was filmed in 1975. Again, it was a night exterior filmed on the sound stage. Huston, by that time, was off in Morocco directing *The Man Who Would Be King,* so a young crew member doubled for him, wearing a safari jacket and gaining height by standing on an apple box, his back to all three cameras. The main camera was looking through the window of a limousine in which Lilli Palmer (playing Zarah Valeska, a legendary actress modelled on Marlene Dietrich) was supposed to be sitting, but Palmer was to be filmed later in Europe, so she was also being doubled. The limousine was being doubled by a rented station wagon.

While the logistics were being worked out, the only serious hitch came when Strasberg insisted that the slap be simulated. Disappointed, Welles sighed, "All right—I'll have to put the same scene into my next movie and find an actress who's willing to be slapped." When the filming began and the "slap" occurred, a female extra standing next to Strasberg laughed, something Welles hadn't planned. "My God!" he said. "That's the strangest thing I've ever seen in my life! Why did you do that?" Strasberg cut in to admit that she had planned the moment secretly, to inject some gray shading into what otherwise could have been a scene of pure male chauvinist antagonism. Welles pondered a bit, then declared, "I like it. Pauline Kael gets slapped, and a woman laughs. *Yes!* We'll keep it!"

[I must reveal here that I contributed to Strasberg's interference with Welles's planning. Before the scene was shot, I mentioned to her what had happened when Welles filmed the scene in which he slaps his Desdemona, Suzanne Cloutier, in

Othello. According to Michéal MacLiammóir's diary of the filming, *Put Money in Thy Purse,* Cloutier continually ruined takes by flinching *before* Welles slapped her. Welles finally told her he would cut the scene before the slap and film the slap separately the next day. But he double-crossed Cloutier by slapping her anyway, without warning. Cloutier told Welles, "Of course I'm very grateful, Mr. Orson, it was the only way to make me do it, but of course I *did* know all the time you were going to hit me: I guess I'm psychic." MacLiammóir praised Cloutier for being "Indestructible," but I was concerned that something similar might happen to Strasberg, and after hearing the story from me, she came up with her own solution.]

With the shot in the can, Welles, roaring with laughter at Strasberg's impudent addition to the scene, dismissed the company for dinner and lumbered toward the door of the sound stage, commanding that it be opened. As the door was rolled back, revealing a brilliant orange sunset over the Hollywood skyline, Welles stared at the natural spectacle outside, took note of the oohs and aahs around him, and muttered to himself, "It looks fake."

The Other Side of the Wind, the first film Welles directed in Hollywood since *Touch of Evil* in 1957-58, chronicles the return of Huston's character, Jake Hannaford, from years in retirement to direct a "with-it" low-budget film full of nudity, arcane symbolism, and radical-chic violence. The loose story format allowed Welles wide-ranging latitude to satirize both the contemporary Hollywood scene and the grand but antiquated postures of Hannaford and his stooges, whose social views verge on the fascistic. Welles's multilevelled approach took what he considered a "revolutionary" narrative style, as complex, in its own way, as his approach to the media-baron protagonist of his first Hollywood film, *Citizen Kane.*

His framing device in *Wind* is a huge birthday party given for Hannaford by the character played by Lilli Palmer. The media are there in force, represented by journalists and critics, and by several television and documentary crews with 16mm and Super-8 equipment. The footage shot by these crews was to be blown up for incorporation into the film, and Welles kept a deliberately haphazard look to all of the party footage, giving it the semblance of *cinéma vérité*. His own crew members operated the cameras at the party, and thus appear in the film. The only member missing is Welles himself; he scrupulously avoided making even a fleeting Hitchcockian appearance on camera. (When a crew member pointed out to him that he was visible in a mirror in one shot, he ordered the mirror tilted away from him, commenting, "I can hear what the critics would say: 'The *auteur* pays homage to himself in the reflection of the mirror.' Oh God!") In contrast to the party scenes are the lavishly composed 35mm film-within-the-film sequences from Jake Hannaford's uncompleted work, also mysteriously titled *The Other Side of the Wind*. It has been suggested that the title itself is a joke at the critics' expense, but Welles never explained what it is supposed to mean.

The shooting style, coupled with the myriad production difficulties, made the filming dizzyingly complex for Graver and his crew, but Graver became a technical wizard in his own right during his years of working with Welles on *Wind, F for Fake*, and many other projects. The labyrinthine texture of *The Other Side of the Wind*, like that of *Citizen Kane*, is Welles's means of expressing the nightmarish dilemma faced by a legendary man being swallowed up in his self-created image and ultimately being destroyed by it—a subject which always obsessed Welles, but never more so than in his later years, when he was acutely aware that every shot he made would be endlessly dissected by film students and scholars around the world. By 1976, it was dismaying to realize that there were already more books *about* Welles than there were films *by* Welles, and *Wind* makes a rather wistful joke on the subject when one *cinéaste* character insists he is doing *the* book on Hannaford. An old colleague of Hannaford's replies, "And I know somebody, somewhere, who isn't." Early in the filming of *The Other Side of the Wind*, Richard Wilson, a longtime Welles associate and a cast member in the movie, asked Welles what the main point of the story was, and Welles told him, "It's an attack on machoism." Despite being a movie director with traces of John Ford, Howard Hawks, and Huston himself recognizable in his personality (not to mention Welles, who named the character Jake because Frank Sinatra used to call him that), Hannaford, Welles said, was really based on Ernest Hemingway, with whom he had an edgy acquaintance. Welles claimed that he had a fistfight with Hemingway during a screening of Joris Ivens's 1937 Spanish Civil War documentary *The Spanish Earth,* when Hemingway, Ivens's collaborator on the film, objected to Welles's delivery of the narration he had written for it. Hemingway then threw out Welles's voice track and spoke the narration himself. According to Welles, Hemingway found his voice-over too flowery and accused him of being a "faggot" from the New York theater. Welles retorted by putting on a mocking swish act, and the fistfight ensued, or so he claimed. Even if the fistfight was an embellishment of Welles's, it's likely that the seed of *The Other Side of the Wind* was planted by that encounter with Hemingway.

In the film, Hannaford is revealed as a repressed homosexual who develops an intense attachment for his young leading man, John Dale, played by Bob Random (who noted, "My entire function in the film is to provide silent visual accompaniment for voiceovers"). Hannaford has always been a Don Juan, with a penchant for seducing his leading men's girlfriends, but in old age the mask starts to slip away, and he is smitten with the leading man. As well as exposing his fraudulent sexual persona—and, by extension, that of the Hemingwayesque "man's man"—Hannaford's possessive impulse reflects the dangerous relationship Welles sees between actor and director, man and god. "Man, they're *real,*" another director character in *Wind* says of Hannaford's characters. "He *made* 'em real; gave 'em existence—he molded the clay—he *conceived* 'em—like a god." To Hannaford, though, as to all of Welles's godlike central characters, this omnipotence is a transitory illusion. The young man slips out of his hands, as all of his characters have, leaving behind only emptiness and death, the foul wind that blows like divine judgment through the rundown Hollywood backlots in the last part of the film. After Dale spurns Hannaford, the old director drunkenly drives off in a sports car he was planning to give Dale, and it crashes. The film follows Welles's favorite narrative structure of starting at the end, with some ironic and portentous narration, and then flashing back to the party. It all occurs the night of July 2, not coincidentally the date of Hemingway's suicide.

From Welles's description of *The Sacred Beasts* script to a French interviewer in 1962, it's evident that while the setting and other details of the story evolved, the Hannaford character remained essentially the same: "There will be a confrontation between my hero, an aging American romantic who is having trouble supporting himself, and an anti-romantic young man of the new generation, 'cool,' who ends up subscribing to romanticism himself and defending the bullfight. This will be a film about death, the portrait of a decadence, a ruin. I will play the part. But don't look for a self-portrait in it. For example, he will be a sadist, and I don't want to be one. When I show cruelty in my films, it's to make you hate it." In the same interview, he observed, "Hemingway and Fitzgerald thought that genius disappears with old age. At the end of his life, Hemingway always tried to prove that he was still young. Fitzgerald, even before he turned forty, was rotted with the same anguish. That attitude is death. It's not something that bothers me."

Some striking parallels could be drawn between *The Other Side of the Wind* and Thomas Mann's *Death in Venice*, which is also the story of an aging artist who becomes obsessed with the beautiful image of a young boy amid the squalor of a dying and once splendid artistic capital. And knowing Welles's lifelong affinities with Shakespeare, it's easy to find variations on the Falstaff-Prince Hal relationship in Hannaford's rejection by Dale and to see echoes of *The Tempest*, particularly since Welles has Peter Bogdanovich, in the role of a young director, quote several lines from that play, comparing Hannaford with Prospero, whose "revels now are ended."

Welles didn't settle on John Huston for the leading role until early 1974, shooting around Hannaford until then. The first day I met Huston on the set, he asked me incredulously, "You've been in this picture for *three years?*" In 1970, Welles told me he had decided against playing Hannaford because he didn't want people to assume it was a self-portrait; he conceded that, despite having someone else in the role, people will still see it that way. When I asked whom he wanted for the part, he said,

"It's either John Huston or Peter O'Toole doing his imitation of John Huston." Huston was a particularly apt choice for the role, not only because of his long personal and professional relationship with Welles but also because his public personality often seemed to echo Hemingway's. Peter Viertel, who counted among his friends not only Hemingway but also Welles and Huston, wrote in his 1991 memoir *Dangerous Friends:* "Orson had always scoffed a little at Huston's personage, probably because he recognized a rival act when he saw one, but before they had finished the first week of working together he fell under the spell of John's charm and larger-than-life personality, feelings that were mutual. John told me that he had enjoyed the experience, one of his last acting assignments, because the movie was 'such a desperate venture.' . . . which made work the kind of perilous undertaking John enjoyed, an adventure shared by desperate men that finally came to nothing."

"Orson does everything," Huston marvelled. "He lights the scene. Holds the camera. He wrote the script. My God, he even makes the sandwiches!"

One of the major changes from Welles's *Sacred Beasts* conception of the story was the addition of Bogdanovich's character, Brooks Otterlake, a rich and famous young director who evokes bitter jealousy and resentment from the struggling older man. As a result of that addition, the Hannaford-Dale relationship became secondary, used mainly as a running counterpoint to the Hannaford-Otterlake relationship. Bogdanovich started out in the film playing Charles Higgam (*sic*), a supercilious critic colleague of Mr. Pister, but after *The Last Picture Show* appeared in 1971, the script was altered to include Otterlake, who has entered filmmaking on Hannaford's coattails, quickly overcoming his mentor at the box office, and is now evading veiled pleas from Hannaford for financial support. The Higgam role was taken over by Howard Grossman, a young Bogdanovich assistant, and the scenes I had done with Bogdanovich we shot again with Grossman.

Otterlake has a Bogdanovich-like penchant for doing imitations, both in person and in his films. "That's what's so nice about Brooksie," Jake says, "I don't have to repeat myself, he does it for me." Before Bogdanovich started the role, it was played by the mimic Rich Little, whom Bogdanovich extolled so highly in his book *Pieces of Time*. Little and Welles clashed, however, and Welles fired him after several weeks on location at an isolated ranch house in Carefree, Arizona. Bogdanovich gamely assumed the role, to the amazement of some members of the company, and later lent Welles his Bel-Air mansion for shooting between February and May of 1975, as well as letting Welles stay in the house long after the end of the shooting. Welles virtually took over the place, almost literally playing *The Man Who Came to Dinner*, and once, when Bogdanovich poked his head into Welles's cutting room, Welles barked at him to get out. Bogdanovich sheepishly closed the door and crept around his house for days without bothering his guest.

The many other *roman à clef* elements in *Wind* also include a Cybill Shepherd character of sorts, Mavis Henscher, played by Cathy Lucas, a blonde teenager from Flagstaff; Mavis comes to the party with Otterlake and is appropriated by Hannaford in a crude sexual power play. It was amusing to watch the combined efforts of two legendary directors, Welles and Huston, failing to extract satisfactory line readings from the novice actress. When the crew tried to impress on her how lucky she was to be playing Huston's girlfriend, she shrugged, "He's kinda old, isn't he?"

The leading lady of *The Other Side of the Wind*, and collaborator with Welles on the screenplay, was the director's companion Oja Kodar. In *Wind* she is the star of Hannaford's film, usually appearing nude or scantily dressed. Welles jokingly explained that he had long had the desire to shoot nude scenes, "but I didn't want to do it under my own name; this way I can pass it off as someone else's work."

Also in the cast is Tonio Selwart, a courtly German actor who, although called "The Baron," bears marked similarities to Welles's former partner, John Houseman. Other reminiscences of Welles's Mercury Theatre days are evident in the casting of old cronies Edmond O'Brien, Norman Foster, Mercedes McCambridge, Benny Rubin, Paul Stewart, and Richard Wilson as what the script calls "The Hannaford Mafia," a group also including Cameron Mitchell and John Carroll. Directors other than Huston and Bogdanovich are in the cast, too: among them, Paul Mazursky, Curtis Harrington, Dennis Hopper, Henry Jaglom, and Claude Chabrol. Marlene Dietrich refused the role of Zarah Valeska, not because of the resemblance to herself (the 1970 version of the script identified the character as Dietrich), but because of the *cinéma vérité* style of the photography. The Strasberg part was originally written for Jeanne Moreau, but Welles, for reasons of his own, did not offer it to her. The production designer for the film, Polly Platt (Bogdanovich's former wife), made a stab at it before Strasberg took it over. There were to be others in this incestuous sort of casting system—notably Joseph Cotten—but they failed to materialize.

There was a noticeable difference between Welles's treatment of the cast and his handling of the crew. With actors, he was capable of infinite patience and delicate diplomacy as he flattered and cajoled them toward his goals, always making them feel like real and valued collaborators. But he was obviously impatient with the technical limitations of the medium ("The camera is a vile machine," he said once) and made extraordinary demands on the crew, often showing a highly authoritative streak in dealing with them. The crew was a young, dedicated, non-union group; Welles would have had a harder time getting such absolute obedience from blasé Hollywood veterans. Most of the crew members were recruited from prior work with Graver or Bogdanovich; among them was production manager Frank Marshall, who later went on to produce films for Steven Spielberg and then to become a director himself. Graver had to turn down many job offers to stay at Welles's side, and like the other crew members he had to put up with extraordinary demands on his private life. But his loyalty was absolute. When he was asked in the mid-1970s why he did not insist that Welles bring the shooting of *Wind* to a rapid conclusion, he replied simply, "You can't put an ultimatum on an artist."

Photographing a film shot largely off the cuff, a film on which the director ordered his script supervisors never to speak to him, Graver managed to maintain a consistency of style, and his function went far beyond the usual cameraman's role. Sometimes Welles allowed Graver to stage and film scenes by himself after giving him instructions; one night during filming in Bogdanovich's house, Graver directed the extras while Welles was off in a bedroom watching Samuel Fuller's *Shock Corridor* on television. Norman Foster and Paul Stewart, both directors themselves, also pitched in to help with the actors, in the absence of an assistant director; when Welles despaired of getting me to understand my behavior in a scene on a bus, he turned to Stewart for help. With a succinct bit of advice from Stewart, I managed my scene in the first take, after which Welles began referring to me as "One-Take Pister."

Welles spent as much time directing the crew as he did directing the cast, closely supervising the lighting and often operating the camera. In one of the drive-in scenes, Graver ingeniously devised a dummy projector reel to cast a revolving shadow over Tonio Selwart, causing Welles to observe, with a mixture of amusement and admiration, "My, we are painting with a fine brush, aren't we?" But Welles also would demand many retakes of most scenes in order to obtain technical and acting perfection, even when, as was his habit in the party scenes, he would instruct the camera operators to make deliberately clumsy movements to simulate the *cinéma vérité* approach. "How was your pan?" Welles would ask an operator at the end of a shot. If the reply was "very smooth," he would order a retake to make it look like the operator was searching for his camera subject.

[Welles was anticipating a style that would become in vogue during the 1990s, both on television and in some feature films, notably Woody Allen's *Husbands and Wives.* Whether Welles would have managed to employ such a style in an expressive manner throughout the party sequences of *The Other Side of the Wind,* avoiding the irritating feeling of constant disorientation and affectation that often accompanies its use by other filmmakers, remains an open question, since he was able to edit only parts of the film before his death. His intention of examining—and satirizing—the media's distorted perceptions of Hannaford, and his plan to intercut the elegantly shot footage from Hannaford's film, may help to validate his visual strategy.]

The crew's dedication to Welles even in the worst adversity can perhaps best be conveyed by recalling what one of them, who preferred to be identified only as "Deep Focus," jokingly called "The Friday Night Massacre." The company had been shooting until 4:00 A.M. in Bogdanovich's house, with two hours of cleaning up left before they could go home, and Welles had scheduled the next day's call for noon. When Graver conveyed the crew's reluctant request for a 2:00 P.M. call, so they could get some sleep, Welles, dead tired himself, lost his patience. "I can't work in this atmosphere, with everybody against me," he ranted, and fired the entire crew, declaring that he was stopping the film and leaving for France in the morning. But when shooting resumed a few days later, all but a handful were back, and not a word was said about the "massacre."

Welles later improvised a scene with Tonio Selwart and Bogdanovich which "Deep Focus" described as "Orson's tribute to the little people." In the scene, which comes at the end of the drive-in screening of Jake's film, Selwart pays tribute to Hannaford's loyal crew people, telling Bogdanovich, "What's important for you now is to get soldiers—good soldiers. . . . They followed Napoleon, they followed Hannibal: They *really* crossed the Alps. They're the real heroes of any story."

For the cast members, being around Welles, Huston, and other colorful personalities in the film made the shooting resemble a floating party, and some of that atmosphere rubbed off on the film, giving it a relaxed, improvisational air. Around his old cronies, Welles frequently became expansive and voluble, swapping elaborate tales about theater, politics, European restaurants, bullfighters, and other favorite topics. And befitting Welles's own gourmet habits, he took great care to make sure the company was well fed, replacing the typical location box lunches with fancy spreads prepared in Arizona by two chefs flown in from Beverly Hills. As the money grew tighter later in the production, however, everyone, including Welles, had to get by on hamburgers and pizza.

In working with his cast, Welles frequently asked for their ideas about dialogue and action before mapping out a shot. But he was also prone to give line readings, usually prefacing

them with, "It's terrible for a director to give line readings, but
. . . " Once, he became exasperated with the way I was reading
my lines in a scene in a moving car, and told me, "You sound
like you're reading from the telephone book! *Think* about what
you're supposed to be saying!" One way or another, he got his
way, yet without making the actors feel like puppets.

Many times over the six-year period, he would tell me,
"Don't act!," explaining that I was usually better with spontaneous reactions on the first take. And when I asked him once
how to play a scene with Strasberg, he replied, "How should
I know? Just do it." As a result, I was thoroughly intimidated,
putty in Welles's hands, but about four years or so into the
filming, a crew member relayed some words of praise Welles
had given my performance during rushes, and I instantly felt
entirely relaxed. For the rest of the shooting, I no longer felt
cowed by Welles's bluster, and was able to enjoy the process
of acting. My biggest problem was maintaining a consistency
of appearance, since I aged from twenty-two to twenty-eight
in the course of the shooting, and my shrinking costume
gradually became laughably worn and obsolete, making me
resemble a character in *American Graffiti*. Somewhere along the
line I lost my green trench coat, and the only substitute I
could find was a black one; after sending Frank Marshall on
a fruitless search through costume houses for a closer match,
Welles told me not to worry about it, because he would tint
the scenes so the color discrepancy wouldn't be apparent.

After being away from the film for more than two years before the 1974 Arizona filming, I arrived on the set twenty-five
pounds heavier, and Welles exclaimed, "My God! He's ma-
tured!" He advised me to keep a day's growth of stubble on
my cheeks to make them seem less filled out. And four separate times during the shooting, I had to shave off a beard and
long hair to get back into character. Welles joked in 1975 that if
the filming went on much longer, he might have to let me take
over the Bogdanovich part "and find a younger Mr. Pister."

Perhaps the most vivid demonstration of Welles's shrewd-
ness in handling actors according to their individual needs
was the tactful way he treated Huston, who, being a director
himself, was always the most docile and obedient of actors.

Since Huston was his peer in age and career stature, Welles obviously had to avoid any appearance of ordering him around, but the finesse with which he molded the performance was marvellous to witness.

Welles wasn't satisfied, for example, with the way Huston turned a lecherous eye on the blonde teenager in one of the Arizona scenes. But rather than find fault with his performance in front of the company, Welles paused for a moment and said, "John, do you know who you remind me of in this scene? Your father." Huston beamed, as he did whenever his father was mentioned. "Oh, really, Orson? Why?" "Because he had that kindly, paternal air—but nobody ever had a higher score." Huston, delighted, picked up on the suggestion and played the scene with a sly, roguish charm that injected the note of irony Welles was seeking.

When I talked with Huston in Hollywood in December 1975, on the eve of the premiere of *The Man Who Would Be King*—the masterpiece he directed during a break in filming *The Other Side of the Wind*—he recalled his experience acting for Welles as "a lark." But then, like so many others, he expressed concern about the progress of the film and Welles's continued problems in raising money. "I'll have to find out where Orson is," he said. "I'm going to call him up and say, 'Why the hell don't you finish it?'"

Epilogue (1996)

As of this writing, twenty-five years after the start of shooting on *The Other Side of the Wind* and ten years after Welles's death, the film still has not been completed. Welles presented two scenes on national television in 1975 during his American Film Institute Life Achievement Award tribute (they can be seen on the videotape and laserdisc editions of that event); other footage has been shown at the AFI's "Working With Welles" seminar at the Directors Guild of America theater in Los Angeles in 1979; in Gary Graver's 1993 documentary *Working with Orson Welles*; and in Oja Kodar's and Vassili Silovic's 1995 compilation film *Orson Welles: The One-Man*

Band. Although shooting on *The Other Side of the Wind* essentially was completed by Welles in 1976 ("There are two or three more shots I'd like to do but they don't really matter," he said), much editing and other postproduction work remains to be done. Although Gary Graver, Oja Kodar, and Peter Bogdanovich remain committed to seeing the project through to release, byzantine legal and financial complications have continued to keep the film in limbo.

Painstaking and exhausting as the process of making the film was, Welles himself still was able to find a certain bitter humor in his struggles to complete *The Other Side of the Wind*. During the shooting of party scenes at Bogdanovich's house in the spring of 1975, I was in another room, waiting to go before the cameras, while Welles was trying to finish another shot. Suddenly I heard the director's booming voice rising above all the commotion: "Who do I have to fuck to get *out* of this picture?"

Filmography

This filmography gives credits for the theatrical films Welles directed, one of the films he made for television *(The Fountain of Youth),* and his pre-Hollywood films, as well as the titles of films in which he acted. It is based on "A Catalogue of Orson Welles's Career," which appeared in the first edition of this book (1972). That "Catalogue"— which drew on sources including Peter Noble's *The Fabulous Orson Welles* (London, 1956), André Bazin's filmography in *Cahiers du Cinéma* (Paris, June 1958), and Peter Cowie's filmography in *The Cinema of Orson Welles* (London and New York, first edition, 1965), as well as much newly collected information—has since been superseded by Jonathan Rosenbaum's virtually complete listing of Orson Welles's work in all media, "Welles' Career: A Chronology," in *This Is Orson Welles* by Welles and Peter Bogdanovich, edited by Rosenbaum (HarperCollins, New York, 1992). Some information from that and other sources, including Bret Wood's *Orson Welles: A Bio-Bibliography* (Greenwood Press, Westport, Ct., 1990), has been used to update this filmography. The reader is referred to Rosenbaum's chronology for information on Welles's uncompleted or unfilmed projects not listed here; his other work in television; and documentary films (other than his own) which he narrated or in which he appeared.

Films as Director

Documentary on St. Peter's Basilica (c. 1924)

As a nine-year-old child visiting Vatican City, Welles shot some footage of St. Peter's, his first experience with filmmaking, according to his account in *This Is Orson Welles*.

Twelfth Night (1933)

Orson Welles filmed most of the dress rehearsal of his Todd Troupers (Todd School, Woodstock, Illinois) production of Shakespeare's play in May 1933. He also played Malvolio, designed the setting, and narrated the film, which was shot in color from a fixed camera position in the auditorium.

The Hearts of Age (1934)

Producer	William Vance
Directors	Orson Welles, William Vance
Script	Orson Welles
Camera	William Vance

With Orson Welles, Virginia Nicolson, William Vance, Edgerton Paul

Filmed (in 16mm) in Woodstock, Illinois, during the summer of 1934. Running time, 5 min.

Too Much Johnson (1938; uncompleted)

Production Company	Mercury Theatre
Producers	Orson Welles, John Houseman
Associate Producer/Unit Production Manager	Richard Wilson
Director	Orson Welles
Assistant Director	John Berry
Script	Orson Welles. From the play by William Gillette
Directors of Photography	Harry Dunham, Paul Dunbar
Editors	Orson Welles, William Alland, Richard Wilson

Joseph Cotten *(Augustus Billings)*, Anna Stafford [Virginia Nicolson] *(Lenore Faddish)*, Edgar Barrier *(Leon Dathis)*, Arlene Francis *(Mrs. Dathis)*, Ruth Ford *(Mrs. Billings)*, Mary Wickes *(Mrs. Battison)*, Eustace Wyatt *(Faddish)*, Guy Kingsley *(MacIntosh)*, George Duthie *(purser)*, Orson Welles *(Keystone Kop)*, John Berry, Howard Smith, Augusta Weissberger, John Houseman, Marc Blitzstein, Herbert Drake, Richard Wilson, Judith Tuvim [Judy Holliday]

Filmed (in 16mm) in New York City and elsewhere in New York in July 1938. Made for a Mercury Theatre stage production of *Too Much Johnson*

(Stony Creek Summer Theater, Connecticut, August 1938), but never edited fully or shown publicly. Running time, approximately 40 min. The only copy of this film was destroyed in a fire at Welles's villa in Madrid in August 1970.

In 1939 Welles assembled a five-minute film from stock footage for use in his vaudeville show *The Green Goddess*, and shot test scenes for one day in Hollywood with actors Robert Coote, Everett Sloane, Gus Schilling, and himself for his abortive RKO feature based on Joseph Conrad's *Heart of Darkness*.

Citizen Kane (1941)

Production Company	Mercury Productions/RKO Radio Pictures
Studio Head	George J. Schaefer
Producer	Orson Welles
Associate Producer	Richard Baer (later Richard Barr)
Production Assistants	William Alland, Richard Wilson
Director	Orson Welles
Assistant Directors	Eddie Donahoe, Freddie Fleck
Script	Herman J. Mankiewicz, Orson Welles (and John Houseman, uncredited)
Director of Photography	Gregg Toland
Assistant Cameraman	Eddie Garvin
Retakes and Additional Shooting	Harry J. Wild
Camera Operator	Bert Shipman
Editor	Robert Wise
Assistant Editor	Mark Robson
Art Directors	Van Nest Polglase, Perry Ferguson
Set Decorator	Darrell Silvera
Special Effects	Vernon L. Walker
Optical Printing	Linwood G. Dunn
Effects Cameraman	Russell Cully
Music/Musical Director	Bernard Herrmann
Song "Charlie Kane"	Herman Ruby
Costumes	Edward Stevenson
Sound Recordists	Bailey Fesler, James G. Stewart
Makeup Artist	Maurice Seiderman

Orson Welles (*Charles Foster Kane*), Joseph Cotten *(Jedediah Leland; also newsreel reporter)*, Everett Sloane (*Bernstein*), Dorothy Comingore *(Susan Alexander Kane)*, Ray Collins *(James W. Gettys)*, William Alland *(Jerry Thompson)*, Agnes Moorehead *(Mary Kane)*, Ruth Warrick (*Emily Monroe Norton Kane*), George Coulouris (*Walter Parks Thatcher*), Erskine Sanford (*Herbert Carter; also newsreel reporter*), Harry Shannon *(Jim Kane)*, Philip Van Zandt (*Rawlston*), Paul Stewart *(Raymond)*, Fortunio Bonanova (*Matisti*), Georgia Backus (*Bertha Anderson, curator of Thatcher Library*), Buddy Swan (*Charles Foster Kane, age 8*), Sonny Bupp *(Charles Foster Kane, Jr.)*, Gus Schilling *(head waiter)*, Richard Baer (*Hillman*),

Joan Blair *(Georgia)*, Al Eben *(Mike)*, Charles Bennett *(entertainer)*, Milt Kibbee *(reporter)*, Tom Curran *(Theodore Roosevelt)*, Irving Mitchell *(Dr. Corey)*, Edith Evanson *(nurse)*, Arthur Kay *(orchestra leader)*, Tudor Williams *(chorus master)*, Herbert Corthell *(city editor)*, Benny Rubin *(Smather)*, Edmund Cobb *(reporter)*, Frances Neal *(Ethel)*, Robert Dudley *(photographer)*, Ellen Lowe *(Miss Townsend)*, Gino Corrado *(Gino, the waiter)*, Alan Ladd, Louise Currie, Eddie Coke, Walter Sande, Arthur O'Connell, Katherine Trosper, and Richard Wilson *(reporters)*, Gregg Toland *(interviewer in newsreel)*, Herman J. Mankiewicz *(newspaperman)*, Jean Forward *(Susan Alexander's singing voice)*.

Filmed at the RKO studios in Hollywood and Culver City, July 22–October 23, 1940. Released May 1, 1941. Running time, 119 min.

Distributor: RKO

Citizen Kane trailer (1941)

During principal photography, Welles directed a trailer for *Citizen Kane*, almost 4 minutes in length and comprised entirely of material not included in the film. (The trailer is included in the Voyager laserdisc edition of *Citizen Kane* and in Gary Graver's 1993 documentary *Working with Orson Welles*.)

The Magnificent Ambersons (1942)

Production Company	Mercury Productions/RKO Radio Pictures
Studio Heads	George J. Schaefer, Charles Koerner
Producer	Orson Welles
Associate Producer	Jack Moss
Director	Orson Welles (additional scenes directed by Freddie Fleck, Robert Wise, and Jack Moss)
Assistant Director	Freddie Fleck
Script	Orson Welles (additional scenes written by Jack Moss, Joseph Cotten). From the novel by Booth Tarkington
Director of Photography	Stanley Cortez
Additional Photography	Harry J. Wild, Russell Metty, Jack McKenzie (for scenes directed by Welles); McKenzie, Nicholas Musuraca, Russell Cully (new scenes and retakes)
Editor	Robert Wise
Art Director	Mark-Lee Kirk
Set Decorator	Al Fields
Special Effects	Vernon L. Walker
Music	Bernard Herrmann (uncredited)
Additional Music	Roy Webb (uncredited)
Costumes	Edward Stevenson
Sound Recordists	Bailey Fesler, James G. Stewart
Narrator	Orson Welles

Tim Holt *(George Amberson Minafer)*, Joseph Cotten *(Eugene Morgan)*, Dolores Costello *(Isabel Amberson Minafer)*, Agnes Moorehead *(Fanny Minafer)*, Anne Baxter *(Lucy Morgan)*, Ray Collins *(Jack Amberson)*, Richard Bennett *(Major Amberson)*, Don Dillaway *(Wilbur Minafer)*, Erskine Sanford *(Roger Bronson)*, J. Louis Johnson *(Sam the butler)*, Charles Phipps *(Uncle John Minafer)*, Dorothy Vaughan *(Mrs. Johnson)*, Ann O'Neal *(Mrs. Foster)*, Elmer Jerome, Maynard Holmes, Edwin August, Jack Baxley, Harry Humphrey *(townspeople outside Amberson mansion)*, Jack Santoro *(barber)*, Lyle Clement, Joe Whitehead, Del Lawrence *(men in barber shop)*, Katherine Sheldon, Georgia Backus *(women in sewing room)*, Bobby Cooper *(George as a boy)*, Heenan Elliott *("terrorized" laborer)*, Drew Roddy *(Elijah)*, Bert LeBaron, Jim Fawcet, Gil Perkins *(men idling in sunshine)*, Henry Rocquemore *(man in apron)*, Nina Gilbert, John Elliott *(guests at ball)*, Helen Thurston *(Lucy's stunt person)*, Dave Sharp *(George's stunt person)*, Jess Graves *(servant in dining room scene)*, Olive Ball *(Mary the maid)*, Gus Schilling *(drugstore clerk)*, James Westerfield *(Irish policeman)*, William Blees *(young driver at accident)*, Philip Morris *(second policeman)*, Hilda Plowwright *(nurse)*, Billy Elmer *(house servant)*; (in deleted scenes:) Mel Ford *(Fred Kinney)*, Bob Pittard *(Charlie Johnson)*, Ken Stewart *(member of George's club)*, Ed Howard *(Eugene's driver)*, Lil Nicholson *(landlady of boarding house)*, B. Emery *(man in boarding house)*

Filmed at the RKO studios in Hollywood and Culver City, October 28, 1941-January 22, 1942 (principal photography); additional scenes directed by Welles, January 26, 29, and 31; retakes, March 10, April 17, 18, 20, and 22, May 19. Released July 10, 1942. Running time, 88 min. (originally 131 min.).

Distributor: RKO

Journey Into Fear (1942–43)

Production Company	Mercury Productions/RKO Radio Pictures
Studio Heads	George J. Schaefer, Charles Koerner
Producer	Orson Welles
Associate Producer	Jack Moss (uncredited)
Director	Norman Foster (and Orson Welles, uncredited)
Script	Joseph Cotten (and Orson Welles, uncredited). From the novel by Eric Ambler
Director of Photography	Karl Struss
Editor	Mark Robson
Art Directors	Albert S. D'Agostino, Mark-Lee Kirk
Set Decorators	Darrell Silvera, Ross Dowd
Special Effects	Vernon L. Walker
Music	Roy Webb
Costumes	Edward Stevenson

Joseph Cotten *(Howard Graham)*, Dolores Del Rio *(Josette Martel)*, Orson Welles *(Colonel Haki)*, Ruth Warrick *(Stephanie Graham)*, Agnes Moorehead

(Mrs. Mathews), Everett Sloane *(Kopeikin)*, Jack Moss *(Banat)*, Jack Durant *(Gogo)*, Eustace Wyatt *(Dr. Haller)*, Frank Readick *(Mathews)*, Edgar Barrier *(Kuvetli)*, Stefan Schnabel *(purser)*, Hans Conried *(Oo Lang Sang, the magician)*, Robert Meltzer *(steward)*, Richard Bennett *(ship's captain)*, Shifra Haran *(Mrs. Haklet)*, Herbert Drake, Bill Roberts

Filmed at the RKO studios in Hollywood, January 6–March 12, 1942, and Fall 1942 (final scene). Originally released in August 1942; revised version released February 12, 1943. Running time, 69 min.

Distributor: RKO

It's All True (1942, uncompleted)

See 1993 listing.

The Stranger (1946)

Production Company	Haig Corporation/International Pictures/RKO Radio Pictures
Executive Producer	William Goetz
Producer	S. P. Eagle [Sam Spiegel]
Director	Orson Welles
Assistant Director	Jack Voglin
Script	Anthony Veiller (and John Huston, Orson Welles, uncredited)
Story	Victor Trivas, Decla Dunning
Director of Photography	Russell Metty
Editor	Ernest Nims
Art Director	Perry Ferguson
Music	Bronislaw Kaper
Orchestrations	Harold Byrns, Sidney Cutner
Costumes	Michael Woulfe
Sound	Carson F. Jowett, Arthur Johns

Orson Welles *(Franz Kindler alias Charles Rankin)*, Loretta Young *(Mary Longstreet)*, Edward G. Robinson *(Inspector Wilson)*, Philip Merivale *(Judge Longstreet)*, Richard Long *(Noah Longstreet)*, Byron Keith *(Dr. Lawrence)*, Billy House *(Mr. Potter)*, Martha Wentworth *(Sarah)*, Konstantin Shayne *(Konrad Meinike)*, Theodore Gottlieb *(Farbright; in cut scenes)*, Pietro Sosso *(Mr. Peabody)*, Isabel O'Madigan

Filmed in Hollywood, Fall 1945. Working title: Date with Destiny. Released May 25, 1946. Running time, 95 min.

Distributor: RKO

In 1946, Welles shot silent-film sequences for use in his play *Around the World*, a musical adaptation of Jules Verne's novel *Around the World in Eighty Days*.

The Lady from Shanghai (1948)

Production Company	Columbia
Studio Head	Harry Cohn
Associate Producers	Richard Wilson, William Castle
Director	Orson Welles
Assistant Director	Sam Nelson
Script	Orson Welles (and William Castle, Fletcher Markle, Charles Lederer, uncredited). From the novel *If I Die Before I Wake* by Sherwood King
Director of Photography	Charles Lawton, Jr. (and Rudolph Maté, Joseph Walker, uncredited)
Camera Operator	Irving Klein
Editor	Viola Lawrence
Art Directors	Stephen Goossón, Sturges Carne
Set Decorators	Wilbur Menefee, Herman Schoenbrun
Special Effects	Lawrence Butler
Music	Heinz Roemheld
Musical Director	M. W. Stoloff
Orchestrations	Herschel Burke Gilbert
Song "Please Don't Kiss Me"	Allan Roberts, Doris Fisher
Costumes (gowns)	Jean Louis
Sound	Lodge Cunningham

Orson Welles (*Michael O'Hara*), Rita Hayworth (*Elsa Bannister*), Everett Sloane (*Arthur Bannister*), Glenn Anders (*George Grisby*), Ted de Corsia (*Sidney Broom*), Gus Schilling (*Goldie*), Louis Merrill (*Jake*), Erskine Sanford (*judge*), Carl Frank (*District Attorney Galloway*), Evelyn Ellis (*Bessie*), Wong Show Chong (*Li*), Harry Shannon (*horse cab driver*), Sam Nelson (*captain*), Richard Wilson (*district attorney's assistant*), and players of the Mandarin Theater of San Francisco

Filmed at Columbia Studios in Hollywood, and on location in Acapulco, Mexico, and San Francisco, October 2, 1946-February 27, 1947; additional shooting, March 10-11, 1947. Released March 7, 1948 (U.K.); May 1948 (U.S.). Running time, 86 min.

Distributor: Columbia

Macbeth (1948)

Production Company	Mercury Productions/Literary Classics Productions/Republic Pictures

Studio Head	Herbert J. Yates
Executive Producer	Charles K. Feldman
Producer	Orson Welles
Associate Producer	Richard Wilson
Director	Orson Welles
Assistant Director	Jack Lacey
Script	Orson Welles. From the play by William Shakespeare
Dialogue Director	William Alland
Director of Photography	John L. Russell
Second Unit Photographer	William Bradford
Editor	Louis Lindsay
Art Director	Fred Ritter
Set Decorators	John McCarthy, Jr., James Redd
Special Effects	Howard Lydecker, Theodore Lydecker
Music	Jacques Ibert
Musical Director	Efrem Kurtz
Costumes	Orson Welles, Fred Ritter (men's), Adele Palmer (women's)
Makeup	Bob Mark
Sound	John Stransky, Jr., Garry Harris

Orson Welles (Macbeth), Jeanette Nolan (Lady Macbeth), Dan O'Herlihy (Macduff), Edgar Barrier (Banquo), Roddy McDowall (Malcolm), Erskine Sanford (Duncan), Alan Napier (a Holy Father), John Dierkes (Ross), Keene Curtis (Lennox), Peggy Webber (Lady Macduff/witch), Lionel Braham (Siward), Archie Heugly (Young Siward), Christopher Welles (Macduff child), Brainerd Duffield (1st murderer/witch), William Alland (2nd murderer), George Chirello (Seyton), Gus Schilling (porter), Jerry Farber (Fleance), Lurene Tuttle (gentlewoman/witch), Charles Lederer (witch), Robert Alan (3rd murderer), Morgan Farley (doctor).

Filmed at Republic Studios in Hollywood in twenty-three days during the summer of 1947. Released October 1, 1948. Running time, 107 min. (later cut to 86 min., but restored to original length in 1980).

Distributor: Republic

In 1950, Welles made a short film, Le Miracle de Sainte Anne, for use in his play The Unthinking Lobster. Among those appearing in the film were Marcel Archard, Georges Baume, Frédéric O'Brady, and Maurice Bessy.

Othello (1952)

| Production Company | Mercury Productions/Marceau Films/United Artists |
| Producer | Orson Welles |

Associate Producers	Giorgio Pappi, Julien Derode, Walter Bedone, Patrice Dali, Rocco Facchini
Director	Orson Welles
Assistant Director	Michael Washinsky
Script	Orson Welles. From the play by William Shakespeare
Directors of Photography	Anchise Brizzi, G. R. Aldo, George Fanto, with Obadan Troiani, Alberto Fusi
Editors	Jean Sacha, John Shepridge, Renzo Lucidi, William Morton
Art Director	Alexandre Trauner
Music	Alberto Francesco Lavagnino, Alberto Barberis
Musical Director	Willy Ferrero
Costumes	Maria de Matteis
Sound Recordist	Piscitrelli
Narrator	Orson Welles

Orson Welles *(Othello)*, Micheál MacLiammóir *(Iago)*, Suzanne Cloutier *(Desdemona)*, Robert Coote *(Roderigo)*, Michael Laurence *(Cassio)*, Hilton Edwards *(Brabantio)*, Fay Compton *(Emilia)*, Nicholas Bruce *(Lodovico)*, Jean Davis *(Montano)*, Doris Dowling *(Bianca)*, Joseph Cotten *(senator)*, Joan Fontaine *(page)*, Abdullah Ben Mohamet *(page to Desdemona)*

Filmed at the Scalera studios in Rome, and on locations in Morocco (Mogador, Safi, and Mazagan) and Italy (Venice, Tuscany, Rome, Viterbo, Perugia, and the island of Torcello), from June 19, 1949, through 1952. First shown at the Cannes Film Festival, May 10, 1952; released in U.S., June 1955. Running time, 91 min.

Distributor: United Artists

Don Quixote (begun in 1955; uncompleted)

See entry for 1992.

Mr. Arkadin (1955)

Production Company	Mercury Productions/Filmorsa (Paris)/Cervantes Films/Sevilla Film Studios (Madrid)
Executive Producer	Louis Dolivet
Production Manager	Michel J. Boisrond
Director	Orson Welles
Assistant Directors	José Maria Ochoa, José Luis De la Serna, Isidoro Martínez Ferri
Script	Orson Welles
Director of Photography	Jean Bourgoin
Editor	Renzo Lucidi
Art Director	Orson Welles

Music	Paul Misraki
Costumes	Orson Welles
Sound	Jacques Lebreton
Sound Recordist	Jacques Carrère
Narrator	Orson Welles

Orson Welles (*Gregory Arkadin*), Paola Mori (*Raina Arkadin*), Robert Arden (*Guy Van Stratten*), Akim Tamiroff (*Jacob Zouk*), Michael Redgrave (*Burgomil Trebitsch*), Patricia Medina (*Mily*), Mischa Auer (*The Professor*), Katina Paxinou (*Sophie*), Jack Watling (*Marquis of Rutleigh*), Grégoire Aslan (*Bracco*), Peter Van Eyck (*Thaddeus*), Suzanne Flon (*Baroness Nagel*), Tamara Shane (*woman in apartment*), Frédéric O'Brady (*Oskar*), Gert Frobe

Filmed in Madrid, other Spanish locations, Munich, Paris, and Rome, during eight months of 1954. First shown in Madrid, March 1955; U.K. release, August 11, 1955; U.S. release, October 11, 1962. Running time, 100 min. (A Spanish-language version, shot simultaneously, used some different actors, including Irene Lopez Heredia as Sophie.)

Distributors: Warner Bros. (U.K.), Dan Talbot (U.S.). British title: Confidential Report

The Fountain of Youth (1958)

Production Company	Welles Enterprises/Desilu
Executive Producer	Desi Arnaz
Director	Orson Welles
Script	Orson Welles, based on the short story "Youth from Vienna" by John Collier
Director of Photography	Sidney Hickox
Art Direction	Claudio Guzman
Editor	Bud Molin
Makeup	Maurice Seiderman

Orson Welles (*host/narrator*), Dan Tobin (*Humphrey Baxter*), Joi Lansing (*Carolyn Coates*), Rick Jason (*Alan Brody*), Billy House (*Albert Morgan*), Nancy Kulp (*Mrs. Morgan*), Marjorie Bennett (*journalist*)

Filmed in Hollywood (in 35mm), May 8-11, 1956. An unsold television pilot, telecast on *The Colgate Palmolive Theatre*, NBC-TV, September 16, 1958. First shown theatrically in 1969 at the Los Feliz Theater, Hollywood. Running time, 25 min. Videotape distributor: Hollywood Video Library (with Peter Brook's 1953 *King Lear*, a television production starring Welles).

Touch of Evil (1958)

| Production Company | Universal-International |
| Studio Head | Edward Muhl |

Producer	Albert Zugsmith
Production Manager	F. D. Thompson
Director	Orson Welles (added scenes directed by Harry Keller, uncredited)
Assistant Directors	Phil Bowles, Terry Nelson
Script	Orson Welles (added scenes written by Franklin Coen, uncredited). From the novel *Badge of Evil* by Whit Masterson [pseudonym for Robert A. Wade and H. Billy Miller] and a screenplay adaptation by Paul Monash (uncredited)
Director of Photography	Russell Metty
Camera Operators	John Russell, Phil Lathrop
Editors	Virgil W. Vogel, Aaron Stell (and Edward Curtiss, Ernest Nims, uncredited)
Art Directors	Alexander Golitzen, Robert Clatworthy
Set Decorators	Russell A. Gausman, John P. Austin
Music	Henry Mancini
Musical Supervisor	Joseph Gershenson
Costumes	Bill Thomas
Sound	Leslie I. Carey, Frank Wilkinson

Orson Welles *(Hank Quinlan)*, Charlton Heston *(Ramon Miguel "Mike" Vargas)*, Janet Leigh *(Susan Vargas)*, Joseph Calleia *(Pete Menzies)*, Akim Tamiroff *("Uncle Joe" Grandi)*, Valentin De Vargas *("Pancho")*, Ray Collins *(District Attorney Adair)*, Dennis Weaver *(motel clerk, "The Night Man")*, Joanna Moore *(Marcia Linnekar)*, Mort Mills *(Schwartz)*, Marlene Dietrich *(Tanya)*, Victor Millan *(Manolo Sanchez)*, Lalo Rios *(Risto)*, Michael Sargent *(Pretty Boy)*, Mercedes McCambridge *(gang leader)*, Joseph Cotten *(coroner)*, Zsa Zsa Gabor *(manager of strip joint)*, Phil Harvey *(Blaine)*, Joi Lansing *(Zita)*, Harry Shannon *(Police Chief Gould)*, Rusty Wescoatt *(Casey)*, Gus Schilling *(Eddie Farnham)*, Wayne Taylor, Ken Miller, and Raymond Rodriguez *(gang members)*, Arlene McQuade *(Ginnie)*, Domenick Delgarde *(lackey)*, Joe Basulto *(young delinquent)*, Jennie Dias *(Jackie)*, Yolanda Bojorquez *(Bobbie)*, Eleanor Dorado *(Lia)*, John Dierkes *(plainclothes cop)*

Filmed at Universal Studios in Hollywood and on location at Venice, California, February 18–April 2, 1957; added scenes directed by Harry Keller, November 19, 1957. Released in February 1958. Running time, 93 min. (1958 release version), 108 min. (longer version released in 1975).

Distributor: Universal

The Trial (1962)

Production Company	Paris-Europa Productions (Paris)/Hisa Films (Munich)/FI-C-IT (Rome)/Globus-Dubrava (Zagreb)
Producers	Alexander Salkind, Michael Salkind

Production Manager	Robert Florat
Director	Orson Welles
Assistant Directors	Marc Maurette, Paul Seban, Sophie Becker
Script	Orson Welles. From the novel *Der Prozess* by Franz Kafka
Director of Photography	Edmond Richard
Camera Operator	Adolphe Charlet
Editors	Yvonne Martin, Denise Baby, Fritz Mueller
Art Director	Jean Mandaroux
Music	Jean Ledrut, and the *Adagio for Organ and Strings* by Tomaso Albinoni (and jazz by Martial Solal, Daniel Humair, uncredited)
Costumes	Hélène Thibault
Sound	Jacques Lebreton
Sound Recordists	Julien Coutellier, Guy Villette
Pin-screen prologue	Alexandre Alexeieff, Claire Parker
Narrator	Orson Welles

Anthony Perkins *(Joseph K.)*, Orson Welles *(Hastler, The Advocate)*, Jeanne Moreau *(Miss Burstner)*, Romy Schneider *(Leni)*, Elsa Martinelli *(Hilda)*, Suzanne Flon *(Miss Pittl)*, Madeleine Robinson *(Mrs. Grubach)*, Akim Tamiroff *(Block)*, Arnoldo Foà *(inspector)*, Fernand Ledoux *(clerk of the court)*, Maurice Teynac *(director of K.'s office)*, Billy Kearns *(1st police officer)*, Jess Hahn *(2nd police officer)*, William Chappell *(Titorelli)*, Raoul Delfosse, Karl Studer, and Jean-Claude Romoleux *(executioners)*, Wolfgang Reichmann *(usher)*, Thomas Holtzmann *(student)*, Maydra Shore *(Irmie)*, Max Haufler *(Uncle Max)*, Michel Lonsdale *(priest)*, Max Buchsbaum *(judge)*, Paola Mori *(librarian)*, Van Doude *(archivist in cut scenes)*, Katina Paxinou *(scientist in cut scenes)*

Filmed at Studio de Boulogne, Paris, at the Gare d'Orsay, and in Zagreb and Rome, March 26-June 5, 1962. Released December 21, 1962 (France); February 20, 1963 (U.S.). Running time, 120 min. (118 min. in English version).

Distributors: UFA-Comacico (France), Astor (U.S.), BLC/British Lion (U.K.).
French title: Le Procès

Chimes at Midnight (1966)

Production Company	Internacional Films Española (Madrid)/Alpine Productions (Basel)
Presented by	Harry Saltzman
Executive Producer	Alessandro Tasca di Cuto
Producers	Emiliano Piedra, Angel Escolano
Production Manager	Gustavo Quintana
Director	Orson Welles
Second Unit Director	Jesús Franco
Assistant Directors	Tony Fuentes, Juan Cobos

Script	Orson Welles. From the plays *Richard II, Henry IV Parts I and II, Henry V,* and *The Merry Wives of Windsor* by William Shakespeare, and (for the commentary) *The Chronicles of England* by Raphael Holinshed
Director of Photography	Edmond Richard
Camera Operator	Adolphe Charlet
Second Unit Cameraman	Alejandro Ulloa
Second Unit Camera Operator	Jorge Herrero
Editor	Fritz Mueller
Second Editor	Elena Jaumandreu
Executive Art Director	José Antonio de la Guerra
Music	Alberto Francesco Lavagnino
Music Conductor	Carlo Franci
Costumes	Orson Welles
Sound Editor	Peter Parasheles
Makeup	Francisco Puyol
Narrator	Ralph Richardson

Orson Welles (*Sir John Falstaff*), Keith Baxter (*Prince Hal, later King Henry V*), John Gielgud (*King Henry IV*), Jeanne Moreau (*Doll Tearsheet*), Margaret Rutherford (*Mistress Quickly*), Norman Rodway (*Henry Percy, called Hotspur*), Marina Vlady (*Kate Percy*), Alan Webb (*Justice Shallow*), Walter Chiari (*Silence*), Michael Aldrich (*Pistol*), Tony Beckley (*Poins*), Fernando Rey (*Worcester*), Andrew Faulds (*Westmoreland*), José Nieto (*Northumberland*), Jeremy Rowe (*Prince John*), Beatrice Welles (*Falstaff's page*), Paddy Bedford (*Bardolph*), Julio Peña, Fernando Hilbeck, Andrés Mejuto, Keith Pyott, Charles Farrell

Filmed in Madrid, Barcelona, and other Spanish locations, September 1964-April 1965. First shown at the Cannes Film Festival, May 8, 1966; released in U.S. March 19, 1967. Running time, 119 min.

Distributors: Peppercorn-Wormser (U.S.), Planet (U.K.). Spanish title: *Campanadas a Medianoche;* U.S. title: *Falstaff*

The Immortal Story (1968)

Production Company	ORTF/Albina Films
Producer	Micheline Rozan
Production Manager	Marc Maurette
Director	Orson Welles
Assistant Directors	Olivier Gérard, Tony Fuentes, Patrice Torok
Script	Orson Welles. From the novella by Isak Dinesen [Karen Blixen]
Director of Photography	Willy Kurant (in color)
Assistant Cameramen	Jean Orjollet, Jacques Assuerds

Editors	Yolande Maurette, Marcelle Pluet, Françoise Garnault, Claude Farny
Art Director	André Piltant
Music	Piano pieces by Erik Satie, played by Aldo Ciccolini and Jean-Joel Barbier
Costumes	
(for Jeanne Moreau)	Pierre Cardin
Sound	Jean Neny
Narrator	Orson Welles

Orson Welles (*Mr. Clay*), Jeanne Moreau (*Virginie Ducrot*), Roger Coggio (*Elishama Levinsky*), Norman Eshley (*Paul*), Fernando Rey (*merchant*)

Filmed in Paris and Madrid, September-November 1966. First shown on French television simultaneously with its theatrical premiere in France, May 24, 1968; and in U.S. at the New York Film Festival, September 18, 1968. Running time, 58 min.

Distributors: Altura Films (U.S.), Hunter Films (U.K.). French title: *Une Histoire Immortelle*

The Deep (1967-69; uncompleted)

Producer	Orson Welles
Director	Orson Welles
Script	Orson Welles. From the novel *Dead Calm* by Charles Williams
Directors of Photography	Willy Kurant, Ivica Rajkovic (in color)

Laurence Harvey (*Hughie Warriner*), Jeanne Moreau (*Ruth Warriner*), Orson Welles (*Russ Brewer*), Oja Kodar (*Rae Ingram*), Michael Bryant (*John Ingram*)

Filmed off the Dalmatian coast at Hvar, Yugoslavia, 1967-9. Working title: Dead Reckoning. Footage shown at American Film Institute "Working With Welles" seminar (Directors Guild of America theater, Hollywood, 1978), and Gary Graver's *Working with Orson Welles* and Oja Kodar's and Vassili Silovic's 1995 compilation film *Orson Welles: The One-Man Band*. Another adaptation of Williams's *Dead Calm* was filmed under that title by director Philip Noyce (1989).

The Other Side of the Wind (1970-76; uncompleted)

Production Company	SACI (Teheran)/Les Films de l'Astrophore (Paris)
Producer	Dominique Antoine
Director	Orson Welles
Script	Orson Welles, Oja Kodar
Director of Photography	Gary Graver (in color and black-and-white)
Assistant Cameramen	Michael Stringer, Michael Ferris

Production Designer	Polly Platt
Production Managers	Frank Marshall, Larry Jackson
Production Associate	Neil Canton
Narrator	Orson Welles

John Huston *(Jake Hannaford)*, Peter Bogdanovich *(Brooks Otterlake)*, Norman Foster *(Billy Boyle)*, Howard Grossman *(Charles Higgam)*, Oja Kodar *(The Actress)*, Geoffrey Land *(Max David)*, Cathy Lucas *(Mavis Henscher)*, Joseph McBride *(Mr. Pister)*, Mercedes McCambridge *(Maggie)*, Cameron Mitchell *(Zimmer)*, Edmond O'Brien *(Pat)*, Lilli Palmer *(Zarah Valeska)*, Bob Random *(John Dale)*, Benny Rubin *(Abe Vogel)*, Tonio Selwart *(The Baron)*, Gregory Sierra *(Jack Simon)*, Susan Strasberg *(Juliette Rich)*, Paul Stewart *(Matt Costello)*, Dan Tobin *(Dr. Bradley Pease Burrr'ghs)*, Cassie Yates *(Cassie)*, Gene Clark *(projectionist)*, Stéphane Audran, John Carroll, Claude Chabrol, Gary Graver, Curtis Harrington, Felipe Herba, Dennis Hopper, Henry Jaglom, Peter Jason, Paul Mazursky, Eric Sherman, Richard Wilson

Filming began in Los Angeles on August 23, 1970. Additional filming, 1970-76, in Los Angeles; Flagstaff and Carefree, Arizona; Connecticut; Spain; Paris and Orvilliers, France. Footage shown at the American Film Institute Life Achievement Award tribute to Welles (Los Angeles, February 9, 1975, and on CBS-TV, February 17, 1975, as part of *The American Film Institute Salute to Orson Welles*, available on videotape from Worldvision); at the AFI's "Working With Welles" seminar (Directors Guild of America theater, Hollywood, January 28, 1979), and in *Working with Orson Welles* and *Orson Welles: The One-Man Band*.

F for Fake (1974)

Production Company	SACI (Teheran)/Les Films de l'Astrophore (Paris)/Janus Film und Fernsehen (Frankfurt)
Presented by	François Reichenbach
Producer	Dominique Antoine
Associate Producer	Richard Drewett
Director	Orson Welles
Screenplay	Orson Welles, Oja Kodar
Directors of Photography	Christian Odasso (France and Ibiza), Gary Graver (U.S. and Toussaint) (in color)
Music	Michel Legrand
Editors	Marie-Sophie Dubus, Dominique Engerer

Orson Welles, Oja Kodar, Elmyr de Hory, Clifford Irving, Edith Irving, François Reichenbach, Joseph Cotten, Richard Drewett, Laurence Harvey, Jean-Pierre Aumont, Nina Van Pallandt, Richard Wilson, Paul Stewart, Howard Hughes, Gary Graver, and the voices of Peter Bogdanovich and William Alland

Filming and editing in France, Ibiza, and U.S., 1972-73. Incorporates material (and outtakes) from a BBC documentary about Elmyr de Hory by François Reichenbach. Alternate titles: *?, Fake, Hoax, Vérités et mensonges (Truth and Lies)*. First shown in September 1974 at the San Sebastian and New York film festivals; U.S. release, 1977.

F for Fake trailer (1978)

In 1976, Welles directed a 9-minute trailer for the U.S. release of F for Fake, with mostly new material (in color), featuring himself, Oja Kodar, and Gary Graver. The trailer (photographed by Graver) was not used by the distributor, and survives only in a black-and-white dupe of the workprint, first shown in public in November 1978 during the American Film Institute's "Working With Welles" seminar at the Directors Guild of America theater in Hollywood. The trailer is included in *Working with Orson Welles* and *Orson Welles: The One-Man Band*, as well as on the Voyager laserdisc edition of *F for Fake*.

Filming "Othello" (1978)

Producers	Klaus Hellwig, Juergen Hellwig
Director	Orson Welles
Script	Orson Welles
Camera	Gary Graver (in color)
Music	Francesco Lavignino, Alberto Barbaris
Editor	Marty Roth

Orson Welles, Micheál MacLiammóir, Hilton Edwards

Filming and editing, Paris and Los Angeles, 1974-78. Incorporates footage from Welles's 1952 film of William Shakespeare's *Othello*. Running time: 84 min. First shown on West German television and later in theaters.

The Dreamers (1980–82; uncompleted)

Welles filmed about twenty minutes of color footage from his uncompleted feature adaptation of two stories by Isak Dinesen, "The Dreamers" and "Echoes," with Oja Kodar as the mute former opera singer Pellegrina and himself as her merchant friend Marcus Kleek. Gary Graver was the cinematographer; shooting took place at Welles's home in Hollywood. Footage appears in *Orson Welles: The One-Man Band*.

Don Quixote/Don Quijote de Orson Welles/Don Quixote by Orson Welles (1992)

Release Version:

Production Company	El Silencio

Producer	Patxi Irigoyen
Associate Producer	Juan A. Pedrosa
Dialogue Adaptation	Javier Mina, Jess Franco
Editor/Head of Post-production	Jess Franco
Editors	Rosa Maria Almirall, Fatima Michalczik
Music	Daniel J. White
General Supervisor	Oja Kodar

Original Shoot:

Producer	Oscar Dancigers
Production Managers	Alessadro Tasca di Cuto, Francisco Lara
Director	Orson Welles
Script	Orson Welles, based on the novel by Miguel de Cervantes
Camera	Jose Garcia Galisteo, Juan Manuel de Lachica, Edmond Richard, Jack Draper, Ricardo Navarrete, Manuel Mateos, Giorgio Tonti, Gary Graver
Editors	Maurizio Lucidi, Renzo Lucidi, Peter Parasheles, Ira Wohl, Alberto Valenzuela
Assistant Directors	Juan Luis Buñuel, Paola Mori, Mauro Bonanni, Maurizio Lucidi

Francisco Reiguera (*Don Quixote*), Akim Tamiroff (*Sancho Panza*), Orson Welles (*himself*); *Dubbing:* Welles and Jose Mediavilla (*voices of Don Quixote*), Welles and Juan Carlos Ordonez (*voices of Sancho Panza*).

Filmed 1955-1973 in Mexico, Spain, and Italy. First shown at the Cannes Film Festival, May 16, 1992. Running time: 118 min. (An earlier assemblage of 35 minutes of footage from *Don Quixote* was shown at the Cannes Film Festival on May 18, 1986.)

It's All True: Based on an Unfinished Film by Orson Welles (1993)

Production Company Paramount Pictures/Les Films Balenciaga/The French Ministry of Education and Culture/French National Center for Cinematography/Canal +/R. Films/La Fondation GAN pour le Cinéma

Producers	Régine Konckier, Richard Wilson, Bill Krohn, Myron Meisel, Jean-Luc Ormieres
Associate Producer/Senior Research Executive	Catherine Benamou
Directors	Richard Wilson, Myron Meisel, Bill Krohn
Script	Bill Krohn, Richard Wilson, Myron Meisel
Camera	Gary Graver (in color)

232 ORSON WELLES

Editor	Ed Marx
Music	Jorge Arriagada
Sound	Dean Beville, Jean-Pierre Duret
Special Consultant	Elizabeth Wilson
Narrator	Miguel Ferrer

Four Men on a Raft:

Director	Orson Welles
Associate Producer	Richard Wilson
Camera	George Fanto (in black-and-white and color)
Assistant Camera	Reginaldo Calmon
Production Assistants	Elizabeth Amster [Wilson], Shifra Haran
Research	Edmar Morel

Manuel (Jacaré) Olimpio Meira, Jeronimo André de Souza, Raimundo (Tatá) Correia Lima, Manuel (Preto) Pereira da Silva (the jangadeiros), Francisca Moreira da Silva (young bride), José Sobrinho (her husband)

The Story of Samba (Carnaval):

Director	Orson Welles
Associate Producer	Richard Wilson
Script	Robert Meltzer
Camera	Harry J. Wild (in color and black-and-white)
Technicolor Consultant	W. Howard Greene
Assistant Director/ Choreography	Herivelto Martins

Grande Othelo, Pery Ribeiro (performers)

My Friend Bonito:

Producer	Orson Welles
Associate Producer	José Noriega
Director	Norman Foster
Story	Robert Flaherty
Camera	Floyd Crosby

Jesús Vásquez (Chico)

The uncompleted three-part Orson Welles film It's All True was produced for the U.S. State Department Coordinator of Inter-American Affairs (Nelson Rockefeller) and RKO. The My Friend Bonito segment was filmed September-December, 1941, in Mexico, and the Four Men and a Raft and The Story of Samba segments were filmed February 9-July 22, 1942, on location in Brazil and at Cinédia Studios in Rio de Janeiro (Manuel [Jacaré] Olimpio Meira was killed on May 19, 1942, during filming of the arrival of the jan-

gadeiros in Rio's Guanabara Bay). The documentary *It's All True: Based on an Unfinished Film by Orson Welles*, was produced from 1985-93 and was first shown at the New York Film Festival, October 1993. (A 22-minute work-in-progress version, *It's All True: Four Men on a Raft*, directed by Richard Wilson and produced by Fred Chandler for the American Film Institute and the National Center for Film and Video Preservation, was first shown at the 1986 Venice Film Festival.) Running time: 86 min.

Distributor: Paramount Pictures

Film performances

1933	*Twelfth Night* (as Malvolio. d: Orson Welles)
1934	*The Hearts of Age* (as Death. d: Orson Welles, William Vance)
1940	*The Swiss Family Robinson* (as Narrator. d: Edward Ludwig)
1941	*Citizen Kane* (as Charles Foster Kane. d: Orson Welles)
1942	*The Magnificent Ambersons* (as Narrator. d: Orson Welles)
1943	*Journey Into Fear* (as Colonel Haki. d: Norman Foster)
	Jane Eyre (as Edward Rochester. d: Robert Stevenson)
1944	*Follow the Boys* (as Himself. d: Edward Sutherland)
1945	*Tomorrow Is Forever* (as John Macdonald. d: Irving Pichel)
1946	*The Stranger* (as Franz Kindler alias Charles Rankin. d: Orson Welles)
1947	*Duel in the Sun* (as Narrator. d: King Vidor)
	Black Magic (as Cagliostro. d: Gregory Ratoff)
1948	*The Lady from Shanghai* (as Michael O'Hara. d: Orson Welles)
	Macbeth (as Macbeth. d: Orson Welles)
	Prince of Foxes (as Cesare Borgia d: Henry King)
1949	*The Third Man* (as Harry Lime. d: Carol Reed)
1950	*The Black Rose* (as General Bayan. d: Henry Hathaway)
1951	*Return to Glennascaul* (as Himself. d: Hilton Edwards)
1952	*Othello* (as Othello. d: Orson Welles)
1953	*Trent's Last Case* (as Sigsbee Manderson. d: Herbert Wilcox)
	Si Versailles m'était conté/Royal Affairs in Versailles (as Benjamin Franklin. d: Sacha Guitry)
	L'Uomo, la Bestia e la Virtù (as The Beast. d: Steno [Stefano Vanzina])
1954	*Napoléon* (as Hudson Lowe. d: Sacha Guitry)
	Trouble in the Glen (as Sanin Cejador y Mengues. d: Herbert Wilcox)
1955	*Three Cases of Murder* (as Lord Mountdrago in the episode directed by George More O'Ferrall)
	Mr. Arkadin/Confidential Report (as Gregory Arkadin and Narrator. d: Orson Welles)
1956	*Moby Dick* (as Father Mapple. d: John Huston)
1957	*Man in the Shadow* (as Virgil Renchler. d: Jack Arnold)
	The Long Hot Summer (as Varner. d: Martin Ritt)
1958	*Touch of Evil* (as Hank Quinlan. d: Orson Welles)
	The Roots of Heaven (as Cy Sedgwick. d: John Huston)
	The Vikings (as Narrator. d: Richard Fleischer)
1959	*Compulsion* (as Jonathan Wilk d: Richard Fleischer)
	David e Golia/David and Goliath (as Saul. d: Richard Pottier, Ferdinando Baldi)
	Ferry to Hong Kong (as Captain Hart. d: Lewis Gilbert)
1960	*Austerlitz* (as Fulton. d: Abel Gance)
	Crack in the Mirror (as Hagolin and Lamorcière. d: Richard Fleischer)
	I Tartari/The Tartars (as Burundai. d: Richard Thorpe)
1961	*King of Kings* (as Narrator. d: Nicholas Ray)
	Lafayette (as Benjamin Franklin. d: Jean Dréville)
1962	*The Trial/Le Procès* (as Hastler, The Advocate. d: Orson Welles)
1963	*The VIPs* (as Max Buda. d: Anthony Asquith)

RoGoPaG/Laviamoci il Cervello (as The Director in the episode *La Ricotta*, directed by Pier Paolo Pasolini)

1964 *La Fabuleuse Aventure de Marco Polo/The Fabulous Adventures of Marco Polo/Marco the Magnificent!* (as Ackermann. *d:* Denys de la Patellière, Noël Howard)

1966 *Is Paris Burning?/Paris brûle-t-il?* (as Consul Raoul Nordling. *d:* René Clement)
Chimes at Midnight/Campanadas a Medianoche/Falstaff (as Sir John Falstaff. *d:* Orson Welles)
A Man for All Seasons (as Cardinal Wolsey. *d:* Fred Zinnemann)

1967 *Casino Royale* (as Le Chiffre in the episode directed by Joseph McGrath)
The Sailor from Gibraltar (as Louis from Mozambique. *d:* Tony Richardson)
I'll Never Forget What's'isname (as Jonathan Lute. *d:* Michael Winner)

1968 *Oedipus the King* (as Tiresias. *d:* Philip Saville)
The Immortal Story/Une Histoire Immortelle (as Mr. Clay and Narrator. *d:* Orson Welles)
House of Cards (as Charles Leschenhaut. *d:* John Guillermin)

1969 *Der Kampf um Rom/The Last Roman* (as Justinian. *d:* Robert Siodmak)
L'Etoile du Sud/The Southern Star (as Plankett. *d:* Sidney Hayers)
Bitka na Neretvi/The Battle of Neretva (as Senator. *d:* Veljko Bulajic)

1970 *The Kremlin Letter* (as Aleksei Bresnavitch. *d:* John Huston)
Start the Revolution Without Me (as Himself and Narrator. *d:* Bud Yorkin)
12+1/Una su Tredici (as Markau. *d:* Nicolas Gessner)
Catch-22 (as General Dreedle. *d:* Mike Nichols)
Upon This Rock (as Michelangelo. *d:* Harry Rasky)
Waterloo (as Louis XVIII. *d:* Sergei Bondarchuk)
Viva la Revolución/Tepepa/Blood and Guns (as Colonel Cascorro. *d:* Giulio Petroni)
The Deep (as Russ Brewer. *d:* Orson Welles, uncompleted)

1971 *A Safe Place* (as The Magician. *d:* Henry Jaglom)
La Décade Prodigieuse/Twelve Days' Wonder (as Theo Van Horn. *d:* Claude Chabrol)

1972 *Malpertius* (as Uncle Cassavius. *d:* Harry Kumel)
Get to Know Your Rabbit (as Mr. Delasandro. *d:* Brian de Palma)
Necromancy/The Witching/Rosemary's Disciples (as Mr. Cato. *d:* Bert Gordon)
Treasure Island (as Long John Silver. *d:* John Hough)

1974 *F for Fake* (as Himself. *d:* Orson Welles)

1976 *Voyage of the Damned* (as Raoul Estedes. *d:* Stuart Rosenberg)

1978 *Filming "Othello"* (as Himself. *d:* Orson Welles)

1979 *The Double McGuffin* (as Himself. *d:* Joe Camp)
The Muppet Movie (as Lew Lord. *d:* James Frawley)

1980 *Going for Broke/Never Trust an Honest Thief* (as Sheriff Paisley. *d:* George McGowan)

Tajna Nikole Tesle/The Secret of Nikola Tesla (as J. P. Morgan. *d:* Krsto Papic)

1980-82 *The Dreamers* (as Marcus Kleek. *d:* Orson Welles, uncompleted)
1981 *History of the World—Part I* (as Narrator. *d:* Mel Brooks)
   Butterfly (as Judge Rauch. *d:* Matt Cimber)
   The Man Who Saw Tomorrow (as Narrator. *d:* Robert Guenette)
1984 *Slapstick (Of Another Kind)* (as Narrator. *d:* Steven Paul)
   Where Is Parsifal? (as Klingsor. *d:* Henri Helman)
1986 *The Transformers* (as voice of Planet Unicron. *d:* Nelson Shin)
1987 *Someone to Love* (as Himself. *d:* Henry Jaglom)
1992 *Don Quixote /Don Quijote de Orson Welles/Don Quixote by Orson Welles* (as Himself and voices of Don Quixote and Sancho Panza. *d:* Orson Welles)

Selected Bibliography

Michael Anderegg, "Orson Welles as Performer," *Persistence of Vision*, No. 7, 1989.

André Bazin, *Orson Welles*, with preface by Jean Cocteau, Editions Chavane, Paris, 1950; second edition, Paris: Les Editions du Cerf, 1972, preface by André S. Labarthe; English translation of second edition by Jonathan Rosenbaum, *Orson Welles: A Critical View*, with foreword by François Truffaut, Harper & Row, New York, 1978, and Acrobat Books, Venice, Ca., 1991.

———, with Charles Bitsch, "Entretien avec Orson Welles," *Cahiers du Cinéma*, June 1958, and (also with Jean Domarchi), "Nouvel Entretien avec Orson Welles," September 1958; English translation of both interviews (abridged) by Terry Comito in Comito's book *Touch of Evil* (see below).

Morris Beja, ed., *Perspectives on Orson Welles*, G. K. Hall, New York, 1995.

Catherine Benamou, "*It's All True* as Document/Event: Notes Towards an Historiographical and Textual Analysis," *Persistence of Vision*, No. 7, 1989.

Maurice Bessy, *Orson Welles*, Editions Seghers, Paris, 1963; English translation by Ciba Vaughan, Crown, New York, 1971.

Peter Bogdanovich, *The Cinema of Orson Welles*, The Museum of Modern Art, New York, 1961.

———, "Is It True What They Say About Orson?," *The New York Times*, August 30, 1970.

———, "The *Kane* Mutiny," *Esquire*, October 1972.

Frank Brady, *Citizen Welles: A Biography of Orson Welles*, Charles Scribner's Sons, New York, 1989.

Simon Callow, *Orson Welles: The Road to Xanadu*, Jonathan Cape, London, 1995.

Robert L. Carringer, *The Making of "Citizen Kane,"* University of California Press, Berkeley, 1985.

———, *The Magnificent Ambersons: A Reconstruction*, University of California Press, Berkeley, 1993.

Juan Cobos, Miguel Rubio, and Jose Antonio Pruneda, "Voyage au pays de Don Quixote," *Cahiers du Cinéma*, April 1965; English translation by Rose Kaplin as "A Trip to Don Quixoteland: Conversations with Orson Welles," *Cahiers du Cinéma in English*, No. 5, 1966, reprinted in Andrew Sarris, ed., *Interviews With Film Directors*, Bobbs-Merrill, Indianapolis, 1967.

Juan Cobos and Miguel Rubio, "Welles and Falstaff," *Sight and Sound*, Autumn 1966.

Richard Combs, "Burning Masterworks: From *Kane* to *F for Fake*," *Film Comment*, January-February 1994.

Terry Comito, ed., *Touch of Evil*, Rutgers University Press, New Brunswick, N.J., 1985 (includes transcription of film).

Peter Cowie, *The Cinema of Orson Welles*, A. Zwemmer Ltd., London, 1965; revised edition, *A Ribbon of Dreams: The Cinema of Orson Welles*, The Tantivy Press, London, and A.S. Barnes, South Brunswick, N.J., 1973; and Da Capo Press, New York, 1983.

Roy Alexander Fowler, *Orson Welles, A First Biography*, Pendulum Publications, London, 1946.

Richard France, *The Theatre of Orson Welles*, Bucknell University Press/Associated University Presses, Cranbury, N.J., 1977.

——, ed., *Orson Welles on Shakespeare: The W.P.A. and Mercury Theatre Playscripts*, Greenwood Press, Westport, Ct., 1990.

Ronald Gottesman, ed., *Focus on "Citizen Kane,"* Prentice-Hall, Englewood Cliffs, N.J., 1971.

——, ed., *Focus on Orson Welles*, Prentice-Hall, Englewood Cliffs, N.J., 1975.

Stephen Heath, "Film and System: Terms of Analysis, Part I," *Screen*, Spring 1975 (on *Touch of Evil*).

Charles Higham, *The Films of Orson Welles*, University of California Press, Berkeley, 1970.

——, *Orson Welles: The Rise and Fall of an American Genius*, St. Martin's Press, New York, 1985.

——, "And Now, the War of the Welles," *The New York Times*, September 13, 1969.

——, "Orson's Back and Marlene's Got Him," *The New York Times*, January 31, 1971 (on *The Other Side of the Wind*).

——, "The Film That Orson Welles Has Been Finishing for Six Years," *The New York Times*, April 18, 1976 (on *The Other Side of the Wind*).

John Houseman, *Run-Through: A Memoir*, Simon and Schuster, New York, 1972.

John Huston, *An Open Book*, Alfred A. Knopf, New York, 1980; Da Capo Press, 1994.

Alva Johnston, with Fred Smith, "How to Raise a Child," *The Saturday Evening Post*, January 20, January 27, and February 3, 1940.

Pauline Kael, with Herman J. Mankiewicz and Orson Welles, *The "Citizen Kane" Book*, Little, Brown, Boston, 1971 (includes shooting script and transcription of film).

——, "Orson Welles: There Ain't No Way," *The New Republic*, June 24, 1967 (on *Chimes at Midnight*), reprinted in Kael's collection *Kiss Kiss Bang Bang*, Little, Brown, Boston, 1968.

Bridget Gellert Lyons, ed., *Chimes at Midnight*, Rutgers University Press, New Brunswick, N.J., 1988 (includes transcription of film).

Barbara Leaming, *Orson Welles: A Biography*, Viking, New York, 1985.

Micheál MacLiammóir, *All for Hecuba*, Methuen, London, 1950.

——, with preface by Orson Welles, *Put Money In Thy Purse*, Methuen, London, 1952; reprinted by Columbus Books, London, 1988.

——, "Orson Welles," *Sight and Sound*, July-September 1954.

Joseph McBride, ed., *Persistence of Vision: A Collection of Film Criticism*, Wisconsin Film Society Press, Madison, 1968.

———, *Orson Welles: Actor and Director*, Harcourt Brace Jovanovich, New York, 1977.

———, "Le Grand Cinéaste: Welles at 52," *The Daily Cardinal* (University of Wisconsin, Madison), July 7, 1967.

———, "Orson Welles Returns from Obscurity," *The Wisconsin State Journal* (Madison), September 14, 1970.

———, "Rough Sledding with Pauline Kael," *Film Heritage*, Fall 1971.

———, "AFI Presents Orson Welles Its Third Life Achievement Award," *Daily Variety*, February 11, 1975.

———, "All's Welles," *Film Comment*, November/December 1978.

———, "Welles' 'Ambersons': Mutilated yet magnificent," *Daily Variety*, July 23, 1992.

Laura Mulvey, *Citizen Kane*, British Film Institute, London, 1992.

James Naremore, *The Magic World of Orson Welles*, Oxford University Press, New York, 1978; revised edition, Southern Methodist University Press, 1989.

———, "The Trial: The FBI vs. Orson Welles," *Film Comment*, January-February 1991.

Peter Noble, *The Fabulous Orson Welles*, Hutchinson, London, 1956.

Jonathan Rosenbaum, "The Voice and the Eye: A Commentary on the *Heart of Darkness* Script," *Film Comment*, November-December 1972.

———, "The Invisible Orson Welles: A First Inventory," *Sight and Sound*, Summer 1986.

———, "Wellesian: Quixote in a trashcan," *Sight and Sound*, Autumn 1988.

———, "Orson Welles' Essay Films and Documentary Fictions: A Two-Part Speculation," *Cinematograph*, No. 4, 1991, reprinted in Rosenbaum's collection *Placing Movies: The Practice of Film Criticism*, University of California Press, Berkeley, 1995.

———, "The Seven *Arkadins*," *Film Comment*, January-February 1992.

———, "*Othello* Goes Hollywood," *The Chicago Reader*, April 10, 1992, reprinted in *Placing Movies*.

———, with Bill Krohn, "Orson Welles in the U.S.: An Exchange," *Persistence of Vision*, No. 11, 1995.

Audrey Stainton, "*Don Quixote*: Orson Welles' Secret," *Sight and Sound*, Autumn 1988.

Robert Stam, "Orson Welles, Brazil and the Power of Blackness," *Persistence of Vision*, No. 7, 1989 (on *It's All True*).

Kenneth Tynan, "Playboy Interview: Orson Welles," *Playboy*, March 1967.

Peter Viertel, *Dangerous Friends: Hemingway, Huston and Others*, Viking, London, and Doubleday, New York, 1992.

Orson Welles, with Peter Bogdanovich, edited by Jonathan Rosenbaum, *This Is Orson Welles*, HarperCollins, New York, 1992.

———, with Oja Kodar, *The Big Brass Ring: An Original Screenplay*, afterword by Jonathan Rosenbaum, preface by James Pepper, Santa Teresa Press, Santa Barbara, Ca., 1987.

——, *The Cradle Will Rock: An Original Screenplay*, edited and introduced by James Pepper, afterword by Jonathan Rosenbaum, Santa Teresa Press, Santa Barbara, Ca., 1994.

——, Letter to *The New Statesman*, May 24, 1958, concerning *Touch of Evil*.

——, Letter to *The London Times*, November 17, 1971, concerning *Citizen Kane*.

——, American Film Institute Life Achievement Award acceptance speech, *American Cinematographer*, April 1975.

——, "My Father Wore Black Spats" and "A Brief Career as a Musical Prodigy," *Paris Vogue*, December 1982-January 1983.

——, "*Touch of Evil*: Orson Welles' Memo to Universal," with introduction by Jonathan Rosenbaum, *Film Quarterly*, Fall 1992.

Richard Wilson, "It's Not *Quite* All True," *Sight and Sound*, Autumn 1970.

Bret Wood, *Orson Welles: A Bio-Bibliography*, Greenwood Press, Westport, Ct., 1990.

——, "Recognizing *The Stranger*," *Video Watchdog*, May-July 1994.

——, "Kiss Hollywood Goodbye: Orson Welles and *The Lady from Shanghai*," Ibid.

Robin Wood, "Welles, Shakespeare and Webster: *Touch of Evil*," in *Personal Views: Explorations in Film*, Gordon Fraser, London, 1976.

Acknowledgments

For the original 1972 edition:

My debts are many, and without the encouragement of several people I would never have finished this book. Orson Welles gave generously of his time and attention to meet with me. Peter Bogdanovich, his collaborator on the book *This Is Orson Welles,* graciously compared notes. I would also like to thank William Donnelly and Michael Wilmington for their discussions of Welles and of everything else in general; Andrew Sarris and Robin Wood, two exceptional critics, for teaching me the trade; Jon Zwickey for his unique perception of Welles and his other insights; Andrew Holmes, Wayne Merry, Thomas Flinn, John Davis, Mark Bergman, and Gene Walsh, for helping me screen movies; Herman G. Weinberg, for his kindness; Gerald Peary, for inviting me to speak about Welles; Marie Garness, devotee of Welles, for her enthusiasm; Wayne Campbell, for a pleasant afternoon of research; Penelope Houston, Ernest Callenbach, and Tony Macklin, for their editorial guidance; Tom Book, Candy Cashman, Ellen Whitman, Mark Goldblatt, Richard Thompson, David Shepard, Milton Luboviski, Jane Mankiewicz, Russell Merritt, and Lawrence D. Cohen, for their advice and interest; Steven Wonn, for his hell-raising; Raymond and Marian McBride, and William and Monica Detra, for keeping the faith; and the members of the Wisconsin Film Society, for watching all those movies.

For the revised edition:

Sections of this book have appeared previously, some in different form, in *American Film, Film Quarterly, Film Heritage, The New York Review of Books,* and *Sight and Sound,* and the editors' permission to reprint is gratefully acknowledged. Parts of Chapters 3, 4, and 12 appeared in *Persistence of Vision,* edited by Joseph McBride, Wisconsin Film Society Press, Madison, 1968.

Ruth O'Hara's enthusiasm for the original edition of this book helped encourage me to undertake this revision, for which she also contributed many valuable suggestions and ideas, as she did on my book about Frank Capra. Her father, Noel O'Hara, also shared his thoughts about Welles and about literature. My children, Jessica and John McBride, always have been understanding of their father's writing career, and I have learned much about life from both of them. In addition to the Welles scholars and critics mentioned in the preface, I also am grateful to Orson Welles, Oja Kodar, Gary Graver, Lou Race, and the rest of the company of *The Other Side of the Wind,* for their companionship in the adventure of a lifetime; the late François Truffaut, Jean Renoir, and Dido Renoir, for our fascinating and convivial discussions of Welles and screenings of his films; Michael Wilmington, for his continuing friendship and stimulating exchange of ideas; Bill Krohn and Myron Meisel, for sharing their knowledge of *It's All True* and other Wellesiana; the late Arthur Knight, for enabling me to see *The Fountain of Youth;* film scholars Christie Milliken and Bart Whaley, for providing me with videotapes of *F for Fake;* Jonathan Fernandez, for enabling me to see the 1992 version of Welles's *Don Quixote;* Florence Dauman, for enabling me to see *Orson Welles: The One-Man Band;* Rebecca Cape and Saundra Taylor of the Lilly Library (Bloomington, Indiana), for the use of photographs from the library's Welles and George Fanto collections; Gary Graver, for the use of his splendid photographs of Orson Welles; Barbara Epstein of *The New York Review of Books,* for asking me to write what became the opening chapter of this edition and providing editorial guidance; and Yuval Taylor of Da Capo Press, for not only keeping my and Michael

Wilmington's *John Ford* in print, but also for making this edition of *Orson Welles* possible and editing it with his customary intelligence and diplomacy. I also wish to thank Jean Oppenheimer, my friend and fellow film critic, for enriching my life with her personal and intellectual companionship.

About the Author

Joseph McBride with Orson Welles in 1978, during a break in the taping of Welles's television talk show pilot in a Hollywood studio. (*Gary Graver*)

Joseph McBride first came to international prominence as a film critic and historian with the original edition of this book on Orson Welles, published under the auspices of the British Film Institute in 1972, when the author was 25 years old. McBride is also the author of a 1977 study of Welles's acting career, *Orson Welles: Actor and Director,* and such other books as the critically acclaimed 1992 biography *Frank Capra: The Catastrophe of Success;* the Howard Hawks interview book *Hawks on Hawks;* and *John Ford,* a critical study written with Michael Wilmington and also published by Da Capo Press. McBride's scriptwriting credits include the American Film Institute Life Achievement Award television specials honoring James Stewart, Fred Astaire, Frank Capra, John Huston, and Lillian Gish, for which he received a Writers Guild of America Award and two Emmy nominations. He covered the film industry for *Daily Variety* in Los Angeles for many years as a reporter and reviewer. His next book is a biography of Steven Spielberg.

Other titles of interest